A MISREPRESENTED PEOPLE

RELIGION AND SOCIAL TRANSFORMATION

General Editors: Anthony B. Pinn and Stacey M. Floyd-Thomas

Prophetic Activism: Progressive Religious Justice Movements in Contemporary America
Helene Slessarev-Jamir

All You That Labor: Religion and Ethics in the Living Wage Movement
C. Melissa Snarr

Blacks and Whites in Christian America: How Racial Discrimination Shapes Religious Convictions
Jason E. Shelton and Michael O. Emerson

Pillars of Cloud and Fire: The Politics of Exodus in African American Biblical Interpretation
Herbert Robinson Marbury

American Secularism: Cultural Contours of Nonreligious Belief Systems
Joseph O. Baker and Buster G. Smith

Religion and Progressive Activism: New Stories About Faith and Politics
Edited by Ruth Braunstein, Todd Nicholas Fuist, and Rhys H. Williams

"Jesus Saved an Ex-Con": Political Activism and Redemption after Incarceration
Edward Orozco Flores

After the Protests Are Heard: Enacting Civic Engagement and Social Transformation
Sharon D. Welch

Solidarity and Defiant Spirituality: Africana Lessons on Religion, Racism, and Ending Gender Violence
Traci C. West

Ecopiety: Green Media and the Dilemma of Environmental Virtue
Sarah McFarland Taylor

Catholic Activism Today: Individual Transformation and the Struggle for Social Justice
Maureen K. Day

Networking the Black Church: Digital Black Christians and Hip Hop
Erika D. Gault

Religion, Race, and Covid-19: Confronting White Supremacy in the Pandemic
Stacey M. Floyd-Thomas

The Contemporary Black Church: The New Dynamics of African American Religion
Jason E. Shelton

White Property, Black Trespass: The Religion of Mass Criminalization
Andrew Krinks

Restorative Justice and Lived Religion: Transforming Mass Incarceration in Chicago
Jason A. Springs

A Misrepresented People: Manhood in Black Religious Thought
Darrius D'wayne Hills

A Misrepresented People

Manhood in Black Religious Thought

Darrius D'wayne Hills

NEW YORK UNIVERSITY PRESS
New York, New York

NEW YORK UNIVERSITY PRESS
New York
www.nyupress.org

© 2025 by New York University
All rights reserved

Please contact the Library of Congress for Cataloging-in-Publication data.
ISBN: 9781479823284 (hardback)
ISBN: 9781479823291 (paperback)
ISBN: 9781479823338 (library ebook)
ISBN: 9781479823321 (consumer ebook)

This book is printed on acid-free paper, and its binding materials are chosen for strength and durability. We strive to use environmentally responsible suppliers and materials to the greatest extent possible in publishing our books.

Manufactured in the United States of America

10 9 8 7 6 5 4 3 2 1

Also available as an ebook

For Rev. Dr. Derrick and Sharron Hills—

For Jennifer—

And for all discerning Black males past, present, and future.

CONTENTS

Introduction	1
1: Charting Relationality in Black Religious Thought	19
2: Black Manhood in the Writings of Alice Walker, Zora Neale Hurston, and Toni Morrison	51
3: James Baldwin, the Black Church, and Queering the Masculinist Oeuvre	82
4: The Relational Turn in Black Male Theologies	104
5: On Black Male (Re)Covery	128
Epilogue: Black Masculinity Otherwise	151
Acknowledgments	161
Notes	165
Bibliography	179
Index	189
About the Author	199

Introduction

I think it is absolutely necessary that black men regroup as black men.... I know whole black men can exist, and I want to see and enjoy them.... I send a prayer to my brothers; that you continue to open to each other and to bless yourselves. Continue to let go of fear. Continue to insist on truth and trust.
—Alice Walker

The Black male stands in relation to others as always vulnerable because his personhood, who he actually is to himself, is not only denied, but also negated by society.
—Tommy J. Curry

When I was a third-year doctoral student, I once had a conversation about whether the scholarship of another Black male scholar and colleague was "anti-Black women." Having read this scholar's body of work and referenced it in my own, I defended his scholarly reputation from the charges of misogyny—mainly on the grounds that his overall project was about humanizing Black men and boys as well as addressing the gender regimes that negatively impact them, as they do Black women and girls. To focus, in this regard, on a humanistic interest in the Black male experience, I reasoned, was not tethered in any way to the devaluing, dismissal, or diminishing of Black women. In response, another Black feminist, who possessed a doctorate, without offering any sustained criticism of my colleague's specific arguments or offering a specific rebuttal, curtly told me to "stay in my lane." This person's arrogance and dismissiveness notwithstanding, that incident has plagued me for years, not simply because of the disrespectful tone, but primarily because of the lack of a real willingness on her part to consider the merits of scholarship that privileges the lives and well-being of Black males by reflecting upon and telling their stories. A few years later, when I was awarded a dissertation fellowship for my research on Black men and theological discourse, another small cadre of Black feminist scholars openly asked why a religious studies project on Black men was worth funding. From then until now, I have reflected upon the intellectual and academic insularity (and hostility) I experienced and what it could or should mean for the future of my work as a scholar of African American religious thought with interests in the ties between religion, race, and gender. The silver lining following these early discomfiting experiences was that they prompted me to take seriously a self-reflexive approach to my research. I was compelled to dive into the realities of my social location as both Black and male, and to examine the ties between this feature of my identity and how this impacted my scholarship. Driven by tensions related to the question of how and why Black males should be privileged in religious and theological discourses, the operative queries I raised were, and remain, apt: What is the *matter* with Black manhood? And what is the substance of Black manhood and Black male identity when considered through multiple prisms and perspectives in African American religious thought and cultural criticism?

This is a book about Black men, gender identity, and possibility. It illustrates the strength and relevance of Black religious thought in curating alternative notions of masculinity for African American males. It may appear odd to some readers to position masculinity and male identity as a topic in religion at all. Primarily, it is critical to note first that *Black* religious thought and experience explodes and complicates the provincialism that designates the canonized, "proper" subject understanding of religion as a field of study. The study of *American* religion has too often been conceptualized in static and unidimensional modalities. In my own work I have found it more valuable, owing to the polyvocal, plural, and ecumenical context of contemporary settings, to adopt approaches to the study of religion that break open confessional categorizations and nomenclatures that position religion and religiosity singularly within Christian and White discursive structures.[1] In the case of Black religion, as both a field of study and a categorization of material religious practice, it is also critical to conceptualize religious experience as expansive beyond the confines of Black Christianity and the Black church. The study of Black religion in America should draw upon theorizations and sources that reflect the uniqueness of African Americans' collective experiences through which they find meaning in response to the vicissitudes of life in an anti-Black society.[2] Following cues from humanist scholar of religion Anthony Pinn, who frames Black religion as a meaning-making process meant to foster a healthier identity and sense of personhood, I position identity formation as religious concern. The (re)creation, reconfiguration, and reimagining of human identity markers, including gender, bears the quality of the religious to the extent that it speaks to the unique drive within all persons that aspires to personal transcendence, fulfillment, and meaning.

Identity formation is a salient feature in the theory and methodology of religious studies. Critical features of human identity include social and material realities such as race and gender. This book gives particular attention to gender identity constructs that center African American males. As a Black male, I adopt a self-reflexive approach, but in doing so I am also implicating myself as a social actor with vested interests in the outcomes and consequences of this line of inquiry. In *Strategic Acts in the Study of Identity*, Vaia Touna and the authors theorize how identity formation is shaped through identification. As a feature of self-construction, identification processes create discursive lines that shape myriad identity options. Social actors who then go on to make identity claims "are also dividing the world into classes of things [by] employing classifications that reflect our interests."[3]

Personal interests, therefore, cannot be divorced from the identity claims and identity *visions* of Black manhood that I bring to this book. In naming my vested interests forthrightly, I can be honest about what this book means and what it accomplishes, given my social location and identity as Black and male. To be sure, dispassion has its place in academic writing, but it can also guise a false neutrality that denies how certain subjects and intellectual tasks come alive for an author. On this score, I also adopt womanist ethicist Katie Cannon's insistence that one "do the work that one's soul must have." The pages to follow are in part for me a humanizing effort in envisioning Black male identity and manhood that run counter to the portrayals, depictions, and imagery that energize racist misandry, within and beyond our various academic spaces and in larger society.[4] In working through (re)presentations of Black manhood to foster new approaches to Black male identity and subjectivity, following Cannon, I envision Black male identity formation as *soul work*—it is a life-affirming praxis that seeks to "give an account of oneself" that both reshapes the scope of Black men and boys' selfhood and resists the splintering and reduction of their selfhood to caricatures and pathologies.[5]

In taking on this soul work, this book locates within Black religious thought, including womanist discourses, interpretive space to proffer alternative conceptions of Black male identity. Stacey Floyd-Thomas writes that as a cultural production, womanism provided Black women "an emerging consciousness that not only provided a new outlook on life but also ushered forth a new epistemology."[6] Central to womanist mechanisms of knowing, as I argue, is a relational orientation grounded primarily in a commitment to Black women's self-actualization and empowerment as well as to the survival of Black women's larger communities. I include womanist *conceptions of relationality* as an informative and instructive interpretive marker in my approach to the envisioning of Black male identity. Womanist relational epistemologies, particularly the conceptual framing introduced in Alice Walker's *In Search of Our Mothers' Gardens: Womanist Prose* and adopted by later womanist and Black male scholars of religion, provides the hermeneutical foundation for this book.

In "Masculinity, Race, and Fatherhood," theologian Vincent Lloyd writes, "Blackness means always being on the wrong side of worldly norms."[7] There is a permanent outsiderism that characterizes Black existence and thus grounds the inability to experience wholeness in oneself—one's humanity, one's identity. Lloyd's commentary on the cursory racial and gender taxonomy in which maleness is synonymous with Whiteness and power furthermore indicates a relational category in which Black "maleness is, in fact, a de-gendered negation of white maleness that is feminine because of its subordinate position to white masculinity," and so on along the race/gender continuum.[8] Too often, topics in gender studies and gender theory are presumed to be the domain of societal and interpersonal issues that singularly impact women. Gender theorist Judith Butler comments at length on the metaphysical and theoretical problems that stem from the presumption of "stable" notions of both women and gender in feminist theory in *Gender Trouble*, noting how fixed and static gender binaries deny the full range of gendered subjectivities.[9] What is often disregarded in gender theory, leading to these conceptual problems, says Butler, is the untethering of sex, race, class, and region from gender identity formation. Gender is not a "free-floating artifice" but rather is situated by "relative point[s] of convergence among culturally and historically specific sets of relations."[10]

When considered along with racial stratification, the meaning and the function of gender for racialized groups render women and men in these demographics illegible or problematically legible.[11] The racial and gender regimes that hold sway in White, Western societies deconstruct Black manhood and woman—resulting in social ostracization outside of the categories of human meaning. For our purposes, what this ultimately suggests is a unique categorical racial taxonomy that renders Black men vulnerable and delimits the life options and prospects for wholeness, including the terms of public perception. It is often difficult to see Black males as vulnerable because of sex and due to the outright relegation of all masculinities to the domain of dominance and power, without accounting for the denial of access to power, systemically, to racially subordinated males. I am sympathetic to Robert Staples's view that "black [men's] subordination as a racial minority has more than cancelled out their advantages as males in the larger society."[12] Like Black women, Black men also bear burdens of what womanist ethicist Emilie Townes has referred to as the racial fantastic hegemonic imagination and its physical, psychological, and ontological regimes of terror imposed upon Black flesh and personhood.[13] The experiences of Black men on this account bespeak a particularized kind of oppression—a gendered and ontic racism that reflects a multidimensional impetus "constantly operating to socialize the public into believing that, given the savage nature of Black men and boys, the various cruelties and stereotypes used to dehumanize them [and destroy them] are accurate."[14]

The ontological, discursive, and social construction of the race/gender matrix ultimately renders Black men irredeemably pathological. Curtis J. Evans's study of the representations of Black religion during the twentieth century also comments upon the nature of this pathologizing, revealing how the racial romanticism of White liberalism contributed to the stereotyping of Blacks as innately religious and emotional, prompting the view that Black religion and culture "was feminine . . . and that blacks lacked the moral and intellectual capacity to achieve manhood."

Manhood here, however, is linked to a universalized category arresting the collective group's lesser civilization.[15] In light of this history, and in light of the racial and gender theories that animate racist ethnologies and that function in some spaces of gender theory in academia, the lyrics from a Stevie Wonder song ring true: we have been a misrepresented people.[16] Black male identity has been overdetermined as innately pathological. Black males are locked beyond the bounds of the ontological and anthropological registers of human being.[17] What I endeavor in this book is in part a response to this misrepresentation and overdetermination, and I spotlight the need for more constructive work on the complexities of Black/male experiences in African American religious thought. In response to the pathologizing of Black manhood and Black male identity, I advocate a broader humanizing cultural project of revitalization and reconfiguration that rejects the destructive and dehumanizing characterizations of Black males by amplifying the humane, the relational, and the communal as hallmarks of Black manhood.

Returning to the Garden: Learning from Alice Walker and Womanists

It may vex some that I began a book on Black males and manhood citing words from Alice Walker. Walker's gender politics, her expansive spirituality, and the coalescence of these facets of her life and work articulated through womanism as a cultural expression and designation of Black women's space may seem ideologically ill-suited, at best. Walker's literary writings and cultural criticism on racial, sexual, and gender-based landscapes in American society and throughout the African diaspora are often met with controversy from male critics. Calvin Hernton once described the source of the ideological and cultural loggerheads between Walker and Black male critics as linked to the growing autonomy of Black women writers, the culturally influential impact of Black women's literature during the seventies and eighties (featuring the self-disclosure of Black women's interior lifeworlds), and the recognition of Black women's writings among the White literary elite.[18] Hernton also linked Black male criticism of Walker to their perception that spotlighting sex and gender oppression within Black communities indicated a counterproductive and counterrevolutionary thrust that sacrificed race loyalty, racial progress, and the cohesion of (patriarchal) Black family structures for women's empowerment. This view was most amplified in the writing of cultural critic and novelist Ishmael Reed, who described the source of Black men's skepticism and disapproval of Walker's depictions of Black life, gender, and sexuality, not only within the novel but also in the 1985 film portrayal of *The Color Purple*: "In the film *The Color Purple* . . . all of the myths that have been directed at black men since the Europeans entered Africa are joined. In this film, black men commit heinous crimes against women and children, and though defenders of Walker's book upon which the movie was based, argue that these creations were merely one woman's story, critics in the media have used both the book and the movie as excuses to indict all black men."[19]

When critiquing the film version of *The Color Purple*, it is natural, following Reed's concerns, to raise larger questions about the gender politics that shape cinematic and dramatic choice. Why do, for example, Steven Spielberg and the cadre of producers and screenwriters not examine the full scope of Walker's portrayals of Mr./Albert and his son, Harpo? As Hazel Carby has illustrated, American film and television have often been mediums through which anxieties and questions pertaining to race, sex, class, and gender are resolved. In this light, *The Color Purple* could be viewed, for good or for ill, as prominent commentary on gender politics among Black women and men in the American South. In the case of Black men and the overall scope of racial representation, however, Carby rejects the male-centric presumptions that set the standard for charting racial progress, but also recognizes how popular culture narratives about Black masculinity function as a site for larger conversations on race and gender.[20]

Some Black women scholars and critics, such as Trudier Harris, spoke to the heart of the identity politics surrounding the novel. Harris claims that "to complain about the novel is to commit treason against black women writers," despite the fact that "there is much in it that deserves complaint, and there are many black women critics in this country who would rather have their wisdom teeth pulled than be accused of objecting to it."[21] The prominence of the film and the novel, as cultural benchmarks that highlight Black women's literary production, effectively silenced voices of dissenting opinion.[22] Harris also criticizes how the "novel gives validity to all the white racist's notions of pathology in black communities."[23] Citing the loose familial units between Black women and men, absentee Black fathers and husbands, and male abusers as commonplace, routinized features of Black experience, Harris's critique on this point would appear to complement those of Reed and other Black men with negative reactions to the film and novel. Yet for all the possible strengths of Reed's insights on race and gender representation, he eventually distracts from these by relying upon problematic invectives against the male allies and supporters of Walker and other women writers, as "bimps and wimps," simplistic epithets toward any man who dares question a "proper" masculine response to cinematic emasculation, defies the norms and standards of male identity and behavior, or seeks to initiate conversations about the embodiment and charting of new parameters for a healthy masculinity.

I am sensitive to the politics of representation that underscores many of the ideological critiques of Walker's writing and views on gender, and in particular on Black men. Where I part company from Reed and other male critics of the period is on the rigidly polemical position taken on Walker's gender themes and how they are to be read. I do not agree with the impression that "many feminists and womanists would like to do away with men altogether and turn the world into a sort of postgraduate seminar of feminism."[24] Is it really fair to suggest Walker had/has misandrist ulterior motives in *The Color Purple* and in other works, to "deliberately [deprive] all the black male characters . . . any positive identity"?[25] Upon a fuller reading of *The Color Purple*, this is not the case at all. I find it more fascinating, following a nuanced approach, not only to consider what may be problematic in Walker's womanism, and its framing of Black men and Black masculinity, but also to try to grasp what is positive and affirmational of Black men's humanity and the capaciousness for growth in imagining an alternative gendered subjectivity.

To be sure, however, Black men have never been the point of departure for what has become womanist discourse or womanist approaches to theology, ethics, or religious studies broadly conceived. Frederick Ware observes that persons who are not Black women, but nonetheless center Black women's experiences, are doing womanist scholarship.[26] Whether or not the work I explore here represents a particular kind of scholarship is not my focus. I'm more interested in delving into the consequences of reinterpreting Black male experience and identity, in part through the intellectual, cultural, and philosophical paradigm of womanist thought. The epigraph from Alice Walker that begins this introduction offers a solid indication of the instructive capability of womanist discourses to inform and shape alternative visions of Black male identity and self-image. There is within womanist thought, including womanist religious scholarship, a relational impetus that constructs a useful frame for reflecting upon new visions of Black masculinity and manhood. Whatever controversies there may be within the overall scope of Walker's writings or gender politics, what I do remain convinced of is her desire to see Black women *and* men embrace healthier mechanisms of relating and self-understandings that position themselves and their communities in a better psychic, social, and communal space for survival and wholeness.

Turning to the opening epigraph featuring Curry's observations on the question of who Black men are and how we define, name, and reclaim ourselves, I believe, supplements Walker's aspirational vision of healthier Black manhood and womanhood. Walker made the claim that "whole black men can exist" during the Million Man March in October 1995. While much of the public opinion on the march was positive, there were some who took issue with the march's spiraling toward sexism, heteronormativity, homophobic assertions of manhood through the exclusion of gay men, and a general denial of the complex array of the markers of manhood that happen to deviate from patriarchal, heterosexual, and Judeo-Christian norms.[27] Walker, however, seemed to be pleased with how the march prompted Black men to name and reclaim authentic masculine space in which moments of recalibrative "regrouping" could then inspire the spiritual energy and creativity that ushered in the courage to imagine more livable futures. Walker's positive tone toward the prospect of evolving, wholesome, loving, and reciprocal embodiments of Black manhood suggests that her writing can be a useful interlocutor for reimagining Black male identity.

For those who read Walker's corpus of writing closely, the vision of Black male growth and the capacity for wholeness should not be particularly surprising. This much is obvious, as we will see, in her portrayal of both the regression and the redemption of Mr./Albert in *The Color Purple*. Walker's conceptualization of womanism bespeaks a foundational philosophical commitment to "the survival and wholeness of *entire people*, male and female."[28] The vision of womanism that Alice

Walker conceives has never been so exclusive that Black men are outright ignored, unremarkable, or irredeemable. While womanists are absolutely "separatists" when it comes to the establishment and need for insulated care communities solely comprising Black women, this should not suggest the kind of antagonism, hostility, and anti-Black-male provincialism that was perceived by Black critics who decried the publication of *The Color Purple*.[29] Walker's call for the embrace of the *entire* person would suggest both a material and an ontological charge. In calling for self-embrace and self-love, Walker's insistence that Black men explore the depth of themselves indicates a commitment to envisioning more livable worlds and futures for Black men in which love of self and a healthier self-regard can ground Black men's transition toward healthier and more holistic states of being (and becoming). Moreover, Walker discloses an optimism in the capacity of Black men to seek out new blueprints and models for Black manhood. If Walker's vision of womanism and relationality was not inclusive of Black men at all, I ask, why suggest Black male wholeness as remotely possible? Why not just castigate us all as irredeemable and let that be the end of the matter?

Obviously, this optimism—this aspiration to higher selfhood and manhood—is not one that Walker and the womanists who follow her are willing to reject. On the contrary, as I argue, womanists, and in particular womanist religious scholars, are not antagonistic toward Black men. True, womanists do not begin and end their work with Black males centered. That is neither their cultural nor their intellectual project, nor should it be. Further, all womanist criticism toward Black males is not rancor. I would therefore say to any critics of womanism, or to critics of this present work, that there ultimately needs to be space for more nuanced openness to both charitability and graciousness in accepting critique. In this work, I engage and reciprocate womanist epistemologies and ways of relating as I work through the quandaries and contestations of Black manhood.[30] In bringing their voices to bear upon Black men from both critical and aspirational postures, I reveal the possibilities and promise of a *shared* discursive and communal revisioning effort that can effectively reconfigure notions of Black male identity. This work is critical because it does not shy away from the problematic facets of some formulations of masculinity in need of critique. It is aspirational because it builds upon an optimistic vision of healthy explorations of masculinity among Black males, while spotlighting the inclusivity and insights of womanist religious scholarship in concert with other literary, critical, and theological sources.

The Intervention of Black-Male-Oriented Scholarship

Alongside the relational foci central to Walker's womanism and as expressed in the womanist religious scholars who are key interlocutors, this book is also premised upon a categorical imperative to humanize and validate Black male experiences. I do not consider this motivation to be opposed to the womanist relational vision. In the same way that womanism is rooted in a liberationist orientation that works to materialize wholeness for women and men, devoting that same energy specifically to Black male flourishing and well-being is, from my perspective, a continuation and extension of womanism's capacity to teach and reach beyond its intended community. Of course, we have at our disposal multiple voices and perspectives from Black-male-oriented scholarship that work to achieve the same ends. In juxtaposing those perspectives with womanist thought, I illustrate the shared humanistic commitments of both.

In *The Man-Not: Race, Class, Genre, and the Dilemmas of Black Manhood*, Tommy J. Curry laments the dearth of scholarship on the empirical realities of Black men and boys as it relates to their particular self-understandings, practices, and even attitudinal postures on gender identity. Too often, says Curry, Black males' identity structures are overdetermined and predetermined by racist and misandrist theories that rely upon unsubstantiated popular culture conceptions of Blackness/maleness as problematic and unworthy of nuanced interpretive approaches that guide our understanding. In describing the intellectual, theoretical, and philosophical approaches to Black male experience as the anchor point of Black male studies, Curry writes,

> Black male studies begins with this premise—this epoche: this declaring of Black male life as worthy of study that arrests/suspends the caricatures of current research described under the rubric of Black masculinity. Black male studies refuses the pathologization of Black men and boys as theoretical advance and proposes the empirically

informed accounts of Black male life—its indisputable value—as the basis to condemn and object to Black male death.³¹

The center of Curry's criticisms that in part inspire the turn to, and the engagement of, Black male studies is rooted in a sustained critique of racist and misandrist caricatures that have shaped perceptions of African American boyhood and manhood. The power of these perceptions relies upon outdated historiographies, ethnological studies, and cultural attitudes that traffic in the presumptions of moral, physical, and ethnic deficiencies of Black males. In addition to the racial and political regimes that give these caricatures staying power, Curry also critiques current methodological and theoretical approaches to the study of Black males as gendered subjects—namely the inability of universal categorizations to account for how "Black males are understood as adaptive and dynamic" subjects and burdened by both race and gender.³²

In writing about Black male identity as a topic in African American religious thought, my objective is also to create discourses that break open the static, constipated, and reductionist terms under which Black males are imagined. The act of reimagining and reinscribing alternative visions of Black manhood involves identity negotiation as a praxis of liberation.³³ Identity negotiation is an agential act of insurrection to the degree that it enables Black males to safeguard, amend, modify, and *create* authentic selfhood in response to varied racial and social orders premised upon an anti-Black calculus. Self-creation, in this sense, speaks to the question of agency and the internal drive that aspires to personal transcendence and a higher meaning above the discursive and ontological impositions of others—an exploding of the limited and bastardized constructions of identity, humanity, and individual purpose that are not of one's own making. I reject the ideological rigidities stemming from the accepted and prevailing truisms pertaining to Black manhood.³⁴

In this rejection, I am aware of certain risks, which in part concern some of Curry's apprehensions about the academically oriented disciplinary prescriptions for thinking and writing about Black men. These risks are of the very same caliber that I believe is traced to the early hostilities I experienced as a graduate student. In reflecting upon these experiences further, I am pressed to wonder to what extent those responses to my research early on were/are inspired by my exceeding the disciplinary bounds against which Black males are "properly" imagined, studied, or reflected upon. In a word, were/are the questions I'm raising—the interpretive schemas I deploy, the interlocutors I engage—deemed insufficient because they don't render Black men sufficiently deficient or pathological? Curry speaks to the charged nature of academic identity politics and censorship in this regard, noting that "to study Black men and boys outside their descriptions as problems is taken to be heresy; any study of Black male vulnerability is taken to be at odds with, and thereby an erasure of, Black female suffering and, more generally, theoretically irrelevant, despite Black males' actual social condition."[35] In this sense, to envision Black manhood beyond the strictures of the pathological and problematic is to disrupt what is presently acceptable and highly regarded in gender theories of Black men, broadly speaking.

While Curry minces no words on the politically contested terrain of Black male identity as a subject of cultural criticisms of race and gender, and specifically cites some segments of feminist theory as culpable in the maintenance of blanket castigations of manhood as inherently pathological,[36] it is his insistence upon the importance of recognizing the *humanity* (and vulnerability) of Black men and boys that I find particularly critical to this present work. Black male studies discourses humanize and recognize the material and interior lifeworlds of Black men and boys in ways that complicate and nuance the telling of their stories and experiences. The humanistic impetus of such work is a welcome complement to womanism's commitment to survival and wholeness. The contrasting aspects of my observation on this point extend beyond mere optimism. As I see it, conceptually, Black male studies is ideologically linked to womanism in its demand for Black males to recover and reclaim their own stories, identities, and humanity. There may of course be a distinction between womanist thought and Black male studies regarding the most powerful route or means of Black males' reclamation and recovery, but the demand as such remains operative in both spaces.

Womanist thought has an instructive capacity in the reimagining of Black manhood, but it remains a discourse and cultural production by and for women of the African diaspora. It is therefore necessary for Black males to draw upon their own discursive spaces, experiences, and historiographies in the re-creation of their identities. It is in this way that Black male studies provides a useful interlocutor in my efforts to reimagine Black male identity from multiple vantage points. In bringing together womanist discourses and Black-male-oriented scholarship, I show how there is space for methodological inclusiveness on the part of those, like myself, who are not womanists. Methodologically, this inclusiveness parallels that of a fine dance. In speaking of the need for a "womanist dancing mind" in the study of the particularities of religion, Emilie Townes suggests that scholarship should be informed by an openness that seeks to know and grasp those worlds, ideas, and persons outside of the ones we know to come to greater understanding and connection.[37] So along with womanist literature and religious thought, I look to Black male religious scholarship, literature, and theologies as sources for further insight on Black men and gender.

In bringing these realms together, the emphasis is not their widely variable ideological, theological, or political commitments but rather how all rely upon a moral, social, and humanitarian vision that promotes wholeness in Black males. While the scope and intended audiences of each realm may differ, this should not suggest that there is no space for overlap or creative exchange. I situate these discourses within what theologians Garth and Karen Baker-Fletcher refer to as a "diunital framework"—a discursive and reciprocal meeting of minds toward a common purpose: the establishment of a relational framework for understanding human selfhood and further, tying this framework to religious, theological, and gender-based discourses involving African American males.

Overview

The chapters in this book chart and explore the implications of relational identity formation as central to a new vision of Black manhood. Because this book is prescriptive and imaginative in its construction and larger scope, the chapters build upon one another sequentially, with each subsequent chapter offering another hermeneutical extension beyond the arguments and approach from the previous chapter(s). The first chapter, "Charting Relationality in Black Religious Thought," analyzes womanism as introduced in the writings of Alice Walker—noting in particular its relational orientations, which are taken up by womanist religion scholars and further, gender-progressive Black male religion scholars.

This chapter also describes "dialogical centralism" as the *methodological relational praxis* that unites Black women and men toward a common purpose: the establishment of a relational framework for understanding human selfhood and wholeness and, further, tying this framework to religious, theological, and gender-based discourses involving African American male identity.

Chapter 2, "Black Manhood in the Writings of Alice Walker, Zora Neale Hurston, and Toni Morrison," offers a literary and character analysis of Black men in Walker's *The Color Purple*, Zora Neale Hurston's *Their Eyes Were Watching God*, and Toni Morrison's *Home*. The characters Mr./Albert, Vergible "Tea Cake" Woods, and Frank Money, respectively, are analyzed on the basis of their representation of Black men who struggle to embody relational identities. In my review of these figures, I advance the argument that within womanism, including literary production, the transformative and wholesome depictions of complex and evolving Black manhood reveal a creative source for reimagining Black male subjectivities that call into question the presumption of patriarchy as central to manhood. Chapter 3, "James Baldwin, the Black Church, and Queering the Masculinist Oeuvre," locates James Baldwin's *Go Tell It on the Mountain* and *If Beale Street Could Talk* within masculinist African American literature. Taking theoretical cues from Keith Clark's *Black Manhood in James Baldwin, Ernest J. Gaines, and August Wilson*, I first argue that Baldwin's work is masculinist in its featuring of complex notions of Black manhood built upon relational identities. Following this, I then address the ties between Baldwin's writings and queer religious discourses due to the capacity of his complex portrayals of Black manhood to rupture easy categorizations of gender by centralizing male vulnerability, cross- and dual-role partnering/parenting models, and less rigid sex and gender roles. Given Baldwin's own upbringing and the religious themes animating his life, I also discuss Baldwin's writing as indispensable for queer religious thought, focusing on how his work advances a critique of sexual and gender mores that find expression in conservative wings of African American Christianity.

The fourth chapter examines the theological visions of Howard Thurman and Martin Luther King, specifically tapping into their respective relational and communal insights. Thurman and King have long been considered central to the cohesiveness of the Black theology project, but what I seek to do is apply the relational features of their perspectives to gender identity formation. I review religious biographies on Thurman, along with *Jesus and the Disinherited*, to foreground the "other-focused" quality of his cultivation of a unique Black spirituality and social mysticism. Through King's writings, speeches, and sermons, I address his idea of the Beloved Community, with further attention to its vision of transformative capacities for both individual and society. This chapter argues that the relational themes central to the religious, social, and theological visions of Thurman and King are useful in their capaciousness to reimagine gender identity and are foundational for a *relational turn* in Black male theologies. The final chapter, "On Black Male (Re)Covery," begins with an examination of psychological and anthropological notions of self and humanity as the base for Black male growth and development. Within Africana intellectual paradigms, I locate, particularly in the writings of Kenyan Christian philosopher John Mbiti and Yoruba feminist theorist Oyèrónkẹ́ Oyěwùmí, anthropologies that stipulate how relationality conditions and nourishes the nature of the human. I introduce these discourses, as relational anthropologies, as a precursor for an ontology of (re)covery. (Re)covery is a self-safeguarding praxis grounded in an ongoing commitment to the renewal of relational selfhood as generative of one's being. I conceptualize (re)covery through insights in pastoral theology and counseling that privilege Black males. Ultimately, this chapter addresses (re)covered Black manhood as a return to that which is essential to the nature of the human but also proactively rejects the limitations and restrictions of domineering and hierarchical notions of masculinity, preferring an evolving, never-quite-finished identity open to reflection and revision, while also grounded in responsiveness and responsibility to others.

In the epilogue, I comment on Black masculinity as a space of possibility. Throughout the book, I work through womanist religious thought, Black male theologies, and Black men's and women's literature—with the goal of illustrating how these various sources all embody alternative expanded conceptualizations of Black manhood. In the process of deconstructing, reconstructing, and (re)covering Black manhood, a lingering question remains: "What is Black manhood at all?" Expanding upon this question further, I take some insights from Victor Anderson's critique of race and his religious philosophy of African American identity and human experience.³⁸ Following Anderson, I argue that transplanting Black masculinity and Black manhood from ideological, cultural, and racial regimes that restrict and dismiss Black male identity and experience provides an opportunity for Black men and boys to be more proactive in reflecting upon the scope of their identities. Anderson's critique of the limited and reductionist religious and cultural arrangements that constitute "authentic" Blackness or that establish the presumed "norms" for the landscape of racial progress assists my efforts to problematize rigid norms and standards for Black manhood. In rejecting the notion that Black male identity is (any)(thing) at all, I apply notions of openness, fluidity, and *possibility* as reference points. Drawing upon Roger Sneed's "ethic of openness" and Ashon Crawley's otherwise discourse foregrounds a way to sidestep the various discursive and cultural traps that delimit Black manhood and instead adopt an alternative hermeneutic that is unbound by rigid ideological and cultural tethers. In linking Black male identity formation to possibility, therefore, I reject "ontological Black masculinity"—the fixity that designates impositions upon Black manhood that deny Black males the agency to name, cultivate, and reimagine their identities on their own terms, and ultimately realize their own drives toward fulfillment, purpose, and flourishing.

1

Charting Relationality in Black Religious Thought

In commenting upon the struggles for liberation among our forebears across the span of African American experience, history, and culture, Christian ethicist Darryl Trimiew observed that "our exemplars were moral paradigms precisely because they did not see themselves as merely individualistic selves. Rather, they tethered their identities completely to the well-being and thriving of their communities, with the understanding that their destinies were interwoven therein.[1] Previous generations across the African diaspora are remarkable because they linked selfhood to a sense of responsibility to and for others' well-being, edification, and fulfillment. As a "responsibilist" self, notes Trimiew, one is tasked with understanding one's role in being responsive to the humanity of others. As an ethical posture and praxis, responsibilism is geared toward the practice of morally just behavior at the individual level—at the macro level pertaining to governance and policy formation, and as a basis for smaller scale community building, particularly among Black faith communities. Nestled within this framework is the concept, and ultimately the aspiration and praxis, of relational selfhood.

This chapter serves as a preamble that outlines Black religious, theological, and cultural underpinnings of relationality as well as the centrality and criticality of this interpretive scheme in the lives and formation of Black male identity. Theorizations of the construction of Black masculinity have long been central to sociologies of race in Black and Afro-American studies. Robert Staples's classic work, *Black Masculinity: The Black Male's Role in American Society*, argued that Black manhood is largely born through conflict "with the normative definition of masculinity."[2] Staples's perspective frames Black masculinity and manhood as a kind of *lack*—suggesting an active gender and racial regime undermining Black men's agency within their familial structures, support networks, and economic and political opportunities. Writing about the socialization of Black males, Leah

Wright Myers cites threats of emasculation, dehumanization, and the impingement of notions of inferiority as critical to Black men's early subject formation within the context of anti-Black racism in America.[3] This, of course, suggests that Black manhood is formed under crisis. The crisis of Black manhood reflects a unique gendered racism that targets African American males, diminishes their life options, and inveighs negatively on the prospects of positive self-image.[4] In his reflections upon Black boys' gender socialization, Staples notes the prevalence of many Black male youths' turn to violence and hyperaggression as authentic markers of manhood. The adoption of antisocial and destructive expressions of masculine identity are not innate to Black males but rather, remain accessible as "alternatives and opportunity structure[s] for other expressions of masculinity [remain] blocked by forces of institutional racism."[5]

There have been several studies on the impact of racial discrimination upon the practice and expressions of manhood among racially subordinated males, in terms of identity formation, attitudinal postures on women and gender, and family structures.[6] What motivates me, however, is the cultivation of new frames and "opportunity structures" pertaining to the expression and embodiment of authentic Black manhood. If it is true, as Staples notes, that alternative conceptualizations of Black manhood are denied or ignored—due to the feelings of powerlessness and disillusionment spurred by racism (and anti-Black misandry)—why not address this dearth of models for alternate Black male subjectivities? I privilege relational constructions of Black manhood as one such possibility in the imagining and envisioning of Black male subjectivity. To this end, the objective of this chapter is to uncover relationality in Black religious scholarship—primarily as cast in the work of womanist scholars in theology and ethics, and Black male theologians. In the perspectives of each, there is a relational emphasis that envisions intersubjective and communal identity. While I do not frame relationality as the singular or exhaustive reference point for Black male identity—nor as proprietary to Black men—I emphasize the relational interpretive scheme to illustrate how Black religious thought may offer new possibilities to recognize, foster, and safeguard new visions of Black male identity.

Dialogical Centralism as Method

In bringing together womanist religious scholarship and Black male scholars of religion, true to the relational themes of this book, I do so with a dialogical impetus in mind. The methodological and theoretical approaches I employ build upon reciprocity and shared exchange, looking to the larger end of self-constitution and identity formation among Black males. My rationale in illustrating the ties and areas of contrast in these realms of Black religious thought is premised upon my admitted bias toward a relational and collaborative hermeneutical approach. I openly admit my bias to be forthright in naming my inclination toward engaging materials in Black religious scholarship that help recover the relational underscoring of the identity formation I envision for Black manhood. It is also important to note, however, that while Black religious voices and scholarship are my primary interlocutors, and intentionally so, the resources compiled in this work were not selected on a provincial disciplinary basis. That is, I have maintained a desire, in my methodological approach, to be open to additional perspectives. In my elaboration upon dialogical centralism, I am particularly indebted to insights in feminist and Christian theological paradigms and womanist theology and ethics.

In *Changing the Subject: Women's Discourses and Feminist Theology*, Mary McClintock-Fulkerson argues that the formation of a more inclusive feminist theology necessitates the rejection of identity politics insisting that women share universal characteristics and instead embraces interpretive schemes that distill discursive power dynamics that shape how people are characterized and treated. McClintock-Fulkerson advocates decentering personal interests while being grounded in an honest appraisal of how all persons, as social and historical agents, make claims about the identities of others that reflect certain interests. This deconstructive approach allows greater awareness of "the role of our own definitions in constructing the other, as well as make us understand that we have no access to what is real outside of our power-laden constructions."[7] What McClintock-Fulkerson's theology and ethics calls for is the acceptance of the full scope of the other as instructive and informative for one's point of view. Moreover, this entails accepting the fullness of and alterity of others sans our own attempts at reducing them to our own interpretive machinations. Attention to actual, concrete others—attention to their unique individuality and perspectives—captures well the basis of dialogical centralism as my method for reading and juxtaposing womanist religious thought and Black-male-oriented scholarship.

The other-directed impetus grounded in attention toward the material and social realities of others is also well articulated in conversational and dialogical vantage points that ground pluralistic approaches to the study of religion and culture. Catholic theologian David Tracy suggests that dialogical approaches assist in constructing space for worldviews and theological frameworks that are inclusive and navigate contemporary societies and cultures and thus represent an ethical posture toward relationality in the present age.[8] Dialogical theologies privilege pluralism and embrace polyvocality—the realities and nuances of which become the vehicle of discourse in which the perspectives and voices of others are validated, recognized, and affirmed. The centralizing of conversation as giving due regard and genuine response to otherness, plurality, and difference illuminates the relational and reciprocal themes within womanist thought.

To revisit again the notion of the womanist dancing mind, which draws upon Toni Morrison's essay of the same name, Emilie Townes observes that the dancing mind approach calls forth an interdisciplinary methodology featuring a mix of religious, ethical, and theological discourses characterized by openness to others—welcoming "the unknown rather than rush[ing] to name it, control it, and dominate it."[9] Embracing difference is grounded within an open-ended exchange between persons and personalities toward the larger end of creating coalitional, multivoiced, and multiperspectival praxis for scholarship and activism in the twenty-first century. The dancing mind—a psychic-relational orientation, weaves and creates *with* the full presence of other voices and thrives in the context of building new futures in which the care for and well-being of others is axiomatic. It is marked by a *thinking with*, rather than thinking against, other persons—other communities. This relational posture demands space for the acceptance of others because in listening to voices other than our own we can "learn from each other's struggles," to "better engage in more rigorous and thoughtful scholarship and action."[10]

In making use of dialogue as method in the reading and interpretation of womanist religious thought with Black male religious thought, a reciprocal (and coalitional) approach is invaluable. Reciprocity is not divorced from standards that cultivate authenticity. Of the nature of reciprocity, Katie Cannon writes, "For me it means giving back in kind and quality, mutually exchanging and being changed by each other's data and resources, paying back what I have received" from others.[11] What I learn from Cannon on this point is simply that true reciprocity is consequential in an intersubjective, interpersonal, and interrelated sense. Reciprocal exchange holds the possibility of a shift in one's self-constitution, self-conception, and self-understanding. Authentic giving of oneself and receiving others breaks open the moments of self-disclosure that reshape and inform our realities as well as those to whom we respond. Although Cannon was describing the work of eradicating perceptions of the incompatibility of collaborative scholarship and citation practices between womanists and White feminists, Cannon's interpretation of reciprocity spotlights the disciplinary congeniality that I seek to model by placing some of the implications of womanist religious thought into conversation with religious and cultural discourses by and about Black males.

As a Black male scholar writing about religion, relationality, race, and gender identity, Cannon's distinction between appropriation and reciprocity presses me to account for not only *how* I read and interpret womanism but also how *I* may be read in the process of dialogue. Along with other Black male religion scholars who are receptive to womanist scholarship, my reading is informed by an instructive and self-reflexive motivation. This simply means that my interpretive scope unfurls kernels of insight, truth, and meaning that reveal the relational orientations of womanist religious thought as an impactful and intervening paradigm through which Black men's self-understanding, personhood, and identity may be reshaped and reenvisioned. Anthony Pinn noted that engaging womanist thought prompted a more vigilant awareness of his embodiment as Black and male and how this shapes moral and ethical obligations among and toward women students and colleagues and generally spotlights features of his everyday existence in the material world.[12] Likewise, in emphasizing the instructive purpose of womanist discourses as central to how I envision and conceptualize Black male identity, my approach avoids absconding from womanist insights with "questionable authority"[13]—which in this case would indicate a failure to consider the transformative capacity of womanism to inform personal and communal conceptions of Black manhood. Cannon's litmus test for reciprocity is measured by ethical responsiveness—one that requires returning that which has been given "from a place of mutual dependence, action, and influence."[14] A truly dialogical and reciprocal impetus underscoring collaborative and coalitional intellectual frameworks cannot be premised upon lip service. Returning in kind what has been cultivated in womanist religious thought and scholarship is exemplified by holding myself and this work accountable to the expanse, reach, and contributions of womanists by thinking through the implications of the discourse for healthier models of self and community in Black male life.

In *My Sister, My Brother: Womanist and Xodus God-Talk* (1997), Karen and Garth Baker-Fletcher talk about the necessity for "diunital thinking" among Black women and men on gender. Diunital thinking "[appreciates] the tensions of difference. It affirms the facticity of contrasts, opposites, and apparently conflicting coexistence."[15] The unison of multiple perspectives and points of view provides for more robust interpretations of society and world and illustrates how identity formation need not be unidimensional but is fluid, open, and evolving. If we are to authentically grapple with the meaning, making, and molding of more liberating spaces for the development of men's and women's selfhood, the process of engagement cannot be one-sided or rely on guesswork about the worlds and experiences of others. This is a call to truly see others, to respond to them, and to remain open to them in all their fullness and complexity. This level of engagement and shared concern reflects a cultural and conversational zeitgeist founded upon the sustained, mutually reinforcing meeting of points of view that are diverse and distinct but nonetheless committed to personal and communal liberation and fulfillment. As I likewise center womanist religious thought to spotlight and reimagine Black manhood along with the voices of Black men, the dialogical focus exemplifies, in methodological practice, a reciprocal interdisciplinarity. While womanist religious thought and Black-male-oriented religious scholarship are independent of one another with different intellectual and ideological commitments, the shared humanistic focus of both can illustrate new intersections for reflection upon Black religious thought, cultural criticism, gender identity, and Black men.

Walking to Canada Together: Womanist Relationality

In her 1983 book, *In Search of Our Mothers' Gardens: Womanist Prose*, Walker outlined her vision of Black womanhood and constructed an unapologetic defense of Black women's agency, health, autonomy, and critical awareness. Walker's innovative creation of an approach to Black women's empowerment issued forth a communal commitment to the uplift and healing of Black women, men, and children. A womanist is the "purple" feminist complement to the "lavender" quality of (White) feminism. Womanism is a representational category and epistemology related to Black feminist sensibilities as expressed in Black women's lives, spaces, and cultures. In an earlier essay that actually predates the publication of *In Search of Our Mothers' Gardens*, Walker contrasts womanism and feminism, noting that "a 'womanist' is a feminist, only more common."[16] Walker's womanism inaugurated "a new way of talking about the relationship between women, social change, the struggle against oppression, and the quest for full humanity."[17] Womanism provided a new lexicon and intellectual, spiritual, and artistic source materials for Black women's cultural expression and is a counterpoint to universalized framings of women's empowerment that decenter experiences of marginalized women of color. However, womanism is also a powerful mechanism through which Black women can name and negotiate their own realities and identities. This is an important clarification because while womanism shares in the analytical resources and categories of modern feminism, it still perpetuates itself through an intersectional focus that is more suited to the social, racial, and sexual experiences of Black women.

While the womanism Walker outlines is strident in its insistence upon Black women's autonomy and even more steadfast in its defense of the integrity of Black woman selfhood, it is the *relational ethos* that I single out as instructive for Black religious thought and constructions of human identity. Walker's articulation of womanism included a four-part definition. Given the ties between the relational and identity-based concerns that underscore this book, of particular note is the second part of the definition:

> Traditionally universalist, as in: "Mama why are we brown, pink, and yellow, and our cousins are white, beige, and Black?" Ans.: "Well, you know the colored race is just like a flower garden, with every color flower represented." Traditionally capable, as in: "Mama, I'm walking to Canada and I'm taking you and a bunch of other slaves with me." Reply: "It wouldn't be the first time."[18]

Walker clarifies the nature of womanist interpersonal relations, namely, the relation of self to oneself and the relation of self to community. In a conversation between mother and daughter, the daughter, true to the "audacious and courageous" character of womanish youth, takes up the task of liberating her community into healthier spaces of being. Walker posits this exchange as a powerful anecdote illustrating Black maternal wisdom, the precocious humanitarian concern of the younger generations to come, and the tenacity of communal love endemic to womanist relational orientations.

I understand relationality in womanist thought to be reciprocal in nature. In this sense, relationality and reciprocity are the base constructs through which I envision human connection and the human self—its actions and movements. This mode of relationality is premised upon intersubjective identity construction in which one is never disassociated from the "other"—whether this other resides within, beyond, or at the borders of one's community of origin. While I take my cues on the importance and depth of this framing of relation from Alice Walker initially, I would now like to give this interpretive scheme added theoretical weight through an analysis of the relational insights from representative thinkers in womanist religious thought, namely theology and Christian ethics. Underscoring my rationale for engaging these sources is the desire to illustrate the instructive purpose of womanist relational insights as a source for approaching identity configuration among Black men.

Traditional Communalism and Womanist Theo-ethics

According to Katie Cannon, womanism has an epistemological bent. It is a particular way of knowing the world and occupying space and place accordingly, in which Black women's moral and social conditions are the point of departure.[19] This way of knowing is relational and grounded within a communal context. In responding to the various crises of our communities as well as formulating positive structures and reflective spaces that give us the resources to survive, relational knowing is rooted in solidarity with others—which Kelly Brown Douglas calls "right relationship."[20] Stacey Floyd-Thomas links womanism and relational epistemology through the notion of traditional communalism, which is considered a central pillar of womanist ethics.[21] Returning to Alice Walker, traditional communalism as a tenet of womanist relationality is evident in the reply of the womanist daughter to the womanist mother in Walker's definition: "Mama, I'm walking to Canada and I'm taking you and a bunch of other slaves with me." Floyd-Thomas observes that womanist ethics frameworks that privilege relationality expand beyond the individual and the solitary. Traditional communalism embraces the "various gifts, identities, and concerns of Black people in general in order to use every resource available to strengthen the community as a whole."[22]

Traditional communalism also features an inter/intracommunal foundation for understanding peoplehood. As the mother in Walker's definition says to the daughter, "The colored race is just like a flower garden, with every color flower represented." The embrace of the diversity and syncretistic quality of human experience and representation is a womanist principle defining how inclusivity is central to its formation of selfhood. Traditional communalism rejects reductionistic and radically individualistic understandings of Black humanity and culture—whether those framings emerge from within the community itself or from those wedded to the distortions of the White fantastic imagination.[23] Communality and relationality provide anthropological foundations for what it means to be a person, a thematic intervention that will be explored in depth in the final chapter. Second, traditional communalism is central to womanist ethics because it provides inclusive space for difference but privileges the foundation for solidarity ethics endemic to survival culture in Black women's experience in an anti-Black and misogynistic society. The moral agency and moral wisdom(s) that emerge from Black women's achievement of authentic selfhood are connective and shared; they are never evoked through solitary means. This is a simple observation, but apt. The communal impulse of womanist ethics generates a cultural and psychic power among Black women and men to negotiate and name their own realities and identities *together* in a society determined to do it for them with insidious motivations. I single out this observation because it illustrates the shared experiences of Black women and men in an anti-Black world that highlights and renders indispensable the need for a coalitional praxis aimed at the negotiation of identity formation.

While the gendered and raced experiences of Black women and men differ, shared experiences of alienation and degradation provide enough overlap such that we are better off linked than estranged as we work to address and respond to the oppressions that impinge upon our lives and kill our souls. However, I am aware of womanists' demand for periodic and strategic separation to foster their health and well-being as well as advocate for themselves and their interests unfiltered. In responding to this demand, however, it is imperative that Black men recognize the prospective risks that naturally arise with any effort to engage and dialogue with Black women on our shared and unshared experiences. By risk I mean dialogical rejection. This is not a rejection of our humanity or integrity, but rather seems more linked to the prospect of a radical demarcation of Black women's space in a manner that necessitates distance from the communities and cultures of Black men.

While some may criticize this constellation or arrangement of womanist space, I affirm it primarily due to its centrality as a tenet of womanist self-love and self-care and due to the need for affirmational spaces in which Black women can make meaning out of the specificity of their lives and generate a liberating praxis that is explicitly responsive to their plight. Cheryl Townsend Gilkes observes that as a revolutionary and life-giving posture that responds to the cultural humiliation and the spiritual and material death of Black women and men, womanism calls forth an overarching commitment to healing, spiritual wholeness, the celebration of life, and righteous struggle.[24] Set-apart space and place for and by Black women offers periodic respite within the everydayness of life through which they can regroup and refocus shared energy as they address and name their realities in full. Walker's womanist call for moderate separatism, "periodically, for health," bespeaks this need.

M. Shawn Copeland's Eucharistic Solidarity

The overarching scope of M. Shawn Copeland's theological writing features the creative fusion of Catholic theology with womanist sensibilities. A significant quality of Copeland's thought focuses on Christian responses to the intersections of race and gender.[25] Copeland's reframing of theological anthropology within *Enfleshing Freedom: Body, Race, and Being* is a work of discursive (re)membering—providing a context for thinking about the Eucharist, solidarity, and Christian community. In the application of his work on identity, otherness, and reconciliation toward the issue of gender, theologian Miroslav Volf observed that the nature of God, not human culture, should provide the primary framework for constitutive relationality among women and men.[26] Copeland explodes and refocuses this line of thought, namely by privileging Black women and Black women's bodies as points of reflection for theological anthropology and as incarnational subjects for Christological discourse. Copeland cites Black women as the "new anthropological subject" in Christian theology.[27] Making the Eucharist a trope for thinking through authentic relationality, Copeland suggests that the bodies of Black women are powerful representations of divine-human contact that uncover the meanings of the body under duress and social stratification and are useful mechanisms of relating that may assist the mitigation of the deadly consequences of this stratification. Central to my concerns, however, is Copeland's use of the *humanum* as a conception of radical human selfhood that is relational in orientation and movement. Before explicitly discussing this element of Copeland's thinking, background on the development of Copeland's notion of Eucharistic solidarity is appropriate.

Nanny, the main protagonist's grandmother from Zora Neale Hurston's *Their Eyes Were Watching God*, observed that "de colored woman is de mule of da world"—pointing to the heavy burdens and brutalization that represent Black women's lot in life. Hurston's portrayal of gender politics in the novel speaks volumes about the extent to which Black and minoritized women are often compelled to shoulder varied forms of physical and emotional labor.[28] I would be remiss not to also point out the dehumanization endemic to such a description of Black women and to reflect upon what this dehumanization might suggest when approached from a theological perspective. What are the material consequences of religious worldviews that validate and nourish anthropologies of Black women (and men) as inhuman beasts? As Copeland notes, the trajectory of Enlightenment and post-Enlightenment thinking is hallmarked by Eurocentric ideas about the superiority of White aesthetics and intellect and the civilizational march toward inevitable cultural dominance at the expense of non-White and non-Western communities. Taking Black women, their bodies, and their humanity as the point of departure, Copeland addresses the distortion of Black women's selfhood through a Christological reading linking the social positionality of Black women and their experiences with those of Jesus of Nazareth.

Citing the theological and ethical problems that accompany theologies that prioritize male and Eurocentric ideals on embodiment, Copeland suggests an alternative reading of the Black female body. The broken body of Christ was "subjugated in empire" and thus is a reminder that "provokes our interrogation of the new imperial deployment and debasement of bodies" who have likewise suffered and died at the hands of empire, whether linked to White supremacy, heterosexism, or misogynist underpinnings.[29] Framing Black women's embodiment as Christological reveals a crucial parallel. Referencing the historical destruction of the bodies of the Black women as the farthest down victims of *American* empire, Black women's bodies specifically invoke the *memoria passionis*—the "dangerous memory" and vivid reminder of Christ's suffering and death. The confrontation of this memory challenges our collective societal amnesia, refuses the cultural neglect of honest assessments of race and gender, and indicts indifference toward the suffering of Black bodies. The dangerous memories as recorded in the gospel writings bear witness to a hallmark of Christian reflection on the life and mission of Christ, specifically as mired in the varied networks of oppressive powers and principalities of his day. The biblical record of Christ's life provides a useful mirroring in the present for interpreting and articulating a theological anthropology of marginalized existence under the weight of a racist and sexist regime.

Womanist articulations of the centrality of Black women's bodies for theological reflection are noticeably apt for contemporary efforts to analyze the meaning and significance of state sanctioned violence against Black bodies and the role of faith communities in response. One gets a sense of this from womanist theologies that augment the cultural and racial critiques that galvanize the grassroots work of Black Lives Matter and other organizations that emphasize racial justice and parity in criminal justice applications. Eboni Marshall Turman, for example, provides a Christological interpretation of the death of Sandra Bland. Bland, a Black woman who died under mysterious and suspicious circumstances in her jail cell after being arrested following a traffic stop, became a symbol of the brokenness of the militarism in American police culture and a moratorium on criminal justice as rooted not in reform but in the functional state-sanctioned terrorism against Black bodies. Turman's Christology of Sandra Bland is at once a theological critique of a racist criminal justice system and a call to remembrance for all broken, suffering, and displaced bodies that have suffered within its regime. In following Copeland's turn to Black women's bodies as anthropological subjects, Turman's framework lays bare the "logics of state-sanctioned neo-crucifixion"—contrasting the body of Jesus of Nazareth with the manifestation of the anti-body, the Black woman.[30] In highlighting the body of Jesus as a painful reminder of the inhumanity practiced upon Black female embodiment and selfhood, Copeland and Turman tie the messianic functions of Jesus's crucified body to the suffering bodies of Black women.

Following Copeland's turn to Black women's embodiment in theological anthropology is her formulation of Eucharistic solidarity. Eucharistic solidarity is a praxis-oriented envisioning of communality that refuses "the dynamics of domination" and provides "a new way of being in relation to God, to others, to self."[31] In grounding theological anthropology in Black women's varied experiences of the burdens of race- and sex-based oppression, Copeland powerfully rethinks the significance of racialized bodies and the divine body in Christian thought—speaking to the salvific consequence of Black flesh.[32] Copeland identifies the theological import of Black women's embodiment by linking it with divine authority. Copeland recalls and reconfigures the "audacious, willful, and courageous behavior" of womanist sensibilities in a way that centers

Black women's bodies as agential—bodies that move, act, and make their weight felt. Centering Black female bodies as proactive subjects transplants the presumption of authoritative White, masculine political and intellectual subject formation and ultimately a compels a "stance that is in direct opposition to most of what passes for culture and thought" in American religious thought and theological studies generally.[33] Copeland speaks to this defiant discursive move: "Bringing these realities together defies all religious, theological, and moral logic, for they signify opposing horizons of meaning. Eucharist and racism implicate bodies—raced and gendered bodies, the body of Christ."[34]

Copeland also adopts the Eucharist to suggest an embodied model of relational solidarity—implicating the movement and *agency* of Black women's bodies in the process of creating this solidarity. Within the Eucharistic gathering, the bodies gather and consume the bread and wine, which represent the body and blood of Christ. Black women establish and situate the terms of relational encounter and "embrace with love and hope those who . . . are despised and marginalized, even as [they] embrace with love and forgiveness those whose sins spawn the conditions for the oppression and suffering of others."[35] Within the Eucharistic framework, it is the initiation of mutuality—of interrelated caregiving, without regard for sex/gender—that is compelling and instructive. Finally, Eucharistic embodied solidarity is helpful insofar as it clarifies and exposes the problems associated with privileging male embodiment. By making Black women the primary agents of this vision of relationality, Copeland highlights the shared subjectivity of all women and men. In the Eucharist, *both* Black male and Black female bodies are living sacraments bespeaking the "real-symbolic unity between what we are as humans, even as the de-creation of Black bodies clarifies the cost of daring to em-body Christ in a morally degraded context of white racist supremacy."[36] Black bodies, particularly Black female bodies, contest racist and sexist ontologies of embodiment. Copeland's Eucharistic solidarity complicates the premium placed on maleness within intellectual, religious, and political spheres and privileges the bodies of Black women as having salvific and Christological authority.

The dynamism of Copeland's framing of solidarity is also underscored by her radical conception of the human self as reciprocal in orientation and movement, which she models after the life and mission of

Jesus Christ. Of Jesus's organic and reciprocal masculinity and embodied spirituality, Copeland writes,

> Through [Jesus's] preaching and practices, living and behavior, Jesus performed masculinity in ways that opposed patriarchal expressions of maleness through coercive power, control and exploitation of "other" bodies.... He nurtured men and women with word and touch, bread and wine, and water and fish. He reached out in compassion to the infirm, and took the lowly and forgotten, children and women to his heart.[37]

For Copeland, Jesus was "the Christ" through the communal character of his embodiment, complicating standard Christological formulations pertaining to the hypostatic union and other categories of the divine/human relationship. Jesus is defined and measured by the ways his life inspired and informs a higher conception of human identity, as "Jesus signifies and teaches a new way of being human."[38] Drawing upon the work of Edward Schillebeeckx, the radical quality of human selfhood outlined in this way is *humanum*.[39]

Humanum is full humanity; its telos is directed toward a higher end to be realized and achieved through the enactment and practice of interrelated and intersubjective identity formation in human life. Humanum is also a process of becoming that enlarges the evolution toward a higher consciousness of human self in relation to God and humankind and "reaches its term in the dynamic realization of human personhood." Copeland notes, "To be a human person is to be (1) a creature made by God; (2) person-in-community, living in flexible, resilient, just relationships with others; (3) an incarnate spirit, i.e., embodied in race, gender, sex and sexuality, culture; (4) capable of working out essential freedom through personal responsibility in time and space; (5) a social being; (6) unafraid of difference and interdependence; and (7) willing daily to struggle ... for the survival, creation, future of all life."[40] The humanum concept yields the following theological pronouncement on the need and value of a reciprocal interpretation of the human self: only among others in self-giving love is human identity found. God in the person of Christ was humanum par excellence, and Black women, whom Copeland situates as at the center of theological anthropology, as they have historically demonstrated the same embodied spirituality and solidarity exemplified in the life of Christ, represent humanum in a way that is instructive for other communities. Copeland's dynamic reading of the relational and reciprocal human self within community "entails recognition of the humanity of the other . . . along with regard for the other in her (and his) own otherness."[41]

The need for mutual, interrelated recognition within the praxis of embodied relational solidarity echoes the subject-to-subject relationality outlined within other perspectives in religious and philosophical ethics.[42] Copeland emphasizes this point by linking the recognition of the other with the principle of relational openness: "The principle of openness flows from this recognition and regard. Openness implies receptivity, that is, a willingness to receive the other and to be received by the other in mutual relationship, to take on obligation with and to the other."[43] Copeland establishes another foundational basis for reciprocal approaches to relationality by identifying the human subject as relational and social in nature and through her framing of a mutualized conception of communal life that recognizes the subjectivity of others and takes an interest in the other's well-being and fulfillment. The Eucharistic solidarity featured in Copeland's perspective outlines an understanding of individual human personality rooted in taking on obligation to others, the significant consequence being the development of a theological anthropology in which humans are most fully human within the context of service and care with and toward others and making this mechanism of relationality constitutive of one's identity.

The Relational Dance: Womanist Process Theology

Process thought, in both religious studies and philosophy, has played a significant role in the development of relationality as key concept of human experience, epistemology, and being.[44] Process thought privileges a *processual* view of material reality, including humanity and the cosmos and, in terms of a religious worldview, also adopts a personalist view of God that shifts, adapts, and is persuasive and persuaded rather than coercive toward human will and behavior. In contrast to more traditional theistic frameworks, process theological discourse imagines an "open and relational" theism in which God is described through the fusion of scientific and metaphysical categories. Theologian

Thomas Jay Oord, who embraces this open and relational paradigm, opines that what makes relational theology from the process perspective distinctive is (1) its affirmation of a personal God who is active and "hands-on" with human creation and (2) the view that God is affected by the actions of human creation.[45] While it is beyond my purview to outline the tenets of process religious thought,[46] describing the perspective briefly is necessary in shifting to the womanist theological perspective of Karen Baker-Fletcher, who is deeply influenced by process understandings of God as relational—this is particularly pronounced in her views on Christology and the environment.

In *Dancing with God: The Trinity from a Womanist Perspective*, Baker-Fletcher carries forth the process-influenced relational perspective and applies it to the nature of Christ. Womanism and the relational framework of process religious thought are ideologically linked, and in particular womanist discourse is a useful addendum to theologies of relationality: "Relational theologies of various types are influenced by and include womanist thought, finding that it enriches and enlivens the work of theology as a whole. . . . My hope is for the womanist theology I and other womanists write to influence all types of relational peoples and theologies around the globe, interculturally, across genders, and beyond all that threatens to divide us."[47] Baker-Fletcher's theology extends process thought, and the relational quality of process thinking is no more apparent than in her assessment of the personal and persuasive nature of God, who remains present and engaged with humanity. While Baker-Fletcher critiques process theism and clarifies her own particularized stance within the two realms of process religious thought in contrast to orthodox Christianity, it is not her rootedness in process thought that stands out. On this score, Baker-Fletcher's proposal and application of a "relational and integrative theology" provides much for consideration.[48]

Baker-Fletcher's attention to God's *responsiveness* to humanity clarifies and offers a theological appraisal of the relational framework I advocate for Black male identity formation. Baker-Fletcher classifies the core character of the Trinity as an essential relation to ground the God/world dynamic. The Trinity, in and through which God is manifest to humankind, says Baker-Fletcher, functions as divine dance. The dance metaphor captures the mode of relation between the distinct persons within the Trinity, as the dynamic among the Trinitarian persons model an ideal of relationality that can be transplanted into the social worlds of women and men.[49] Early Christian thought conceptualized this modality of relation within the Trinity through the notion of the *perichoresis*. Perichoretic imagery underscores the distinction of each member of the Trinity but also emphasizes its cohesion through relation. In the likeness of a good dance, the trinitarian persons—partners—are "mutually constitutive" of one another; each shares in and participates with the sharing and participation of the other.[50]

The relational character of the Trinity—the sharing, the mutuality, and the linkage of the individual to the communal—is applicable to the relational character of human experience and identity formation. As Baker-Fletcher notes, theology "is always about what God does in creation and in the midst of all peoples."[51] What human communities do in response to God grounds the nature of relationality, but the relationship is broken. Humans are estranged from God and one another because of "separation, violation, conflict, and disharmony."[52] Estrangement would appear to be the ontological categorical description of the state of humanity in the aftermath of its predilection for anti-relational modes of being. Baker-Fletcher's naming of this consequence as estrangement echoes Howard Thurman's assessment of hatred in *Jesus and the Disinherited*: "Hatred destroys finally the core of the life of the hater. While it lasts, burning in white heat, its effect seems positive and dynamic. But at last it turns to ash for it guarantees a final isolation from one's fellows. It blinds the individual to all values of worth, even as they apply to himself and to his fellows."[53]

Human communities have failed to live with one another authentically, affirmationally, and reciprocally because the relational identity shared in God's own nature is ruptured. Relationality is disregarded in favor of what Marcia Pally refers to as undue separability.[54] Separability, ontologically considered, is the tendency to imagine one(self) as disconnected from others outright. As God is relational and connective vis-à-vis God's tethering to humanity and the world, it is the task of human beings to embody and practice the same mode of relationality as the image of God (*Imago Dei*). For women and men, to be sure, embodying a deeper sense of relationality as central to identity formation is not mimicry of this divine impetus. What Baker-Fletcher's framing presses us to aspire to and, hopefully, embody is a deepening of our sense of self-fashioning and self-understanding—a more sustaining and connective manner of seeing self in relation to other and the whole of creation.

Relationality in Black Male Religious Discourses

At this juncture of the chapter it is important to follow up womanist insights on relationality with the perspectives of Black male religious perspectives that are influenced by and engage womanism as an instructive, transformative, and impactful discourse for Black men. This part of the chapter not only provides a sense of the breadth of the collaborative work and mutual engagement between Black male scholars and womanism but also preserves the dialogical impetus for engaging womanist scholarship in a reciprocal approach rather than mere appropriation. I have chosen to spotlight Black male scholars who've provided a significant analysis of womanist religious thought and literature to discuss nuances evident in their respective relational insights. On this basis, I review the theologies of Garth Baker-Fletcher and Dwight Hopkins. Engaging their work is illuminating because both of their perspectives wrestle with the meaning, purpose, and function of the human self in relationship. I illustrate how Black male theological perspectives are valuable to relational constructions of Black manhood in that they encroach upon the importance of articulating more robust notions of human selfhood as a critical feature of Black religious thought.

Xodus Manhood

Part 1 of *Xodus: An African American Male Journey* is aptly titled "Conversations, Deconstructions, Reconstructions." These categorizations perfectly capture the dialogical, aspirational, and reconstructive tasks of identity formation that ground many of the motivations that have inspired this book. In the case of Black women and men, the racist perception of their (non)personhood indicates a tragedy of misrepresentation, often intentionally and insidiously so. As Black women have been forced to survive (and thrive) amid ontological and material assaults that have introduced them to the gamut of identity distortions, Black men too have been linked to similar but distinctive modes of marginalization. Seeking an alternative way forward for Black male identity formation and fulfillment in contrast to the Eurocentric frames that dictate gender norms, religious meaning, and mythologies that "dis-member" Black and African personhood, Garth Baker-Fletcher proposes a "remythification" that "boldly asserts the right of Afrikans to create and propagate new myths to re-member within our psyches and our cultures what has been disremembered for too long."[55] Xodus theology and manhood is the result of Baker-Fletcher's schematic and interpretive shift.

Xodus discourse forms the basis for a decolonized theological, ethical, and interpersonal intervention for African American manhood and the collective Africana community. At the individual level, Xodus awakens Black men to a new awareness—to their community, their movement in the world, and the consequences of that movement. Honoring the memory of Malcolm X (among many other "elders"), Baker-Fletcher posits Xodus as psychospiritual liberation—a revolution for African American manhood that reconfigures and brings into being new modes of selfhood that reject and resist Euro-domination by embodying relationality, community, and social solidarity as an interpersonal and cultural praxis. Xodus is "Sepia-centric," privileging the internal and spiritual "process of moving from Euro-Space to Us-Space."[56] Xodus space and identity formation inaugurate a reorientation of values that more authentically reflect the life options and cultural vitality of African Americans. Central to the interdisciplinary and multireligious sources that build Baker-Fletcher's theological and ethical vision are Black women's literature and narratives, womanist thought, Afrocentric Christian theology and ethics, and pan-Africanism.

While Xodus sensibilities deconstruct Euro-conceived anthropologies of selfhood and humanity, it is the relational underscoring of Baker-Fletcher's understanding of human identity and notions of power that elicits particular attention. Living into Xodus identity and selfhood necessitates an initial "awakening"—the realization of the necessity to shed the values of Eurocentrism and thus move toward a new self-conception and identity that is rooted in the communal orientations that privilege the liberation and fulfillment of all. Xodus is marked by both individual and communal liberation, and the awakening process signals an internal, psychic, and spiritual shifting from the delimitations of White hegemony, specifically those grounded upon radical individualism. Regarding questions of male identity and manhood, Baker-Fletcher cites Euro-dominant epistemological and cultural foundations as being out of sync for African and African American men's flourishing and wholesomeness. The significant feature of Euro-dominance that Baker-Fletcher indicts is the misguided lust for power and control as central to self-identity. Traditional understandings of power in *White*, middle-class male structures are rooted in mastery, control, coercion, noncooperation, and hierarchy. This is "false power"—a power that diminishes others, is wielded in an elitist posture, and retards rather than advances equality and justice. What is needed, in terms of a theo-ethical response, says Baker-Fletcher, is a redefinition of power that is communal, cooperative, and mutually reinforcing and affirming as a cultural norm for everyday life and particularly as a feature of African American males' self-constitution.

"Xodus power" is relational power. This is a power that shares with others and privileges a spirit of shared concern for the edification, growth, and dignity of those in relationship. Black men cannot embrace and fully authenticate this modality of relationality without the disavowal of all mechanisms of being that are not grounded in intimacy, cooperation, and empathy. On this score, Baker-Fletcher proposes, in true dialogical, collaborative, and cooperative fashion, "taking our sisters seriously." Reorienting manhood toward genuine relational power, from an Xodus perspective, begins with a willingness to practice intentional listening to the stories and experiences of others—while being open to what is shared and heard. This listening and reception "is open to instruction, correction, criticism, and praise because its intent is to upbuild community" and is therefore "able to take the concerns, criticisms and pain of the sisters seriously."[57] The reorientation of values and conceptions of power in constructions of Black manhood and community, along with a dialogical impetus that is inclusive of Black women's humanity and wisdom, provide the necessary tethering of Xodus relationality to the influence of womanist thought. In this sense, this mode of listening occasions shared power.[58] Baker-Fletcher notes that the deconstruction of traditional models of Black manhood that are not conducive to Black life requires a "new form of shared power that requires openness, vulnerability, and readiness to change."[59] Critical listening—

the deep acknowledgment and reception of Black women's stories and experiences—can provide Black men the wherewithal to acknowledge and critique sexism.

As an Xodus principle, listening-as-relating is a significant practice for cultivating a relational/communal identity. As Baker-Fletcher writes, "Such listening becomes a way of becoming our best self"—a self that is internally and externally connected to the well-being, care, acceptance, and affirmation of others."[60] Essentially, Baker-Fletcher calls for the creative fusion of antiracism and antisexism as central to Black male identity formation. "[Womanism] calls for a community-wide vision of liberation, an inclusive norm that values and honors the unique experiences of Black women as well as Black men, and challenges African American males to work on our sexism as strenuously as we have worked to eradicate racism."[61] Building upon extended conversation with womanist religious scholars, Baker-Fletcher offers "Bodyself" and "liberatory partnership" models in order to articulate the relational dimension of the micro and macro implications of Xodus sensibilities in African American male life.

Bodyselfhood and liberatory partnership are pillars of Xodus manhood and Xodus relationality, as both present new conceptualizations of Black male identity within the context of community. The Bodyself is a "self-in-the-making, open to reform, challenge, criticism"—it is a processual, evolving interpretation of Black manhood rooted and grounded in the mutual, interconnected attributes previously described. Baker-Fletcher envisions the Bodyself as an *ideal* of manhood that one puts into practice and develops (and redevelops) over time, courageously taking up the challenge of discovering and embodying new ways to be male that trouble gender values and ideals socialized as acceptable and the "only way."[62] Baker-Fletcher's Bodyself model highlights Black manhood and personhood that thrive within relationships of egalitarian partnering, the sharing of resources and experiences, and the rejection of patriarchy and heteronormativity. Within an Xodus framing, men who embrace Bodyselfhood turn from nuclear-model notions of family, marriage, and fatherhood, in that such constructions of manhood relegate women and intimate partners to the private sphere and privilege male-as-head mindsets in familial and social arrangements and, as such, must be condemned as unacceptable standards for full communal liberation.[63]

There is evidence that the Bodyselfhood ideal is a cultural feature of Black male attitudinal postures toward ideas of manhood. Andrea Hunter and James Davis's study of African American men's definition of manhood found evidence of articulations of gender identity grounded in largely positive and relational values that are multidimensional—emphasizing responsibility and accountability, partnering/parenting, and spiritual and religious fulfillment. These men's framings of manhood showed marked contrasts with other common and stereotypical perceptions, which typically feature, among other traits, a preoccupation with physical strength, aggressiveness, and competition.[64] There is also evidence of racial and ethnic variations in perceptions of gender identity. Emily Kane revealed that African American women *and* men held greater egalitarian gender role attitudes in contrast to Whites and Latinos—noting that sensitization to racial disparity in part leads Black women and men toward greater commitments to gender equality than practiced by Whites.[65] Such ethnographic research provides a needed intervention against the unidimensional perceptions of Black men as intimate partners, spouses, and fathers.

As a cultural practice, the cultivation of Bodyselfhood within Xodus relationality also creates private and public discursive spaces that are of use to Black faith communities. This is an important intervention in light of womanist critiques of Black churches and, in particular, how those spaces cultivate ministries and gender paradigms that disfigure the personhood *and* leadership capacities for Black churchwomen.[66] Bodyselves within the context of ecclesial space eschew "sexist biblical hermeneutics that construct the roles of women to the private sphere of domestic concerns."[67] Baker-Fletcher illustrates the interconnected nature of right relationship within Xodus notions of relationality and community; he is unwilling to accept any notion or practice of relationship that fails to accept the complete humanity and personality of Black women. As Black churches are key components of both the dissemination and overturning of biblical interpretations of sex and gender that promote the unquestioned "headship" of men, whether within the church or the larger community, Baker-Fletcher implores Black men and women to become acquainted with Black religious scholars whose work is founded upon sexually inclusive scholarship.[68]

On a practical level, Xodus masculinity is also useful as a response to a new era of public life that features the high influx of women into the public domain, competing for jobs and economic resources that men once monopolized. Intersectional foci in liberation movements, along with greater visibility of women's issues, have worked in tandem to "[release] women from a self-understanding that confined their aspirations to the raising of children, flooding the public sphere with highly motivated and educated women."[69] The cultivation of Xodus sensibilities in the relational identities of men enables the development of a new consciousness about the nature and function of masculinity and manhood within egalitarian partnership. It is important, also, to distinguish how Baker-Fletcher understands "partnering"—as this language lends itself to the perception that he situates heterosexuality as the norm. Liberating, or liberatory partnership, is at the heart of egalitarian partnering. Xodus framings of manhood call for the rejection of all sexist norms, including the rendering of homosexual partnering as abnormal. Partnering encompasses all the modes of relating, living, and loving that are considered beyond the bounds of heterosexuality. Xodus space gives Black men a different reference point for self-identity within community and further enables Black men to deconstruct those ideas about community that serve to subordinate women, gays, and lesbians and prevent them from realizing their full potential, both in private spheres and within the larger spaces of communal life. Becoming Bodyself sensibilities, which feature an organic, connected view of Black male selfhood in relation to Black women within the context of community, give Black men the incentive and the cultural means through which they can reimagine and refashion for themselves new masculine identities unburdened by the restrictions of traditional and/or Eurocentric norms.

The Xodus commitment to right relationship through Becoming Bodyselves is connected to partnering that likewise engages in the praxis of deconstructing, through faithful action, misogynistic underpinnings of relationality. Liberatory partnership "means aiding each other in ongoing self-critical process that creates healthy Becoming Bodyselves."[70] As liberatory partnership requires embodied presence and the establishment of open, mutual, and reciprocal lines of communication, Xodus partnership is committed to this ideal of dialogue and engagement and seeks, in a collaborative and coalitional spirit, the insights of womanists and other Black women in churches and communal spaces. Xodus liberatory partnership advocates a radical form of community that extends itself beyond the provincialism of male-dominated spaces and speech and works to build sites "where Black women and men can hear each other's pain, insecurities, sufferings, and longings without reproach, fear, or intimidation."[71] As an addendum, I would note that creating dialogically engaged spaces also extends itself to gay, lesbian, queer, and trans communities—reciprocity within the context of communal space cannot be established in truncated ways that ignore and downplay the equally real and equally valid experiences and insights of multiple sexual and gendered identities.[72]

Reciprocal exchange, where one can receive the experiences and feelings of others mutually, provides men the opportunity to be transformed through acceptance and acknowledgment of the various lifeworlds of women. Liberatory partnership is founded upon genuine, life-giving space within which people realize their full potential in the hope of becoming their best selves while seeking and encouraging the full potential of others. As Baker-Fletcher notes, the process of creating liberatory partnerships within churches and the larger community is a unique responsibility for Black men. There is a pervasive perception that Black men remain silent in the face of sexism and misogyny—often downplaying these realities in favor of a race-central political approaches.[73] In light of this, Baker-Fletcher's turn to relational models like liberatory partnership can assist with shifting the feelings of unsupportiveness and isolation felt by Black women while also prompting a greater sense of urgency and agency on the part of Black men as we work to not only live into fuller identities but also bridge some of the disconnects that rupture cohesion and solidarity. Owing to its dialogical and reciprocal commitments, liberatory partnership as a shared cultural project can compel, inspire, and provide a model for Black men to create safe spaces therein "for women to be fully human."[74] Baker-Fletcher pushes for a more proactive relational stance, as an Xodus praxis of partnership, that eschews easy answers to ethical obligations regarding women and rejects half-hearted and cursory investment in the creation of liberating spaces for women and men.

Xodus frameworks offer a useful and needed intervention in Black religious scholarship due to their specific tethering of visions of Black manhood to the uplift, support, and affirmation of Black women's historiographies and interior lifeworlds. Often, men are implored to "be better." Be better in the treatment of women. Be better as fathers. Be better as romantic partners. I cannot disagree with these pointed requests. However, I would add only one bit of clarity, given my reading of Xodus theology and ethics: *relate better*. Right relationship, when embraced as central to one's identity and purpose for being, occasions the possibility for transformative social and interpersonal exchange on all fronts. Xodus relationality, as a mechanism that uplifts and reshapes Black manhood, provides Black men the cultural and spiritual inspiration to reclaim a natural and connective identity that is responsive and morally obligated to others. Relational Black male identities rely upon the "community affirmation of both men and women included together in the decision making as well as practical work" toward the realization of more livable futures.[75] Perhaps in realizing a more livable world and hoping for more sustainable futures for women and men—grounded in reciprocity and shared, mutual concern—the Xodus vision of antisexist Black manhood is a powerful testimony toward that end.

The Values of Connectedness

Womanist scholars have long looked to Black women's literature for theological insight and religious, ethical, and moral values. As Katie Cannon reveals in *Black Womanist Ethics* (1988), Black women's literary traditions offer unique vantage points through which Black women can interpret the sociocultural patterns of Black communal life and investigate the moral struggles unique to their experiences as Black women. Black women's writings provide examples of the Black woman as moral agent. These sources illustrate how Black women's lives reveal a repository of ethical values driven by the struggle to survive interlocking oppressions, while holding on to courage and dignity in a world determined to destroy those attributes.[76] As a central pillar of womanist thought, Black women's literature foregrounds the centrality and special insider status of Black women within the ebbs and flows of Black communal spaces. This means that ethical insight and moral wisdom come not from the dictates of high virtue theory but more likely from the religious and cultural experiences of "the suffering faces of those who are truly just a sister away."[77]

Dwight Hopkins's theological scholarship spotlights the importance of engaging womanist religious thought. Adopting the above-noted womanist hermeneutic regarding the constructive imperative of drawing upon Black women's literature, Hopkins turns to Toni Morrison to unpack the *values of connectedness*, which I cite as another salient relational orientation useful for Black men's self-identity. In his description of Black women's "spirituality of funk" in *Shoes That Fit Our Feet: Sources for a Constructive Black Theology*, Hopkins argues that it is life experience and societal navigation of Black poor women that occasion the formation of an ethical and communal sensibility to foster individual and cultural liberation.[78] Through an interrogation of the folk religious practices of the enslaved and Black women's embodied spirituality, Hopkins sets the terms for the development of Black theological discourses that resonate with contemporary African American religious experience. Beyond African / African American folk tales, Hopkins draws specifically upon Black women's spirituality, as developed within the literary writing of Toni Morrison. Morrison's fiction serves as a critical source for interpreting Black religious experience due to its mapping of "the resources for survival and freedom" over against the othering of Black women. The dehumanization of Black women, a process Morrison refers to as "the Thing," characterizes an ontic space of lack—a "demonic, sterile, and life-denying spirituality that oppresses poor Black women" and renders them essentially outside the zone of humanity and agency.[79]

Morrison notes that Black women have become adept at retrieving the inner resources and convictions that assert autonomy and full personhood, which she refers to as "the Funk," comprising "women's spirit of liberation," and is "found in values and traditions used by poor Black women in order to survive and free themselves from the evil grip of the Thing."[80] In Morrison's writings, Hopkins notes that womanist spirituality entails Black women's connectedness "to the poor black woman herself; to her immediate community; to her broader community; and to nature."[81] Of womanist self-connected spirituality, Hopkins notes that healthy selfhood in Black women is the precursor to a more wholesome response to the extended community. The value of internal, spiritual connectedness resides in the power it cultivates to love herself into healthier modes of connection and relationship with others. Ultimately, the value of self-connectedness empowers poor Black women to re-create themselves away from the dictate of Whiteness, the limitations of poverty, and male chauvinist demands, and toward the self-authority to be free granted by God's spirit.[82] This mode of connectedness unpacks the spiritual underpinnings that enable Black women to resist the "pressures of harmful forces that would isolate black women from those whom they cherish in their close spiritual bonds."[83] Clinging to the ties that enabled the survival of Black families during and following slavery, the communal connectedness of womanist spirituality is conceived in mutuality and extended toward Black women's immediate community— "their families, their relation to other Black women, and their intimate dynamics with Black men."[84]

What is additionally interesting about womanist connectedness as a relational hermeneutic is the posturing of Black women's othermothering / mother-wit communities as a feature of survival culture that enables the navigation of multiple dehumanizing features of everyday life. The cultivation of relationality in this way, which becomes central to one's own sense of self and identity, privileges individual and interpersonal subjectivities in ways that nourish the capacity for survival and fulfillment. Emilie Townes captures womanist connectedness in the following from a poem: "They came because they had no choice, to form a we that is many strong and growing."[85] The formation of a "we" prioritizes and valorizes Black women's strength in numbers as a powerful prophylactic offering survival and resistance. As a manifestation of intersubjective solidarity, connectedness shifts from the mundane to become a strategy of resistance insofar as it promotes collective healing, self-reconstitution, and renewal in navigating the thorniness of various oppression(s).

Connectedness, which Hopkins frames as a new constructive source and norm for Black liberation theology, highlights some of the themes of relationality and reciprocity previously noted. Connectedness emphasizes a "when one wins, all win" approach to human relationships—that is, a relational ideal in which people maintain individuality, integrity, and self-worth without denying the value of others. Analyzing Morrison's *Sula*, for example, Hopkins emphasizes the relationship between Nel and Sula, notably the depth of their friendship, as a model of "woman-to-woman connectedness"—illustrating "how to be with someone else and not smother the person in the process."[86] Such bonding experiences cultivate a respect for the selfhood and humanity of others—an awareness and acknowledgment of other selves' integrity. In drawing upon this dimension of womanist relationality, Hopkins likewise advocates for the envisioning and mapping of Black theological discourses that are sensitive to Black female epistemologies *and* to the realities of sex and gender restrictions to be accountable to the voices of oppressed and silenced communities.[87]

Hopkins's turn to Black women's spirituality and the values of connectedness spotlights a relational construct that can inform the reconfiguration of Black male identity, but Hopkins is also spotlighting the need for insurgent solidarity in a world that denies the humanity and agency of Black women and men and ruptures authentic community making. One takeaway from the values of connectedness for Black men, as Hopkins suggests, is the formation of a new relational praxis with Black women, with our communities, and within ourselves. This modality of connectedness as outlined within womanist spirituality and relationality "has potential, with the just cooperation of Black men, to foreshadow a new example of black female-male vibrant complementarity."[88] Nancy Lynne Westfield's study of Black women's religious gatherings in *Dear Sisters: A Womanist Practice of Hospitality* focused on the question of resilience—the spiritual tenacity that enables one to "keep on keepin' on" in the midst of struggle. Resilience represents staying power—an ethical and religious posture toward the world meant to protect one's integrity, dignity, and humanity regardless of the countervailing forces. The concealed hospitality groups in Westfield's study enabled the women participating to cultivate resistance and resilience communities in which shared commitment to wholeness, reciprocal affirmation, and empathic pathways of sharing assisted their capacity to withstand and respond to the difficulties of their lives.[89]

In focusing on the uniqueness of Black women's spiritual lives, Hopkins's emphasis on the connectedness illustrates the value of incorporating and reciprocating the organic spirituality of Black women's interior worlds into our perspectival and personal being. Black women's spirituality, to be sure, need not be confined to particular religious communities or creeds. In the expansion of the notion of spirituality on this score, I concur with Marla Frederick, who ties Black women's spirituality to proactive and praxis-oriented interventions grounded in healing, self-(re)creation, and personal growth.[90] The values of connectedness that Hopkins espouses represent an ideal of self-constitution and the mapping of communal space that thrives in the effort to reimagine one's self, place, and space but harkens to a tradition of Black women's spiritual and cultural survival. In its instructive implications for Black men, the embrace of relational identities that feature an abiding sense of connectedness places a particular emphasis on responsiveness. Connectedness calls for a higher, more intentional embrace of and response to the interior worlds and external experiences of those normally outside the bounds of our immediate registers of knowing, being, or doing. As creatures of habit, we are all, each of us, locked into our own ways, and it is often difficult to reimagine ourselves differently. The embrace of this relational orientation is processual and is not an easy undertaking. What I argue, however, is for recognition of the possibilities and promise related to an imaginative and open-ended turn in how we see ourselves and refashion our identities—beset as the process may be by setbacks, misgivings, and conversational/dialogical growing pains. The values of connectedness do not represent any final, end-all resolution to these matters but do hold possibilities for pushing the boundaries of the meaning, scope, and interpretation of Black manhood.

Conclusion

In his classic essay, "Many Thousands Gone," James Baldwin laments that Black embodiment and being (which he frames in the masculine) is often lodged within the narrativization of (White) American imaginaries: "The Negro in America . . . is a series of shadows. . . . One may say that the Negro in America does not really exist except in the darkness of our minds."[91] The consequence of the racialization and pathologizing of Black women and men's humanity in this way prompts a loss of identity. Emilie Townes, addressing Baldwin's reading, notes that identity loss has far-reaching consequences beyond the most immediate victims—bespeaking the generational and futuritive implications of the afterlife(lives) of anti-Black racial apartheid. Townes shifts the concern of identity loss toward an analysis of perceptions of Black manhood, ultimately favoring a theo-ethics of memory/countermemory as a mechanism of recovering Black manhood and humanity from the throes of anti-Black publics, propaganda, and policies.

First articulated in *Womanist Ethics and the Cultural Production of Evil*, Townes's notion of countermemory opens space to reclaim Black womanhood from racial stereotypes generated by the White imagination and that arrests and renders proprietary Black female identity—thereby banishing Black womanhood into obscurity and limbo.[92] Townes turns her attention to Black manhood as subjected to the same discursive regimes in another essay, "Vanishing into Limbo. Part II: Black Men as Endangered Species . . . Not." Townes declares quite forthrightly, "We must name ourselves with precise righteousness."[93] Townes recognized the moral and ethical problems that result when both Black and White societies accept racial (and gendered) caricatures as proxy status for Black (in)humanity and therefore advocates larger, overarching cultural revisionist and refashioning projects that enliven and refresh Black humanity and rescue it from the agency-killing and soul-diminishing ethos of White supremacy. The power of naming is a political and agential act, and it is not one bereft of larger psychic implications. The "righteousness" endemic to self-naming, it seems, harkens to Audre Lorde's prophetic warnings about the impositional nature of the fantasies and gazes of others upon one's personal identity.[94]

As illustrated throughout this chapter, womanist religious thought and womanist conceptualizations of relationality serve as windows of cultural countermemory that positively impact the envisioning, perception, and scope of Black manhood and Black male identity. The use and power of cultural memory projects to upset the racial and gendered status quo provide wherewithal to indict all knowledges and accepted truisms about Black male personhood that are found to be "partial, incomplete, and unbefitting of our integrity, worth and dignity, as human gifts."[95] In working through the insights of Black and womanist religious discourses on relationality, personhood, and identity, I furthermore posit that their perspectives ultimately function as countermemory narratives that go against the grain of popular mythologies of African American manhood by calling forth a new identity framework for understanding Black male existence. While the caricaturing of Black men and boys weighs heavily upon my personal and intellectual dispositions, ultimately my intervention is grounded in an imaginative and self-reflexive pursuit that I would like to see Black men embrace rather than be so concerned about offering apologies in the face of perceived slights against Black manhood. We can and should defend our(selves). However, this defense cannot lose sight of the imaginative and self-reflexive motivation that pushes us to embrace more robust conceptualizations of our humanity as we look toward more livable futures and toward stronger relationships with others in our communities.

2

Black Manhood in the Writings of Alice Walker, Zora Neale Hurston, and Toni Morrison

I'm satisfied this the first time I ever lived on earth as a natural man. It feel like a new experience.
—Albert, *The Color People*

The sites and sights of Black manhood and the (re)presentation of Black manhood have long been central to the cultural projects in African American life, thought, and political organization. In *Constructing the Black Masculine: Identity and Ideality in African American Men's Literature and Culture, 1775–1995*, Maurice O. Wallace wrestles with how Black men have negotiated the racialized gazes of White society. Wallace's study on the politics of Black men's representation, which privileges the mediums of photography and literature, explains how Black men both embody and survive the tensions of the racial gaze, but also contest the "disjunction of race and manhood in American culture" in order to realize an authentic masculine subjectivity.[1] What inspired Black men's contestation over the reins of their portrayals, depictions, and perceptions of their manhood, says Wallace, is grounded in an ontic squeeze. "Black masculinity is . . . a key site of [ideology and] ideological representation" upon which competing ideals and identity frames are played out.[2] The jeopardy of Black men caught within the modern and postmodern racial vision is linked closely with the terror of "enframement"—being relegated to the scope of gazes, the reductionism, and the "bankruptcy of vision" that fixes Black-and-male otherness in the White, American imagination.[3]

As Wallace suggests, there has been and remains a long-established subversive quality to Black men's varied collective and individual responses to the many forms of racialized enframement of their bodies and being. Several studies have outlined, for example, Black men's attitudinal postures, psychological adaptation, and other coping and survival mechanisms meant to parry the onslaught of discursive bullets that short-circuits their agency, personhood, fulfillment, and freedom of expression within the racist gaze.[4] The representation of African American men remains a contested issue in larger cultural discourses in part because of America's racial legacy of minstrelsy as well as a culture of hypersurveillance weaponized against Black men, who are perceived as threat qua threat. Past and present generations of Black men have taken it upon themselves, therefore, to reclaim their identities from these ideological and cultural regimes, often using the resources and institutional structures of the Black community to do so. Martin Summers concurs with this observation, illustrating how twentieth-century Black men in urban cities were able to articulate a distinctive gender subjectivity in contrast and in opposition to White masculinity against the backdrop of migration, immigration, and a shifting industrial and vocational sphere and amid discourses about the terms of authentic citizenship.[5]

I began this book mapping the relational turn as a feature of Black religious thought. Taking my cues from the relational orientations of Alice Walker's mapping of womanism and extending these insights further within womanist religious thought and Black male theological discourses, these sources provided the necessary architecture for building an interpretive approach emphasizing a new norm in Black religious thought broadly, but that gives particular attention to gender identity formation. I now shift to an examination of Black women's literature, which is indispensable to interpreting Black women's culture. In particular, I am interested in what Black women writers have said and think about Black manhood. In other words, how have Black women writers represented Black men, and what does their portrayal suggest about notions of manhood and how wholesome Black male identities are formed? This chapter considers the representation of relational Black male identities through a literary analysis of womanist-identified literature, namely *The Color Purple*, *Their Eyes Were Watching God*, and *Home*.[6] Before delving into this review, there are some areas of methodological clarity needed both for organizational purposes and to accent my concerns on representation.

A Note on Womanist-Identified Literature

In attempting to adopt the appropriate terminology to classify the novels under review, a question guiding this analysis is prominent: Are these works womanist literary sources, or are they best characterized as *womanist-identified* literature? I lean toward the latter, in the interest of being as accurate to the worldviews of the authors as possible. The nomenclature of this distinction is lodged within my desire to be responsive to what Valethia Watkins refers to as the Black Feminist Revisionist History Project (BF-RHP). This ideological and discursive sleight of hand, notes Watkins, treats Black women and their cultural productions "as if they are a homogenous group when, in reality, they are diverse in their political consciousness, perspectives, ideas, and commitments as any other group."[7] As a matter of discursive construction, BF-RHP is problematic because it misguidedly tethers contemporary notions, such as "womanist" or "feminist" motivations, to earlier generations of Black women for whom such ideological classifications may have been inappropriate or possibly unrecognizable. Emilie Townes addresses this problem, noting the confessional appropriation of womanism undertaken by individual by Black women:

> The use of the term womanist to describe a theorist's or practitioner's work is one of avowal rather than denotation. . . . This provides an organic undertaking of constant self-reflection in the context of the "doing" of one's vocation and avocation . . . the womanist is not free to name others as womanist if this is not a term they claim for themselves. For example, describing Black women from the nineteenth century as womanists is inaccurate. Although many like Ida B. Wells-Barnett, Sojourner Truth, and Anna Julia Cooper employed an interstructured social analysis in their activism, none of these women claimed the term womanist for herself. At best, and most faithfully, these women embody nascent womanism that provides a rich framework for womanists of this era to flesh out.[8]

In looking to our Black women forebears in their varied intellectual, social, and religious milieus to construct a useable past shaping present-day intellectual and ideological interests, it is important to avoid the temptation to make easy categorizations that blur the distinctions of past and present articulations of Black women's identity markers.

To many readers such a concern may strike one as splitting ideological hairs, but given the deeply politicized and contested issue of naming in Black feminist and womanist discourses, I strive to remain sensitive to, and aware of, the quagmire. Patricia Hill Collins maintains that in the process of claiming feminism and womanism as prominent ideological and/or political categories that ground Black women's efforts to construct self-identity, many Black women ultimately "see little difference between the two since both support a common agenda of Black women's self-definition and self-determination."[9] The point in bringing attention to the issue is simply to illustrate methodological openness in any reflection upon Black women's literature or cultural productions. Respecting the ideological and descriptive agency that underscores Black women's writings is primary in embracing Black women's voices, but it is also important because it assists the recognition of political and social worlds within which these women write and further appreciates how they have made contributions, on their own unique and distinctive merits, to Black intellectual discourses. Hurston's case is particularly interesting in this regard, as the tense ideological battles between herself and other Black male Harlem Renaissance writers on the issue of artistry versus protest-oriented fiction writing has been well documented.[10] Ultimately, the naming and other characterizations Walker, Hurston, and Morrison advocate is best articulated on their own terms, and I have no wish to be a proxy for them in this chapter.

In my use of "womanist-identified literature" as the category of choice, I do so to categorize the canon of three Black women writers who frequent the scholarly, creative, and imaginative palate of self-identified womanist scholars of religion. In the case of Alice Walker's *The Color Purple*, designating it as womanist literature is appropriate because Walker has written at length about the aptness of this description for her writing. But in the case of Morrison and Hurston, the question of how to classify their writings without overstepping or misrepresenting its ideological foundation presented a challenge. Katie Cannon's *Black Womanist Ethics* grounds many of my considerations here and specifically prompted the use and designation of "womanist-identified" to discuss the approach to Morrison and Hurston's writings.[11] Cannon notes that in the case of Hurston and other Black women writers, they provide rich resources for wisdom and an ethic of survival that can be practiced by Black women and men.

Specific to Hurston, Cannon finds a reservoir of dignity, grace, and courage that is a useful foundation for a moral agency that centers Black women's examples—a moral agency that can be embodied and practiced as a means of developing an identity that is connective and embraces others as constitutive of oneself. Hurston and Morrison centralize Black women's agency and lives as resources and models for liberative, relational living and therefore bring to life the womanist themes that Walker envisioned, so much so that later womanists embrace their literary writings to augment the ties between womanist thought and religious thought. With the clarification of these works as womanist-identified (while holding in tension the concerns regarding their possible misrepresentation as womanist novels) now stated, I explore the portrayal of Black men in the novels on more firm ground, acknowledging the possible representational pitfalls in such a framing, while illustrating the political impetus that often impacts the process of discursive ideological categorization and cultural production.

The Black men chosen for review all emerge in Walker, Hurston, and Morrison's novels as representations of relational Black male identities. The central characters that guide my analysis are Mr./Albert, Vergible "Tea Cake" Woods, and Frank Money, respectively. Of these examples, I single out the following thematic attributes, respective to each: (1) inter/intrapersonal reflection and reform grounded in organic Black manhood; (2) the embrace of compound subjectivity; and (3) living into personal and communal fulfillment through care ethics and attention to the well-being of others. Looking to the characters as tropes for relationality in Black male life is by no means an admission that they are without flaw, though seamless, unambiguous perfection is not the point. What drives my interpretive approach, specifically, is the extent to which these novels' portrayal of Black men assists efforts to reimagine Black manhood as a space for relational self-constitution. What results, therefore, when womanist-identified literature envisions and outlines the cultivation of positive and affirmative Black male identities? Womanist-identified literature reveals an endeavor to truly see Black manhood in an aspirational and inspirational light—potentially reinvigorating a positive resonance among Black men who likewise seek new mechanisms of understanding their identities. In making such a pronouncement, I must address some areas of tension considering the critiques of Black male studies regarding disciplinary silence and the perception of shaming scholarly voices and perspectives that center Black men.

In speaking on the disciplinary morality of the humanistic disciplines in academia, Tommy Curry critiques how the study of Black men and boys beyond the realms of pathology, defect, and cultural maladjustment often finds no quarter in current academese. Specific to my own objectives in this present work, I am keen to Curry's observations on what is deemed acceptable in any analysis that centers Black men. In this view, Black male life can be intellectually valid as a subject of study only when the methodological and theoretical scope deployed is from the vantage point of Black feminist paradigms that problematize the entire scope of Black masculinity. Such a critique clearly implicates my project, as it engages womanist religious scholarship and literature partly for its theoretical approach. While Curry's critique on the delimiting prowess of disciplinary regimes pertaining to Black male lives as subjects of study is well taken, I do not think the collaborative, dialogical, and *ideological* interdisciplinarity for which I advocate should be dismissed.

In womanist discourses, with its commitment to the wholeness and survival of Black women and men, there is a sustained bias toward the privileging of Black women. However, I remain convinced of its capacity to proffer an instructive and liberating "good word" to Black men as they endeavor to realize healthier spaces of being. In contrast to the many and constant gender moralities of our day that deem Black men problem men in toto,[12] womanist thought offers complex and nuanced visions of Black manhood that do not fall prey to the caricatures of either racist misandry or emasculation. I illustrate this same aspirational vision within the context of womanist-identified literature. In the pitfalls and promise of the male characters reviewed, I lay bare the ambiguities of each, juxtaposed with holistic and relational ways of being (male) to uncover the literary challenge each poses to us in the present in our efforts to dismantle the presumption of dominance, coercion, pathological control, and imbalanced relation often imagined as central to what it means to be male.

Alice Walker's Natural Men

James Baldwin's essay "To Crush a Serpent" indicts Christian fundamentalism in American culture for its rigid interpretation of embodied sexuality, an ethos of overt racism as indicated in the conservatism of the religious right, and its negative impact on notions of communal and embodied salvation. Baldwin's soteriology troubles the pietistic, individualist Christian soteriology in American evangelicalism. In contrast to the focus on the singular rapture of one's soul and "getting right with God," Baldwin situates salvation as a social process built upon the recognition of personhood. Salvation, says Baldwin, "is the beginning of union with all that is or has been or will ever be" and "connects, so that one sees oneself in others and others in oneself."[13] Salvation is a *relational* issue—its realization is dependent upon the recognition of shared selfhood with others. Baldwin's relational arrangement of salvation offers a marked contrast with what he cites as the puritanical and anti-body dimensions of conservative, fundamentalist Christian soteriology:[14] "The prohibitions that suit the fundamentalists best all involve the flesh," and "sin is not limited to carnal activity, nor are the sins of the flesh the most crucial or reverberating of our sins."[15]

In preserving the integrity of the body, Baldwin fosters a theology and Black spirituality of the flesh that embraces the absolute unity between God and the embodied character of human life. The incarnational underscoring of Baldwin's interpretation of salvation thus allows space for a theology of body that is inclusive of, and receptive to, the varieties of sexual and gender identities.[16] It is my view that the interrelated, communal tenor of Baldwin's articulation of his concept of salvation is likewise a useful interpretive tool in our reading of Black male identity in womanist-identified writing. As Baldwin notes, "Salvation is not separation. It is the beginning of union with all that is or has been or will ever be."[17] In contrast to Baldwin's soteriological description, anti-relational mechanisms of identity formation are not rooted in norms pertaining to mutuality, collaboration, or reciprocity but rather are practiced through norms of control, coercion, abuse, and alienation.

The anti-relational features within Mr./Albert's portrayal in *The Color Purple* presume hierarchical arrangements and practice value judgments tethered to male and female bodies and being, with ultimate favor and value assigned to men. Another way of describing this problem is captured by the notion of "pathological/toxic masculinity"; however, because I explore this topic through Black men, I am not comfortable using this phrasing, as Black men are already read and interpreted at base as pathological—for both their Blackness and the tandem of their identity as Black *and* male. To avoid the racial and gendered loggerheads that filter perceptions of Black male personhood in damaging constructs, I simply speak broadly of anti-relationality as a construction of Albert's particular understanding of himself as a man and how this understanding was manifest within his larger community and as displayed in his relationship with Celie. Albert's embrace of anti-relationality privileged coercion, domination, and control in lieu of authentic partnership. His ideal of manhood failed and fails, in the dynamic with Celie, and arguably with other women, because he could not see the humanity and agency of women. He could not reciprocate or embody a relational identity because he didn't see her humanity as connected to his own. The devaluation of Celie and women generally consequently aided the destructive capacity to do harm to self and other. These represent modes of "relating" (which aren't actually relating) characterized by dominance, hierarchal assertions of control, and a disregard for the subjectivity and agency of women.[18]

In Albert's case, there are glaring displays of these features with additional implications. The domination, coercion, and control he practices feature the tragedy of physical and ontological violence and prompt a generational trigger effect in other men. Alice Walker's attention to Celie's sexual, marital, and mental abuse at Albert's hands provides poignant commentary on the environmental and societal traumas that impact Black womanhood in the form of domestic violence. Albert enacts physical violence and control over Celie—bespeaking a generalized disregard of her personhood, bolstered by an inclination toward dominance. His efforts here are based upon his desire to make Celie conform to his standards of domestic control: "She my wife. . . . Plus she stubborn." Celie, the stubborn wife in need of a man's validation and control and, when necessary, a beating, is frozen into the patriarchal assumptions of Albert's conception of marriage, relationship, and womanly domesticity—illustrating Celie's ontologically static positionality. Walker also points to Albert's relationship with his son, Harpo, as being impacted by Albert's embrace of anti-relationality. By way of a parental ripple effect, Harpo embraces the same framings of identity and relationality with his wife, Sofia, indicating the generational recycling of anti-relationality. As Sofia says of Harpo, "He don't want a wife, he want a dog."

I highlight Albert's example due to his overall development by the novel's end—namely, for his eventual adopting of a relational understanding. Albert's recognition of this need for an about-face—a self-reflexive need to model and practice right relationship—can inform our understanding of relational identity formation. Kelly Brown Douglas cites right relationship as "a womanist way of relating to their families and men," emphasizing communal wholeness through: "1) a communal understanding of family, 2) a willingness to do what was necessary for the well-being of the family/community, 3) female networking and cooperation, and 4) a reciprocal relationship of equality and respect with their men/husbands."[19] The familial underscoring Douglas ties into wholesome relationships helps unpack the reformation of Albert's masculine identity. Albert's gradual embrace of relational selfhood was in part a consequence of the efforts of a family member as well as recognition of the need for a different kind of relationship with Celie. Albert, with the help of both Harpo directly and Celie indirectly, and through the process of his own discernment, learns to embrace a relational framing that thrives on openness, mutual care, and a desire for the well-being of others. Illustrating right relationship, Harpo emerges as an interesting figure in the saga of Albert's redemption—becoming a humanizing influence.[20] It is vital to emphasize Harpo's role in Albert's recuperation and healing after falling ill as well as his prompting of Albert's actions that lead to reconciliation with Celie.

As we learn from Sofia, Albert, in the aftermath of Celie's departure, becomes a recluse—"shut up in the house so much it stunk." Harpo eventually forces his way into the home and begins the practice of caretaking for his father, which reveals the extent of Albert's vulnerability as well as troubles and defies some of the stereotypical conceptions of masculine identity as invulnerable, invincible, and lacking emotional depth. Sofia notes, "Harpo went up there plenty of nights to sleep with him . . .

one night I walked up to tell Harpo something—and the two of them was just laying there on the bed fast asleep. Harpo holding his daddy in his arms." Harpo, the son, therefore, becomes a parent figure to the father—nurturing, feeding, and bathing. When Celie notices Albert's rejuvenated appearance, most apparent are the external results of Harpo's care. There is one specific facet of Harpo's influence upon Albert that prompts his physical restoration and health worth noting further. Celie questions the source of Albert's new health, and for Sofia the reason is obvious: "Harpo made him send you the rest of your sister's letters. Right after that he start to improve. You know meanness kill" (225).

Harpo therefore must be credited with having a hand in the reversal of Albert's misfortunes as well as reconciliatory efforts toward Celie—all of which is part and parcel of his overall redemption. Despite this, Harpo is a victim of his and Albert's anti-relational excesses, as he exhibits the very same tendencies and anti-relational behaviors as Albert—notably the beatings of Sofia, prompting their estrangement. Not to trivialize or dismiss this element of Harpo's contradictory behaviors, nursing Albert to health, providing wise council, and his own eventual reconciliation with Sofia through a reimagining of the nature of marriage, reflect Alice Walker's attention to both the contradictory and the transformative aspects of their identity formation. Walker's portrayal of Harpo and Albert's growth demonstrates the holistic vision in womanist thought that sees men as capable of engaging the practices of right relationship. Like Albert, Harpo is a work in progress, not all terrible, not all wonderful. By the novel's end, he makes efforts to reconcile himself with Sophia after years of estrangement and abuse. Whether his actions on the part of Albert's rejuvenation prompted this reconciliation is not completely explicit. While Harpo is not the central figure for this reading of the shifts and evolution of Black manhood in Walker, in centralizing Albert's efforts toward transformation, Harpo's participation in Albert's process toward redemption and toward a greater relational identity must be acknowledged.

Most indications of Albert's self-reflexive responsiveness to the needs for shifts in practice of a relational identity become evident through private interactions with Celie. In one of Celie's letters to Nettie, she discusses the prospect of hating Albert for what he's done to separate Celie and Nettie. I quote Celie's feelings at length:

But I don't hate him.... After all the evil that he done I know you wonder why I don't hate him. I don't hate him for two reasons. One, he love Shug. And two, Shug use to love him. Plus, look like he trying to make something out of himself. I don't mean just that he work and clean up after himself and he appreciate some of the things God was playful enough to make. *I mean when you talk to him now he really listen,* and one time, out of nowhere in the conversation us was having, he said Celie, I'm satisfied this the first time I ever lived on Earth as a natural man. It feel like a new experience. (260, emphasis added)

Celie's thoughts and recollections here are interesting in that Shug Avery is cited as a source of shared concern, love, and connection between the formerly estranged Celie and Albert. Shug was the primary factor in their path toward embarking upon a mutual friendship. Their connection through Shug prompts Celie to observe that Albert "seem to be the only one understand my feeling" (259). Celie's own words indicate Albert's improvement, not simply in terms of domestic upkeep ("he work and clean up after himself") but particularly in his capacity to be a partner. I speak of "partner" here to indicate the status of their new friendship. Albert, in contrast to his previous dealings with Celie, "really listen." Celie's observation suggests an intentional attentiveness from Albert with moral implications.

P. Sven Arvidson observes that attentiveness requires focusing on another "as the theme of ... ongoing attending life."[21] Attention is premised upon an ethical posture that centralizes the well-being of others and extends beyond mere acknowledgment. Attention, as Celie suggests, entails seeing the "whole being," which is one's full self, unadulterated, unaltered, and unminimized. Within the overall sphere of Albert's attention, Celie became, even if momentarily, the focal point. Albert pays attention to Celie, and in doing so he receives the fullness—the wholeness, of Celie's voice, her experiences, desires, personality, and alterity. Their conversation(s), rooted in a mutual process of reception and attention, achieves a "moral moment."[22] Because Albert listens, he does not "single out some item in the sphere of attention which is anything less" than a full recognition of Celie and her personhood.[23] The moral and reciprocal implications of Albert's attention to Celie are solidified on these grounds because he accepts the whole and not the part—the total and not the partial. In this moment of moral recognition, Albert, as a work in progress and not fully embodying a relational identity, is able to share and receive with Celie, and in doing so, they endure and be-come together as two subjects.[24]

Also illustrative of Albert's intentional push toward a different imagining of his identity as a man are the examples of his acknowledgment of change and self-growth. Unprompted, as Celie recollects, Albert expresses a joy in his feeling like "a natural man" (260), which I interpret as a moment of recognition from Albert on the transformative capacities of relational identity. In becoming a "natural man"—organic and connective—Albert had to come to terms with the destructiveness of his behaviors. Sofia was right. Meanness did kill—it killed "Mr.," the representation of the identity that Albert embodied but learned to eschew by living into relational identity unbound by patriarchal hierarchical arrangements. More than mere title, "Mr." is a symbol for the embrace of hierarchical patterns of relating that reified patriarchal mores situating men as permanent authority figures over women's lives. In attempting to transition toward and become a natural man, Albert realized he couldn't remain "the fool [he] use to be" (271). As a natural man, Albert embraces growth and maturation and most of all embraces him(self) as a relational being.

But there is still deep womanist wisdom that should also arrest our attention. As Sofia said to Celie, "meanness kill," which I do not take as a trite altruism. Sofia's critique of the abject futility of meanness directly indicts personal dispositions and practices of identity formation linked to anti-relational mechanisms of being and behavior. Sofia's recognition of the consequences of meanness—for both the community and the individual—comes into greater focus when tied to Albert's declining health and his improvement once he began treating Celie humanely. One may also consider how this meanness is deadly beyond both Sofia's wisdom and Alice Walker's literary imagination. While meanness provides a way of talking about anti-relationality, it might also be helpful to consider how the consequences thereof do palpable material harm to Black men's livelihood and health. Albert's health and social well-being improved alongside his heightened relational self-understanding. His descent, marked by isolation, despair, and hitting the proverbial rock bottom of life's misfortunes, prompted a recalibration of self; he learned to reconcile himself to family—to community, to Celie. Albert's gradual, ongoing effort to reform his identity is grounded in a reconstructed relationship with his son and his efforts to rebuild his relationship with Celie through shared experiences and emotional outpouring that create the possibility for corrective self-reflection on the destructive components of his masculine identity. The "natural man" transitioning that Albert mentions and attempts to embody reflects an imperative in the self-reflexive dimension of masculine reconfiguration—pushing for Black men to "rethink their own masculinities and sexualities in order to create more productive relationships within the Black community."[25]

Albert can serve as a fictional representation of a transitioning Black manhood that assists our efforts to reconfigure pathological practices tied to male identity formation. A praxis of manhood grounded in control, domination, aggression, violence, and the subordination of others, particularly women, is unsustainable and unhealthy. It is destructive to male selfhood, and it is destructive to the ties of human connection. It is destructive to male selfhood because it denies and short-circuits authentic growth and personal expression. It is destructive to connection because it prompts men of all backgrounds to rely upon an ethos of dominance rather than communal ties as a way of experiencing others. "Natural Man" identity, which is an understanding of self that is more organic and receptive of nonhierarchical arrangements of relating to others, thrives within the contexts of egalitarian partnering, openness, and self-reflection. Eschewing the façade and puniness of male identity formation rooted in control over others can compel one toward the prospect of human enlargement—a calling to exhibit a notion of self and community beyond where we currently are and beyond what we currently practice. Domination, aggression, and violence cannot and do not make men larger, freer, more loving, and more relational. The turn to Albert provides a useful illustration of the possibility of Black men taking on, and reconstructing, new identities and mechanisms of relating.

Watching for an "Us": Tea Cake's Compound Subjectivity

In the foreword to Robert Hemenway's groundbreaking biography of Zora Neale Hurston's life and literary contributions, which outlines her early experiences, her personal and professional relationships, and the motivation and creative push behind her artistic achievements, Alice

Walker notes that the most characteristic feature of Hurston's work was "racial health—a sense of Black people as complete, *complex*, undiminished human beings."[26] Hurston's desire for an unfiltered portrayal of Blacks as full humans as indicated throughout the corpus of her work reflects an unapologetic race pride and an intimate connection with, and passion for, the masses of African Americans. Hurston, in contrast to Black male contemporaries of her time, did not position her literary style and conception of African American life as the prototypical "protest novel" of the Harlem Renaissance artistic and intellectual era. Hurston carried forth her modus operandi regarding the organic and earthy portrayal of Black life in her best-known work, *Their Eyes Were Watching God*. In particular, the novel presents a Black woman's coming of age and living and loving in the midst of her "folk"—the complex and contradictory ebbs and flows of Black life and love in the twentieth-century American South.

Critics and Hurston scholars have been particularly keen on addressing gender politics in her writings, namely Hurston's portrayal of the negotiation of male and female roles in twentieth-century Black communities.[27] My point of departure centers on Vergible "Tea Cake" Woods, the third husband of the novel's protagonist, Janie Crawford. Through Tea Cake, I emphasize the framing of compound subjectivity, a second feature of relational identity formation. I understand compound subjectivity to be a relational posture steeped within the reciprocal and mutualized recognition of the agency of other persons—the embrace of compound subjectivity within relationships neither alters nor diminishes the weight of another person's occupation of time and space. Tea Cake, in contrast to Janie's previous relationships/marriages, embodies this disposition toward Janie; however, his failures to fully live into this relational ideal manifest in violence toward Janie. This feature of their dynamic, of course, renders impossible any simple, romanticized reading, and it is therefore critical to hold in tension the problematic *and* the positive in Tea Cake's portrayal. In considering Janie's overall development and experiences within the plot, the characteristic feature of her interpersonal experiences with men involves varying degrees of their attempts at coercion, control, and silencing. Tea Cake, however, makes more of an effort to see Janie as an actual partner. It is my argument that Tea Cake provides a useful lens into compound subjectivity in relationships as a feature of his identity.

After a loveless, controlling marriage to Logan Killicks, and in the wake of her second husband's death (he, too, proved to be controlling), Janie was disinterested in the prospect of either marriage or romantic involvement: "This freedom feeling was fine. These men [new suitors] didn't represent a thing she wanted to know about. She had already experienced them through Logan and Joe." The first marriages failed because both men "insist too severely on Janie's obedience to them and to conventional sex-role and class-role stereotypes," while devaluing Janie's personhood and voice.[28] Janie envisioned for herself relationships based on partnership—relationships where she could still maintain her self-integrity. She plainly states this egalitarian desire while indicting the second husband, Joe Starks, on his deathbed, lamenting that her own mind, voice, intelligence were lessened to be "Mrs. Mayor Starks": "All dis' bowin' down, all dis obedience under yo' voice—dat ain't whut Ah rushed off down de road tuh find out about you."

A relationship and marriage based on equality becomes a possibility with Tea Cake in his acceptance of Janie's freedom and humanity, especially, as I illustrate, within spaces commonly deemed masculine or male-dominated. It is Tea Cake's inclusion of Janie into these spheres that I suggest is meaningful for this embrace of Janie's subjectivity alongside his own. My thinking on this feature of Tea Cake's development parallels that of Mark Anthony Neal, who actually goes further than my purview by suggesting that Tea Cake's capacity for attentiveness, non-possessive love, and reciprocity in his relationship to Janie provides a trope for Black male feminist manhood. Neal observes that Tea Cake's fluid and malleable gender role politics exhibited in his relationship with Janie unsettled the presumptions of Black male privilege and dominance central to Hurston's era.[29] Further, as SallyAnn Ferguson notes, "Tea Cake genuinely encourages Janie to discover and realize her inner self."[30] Part of the discovery of Janie's inner voice and self-assertion is introduced through her inclusion into presumed masculine activities, namely checker games and gun shooting. The question is not whether these are masculine spaces; this much is obvious given the social and gender conventions for male and female behavior during the early twentieth-century context in which the novel was written. My concern is what Tea Cake accomplishes by inviting Janie to participate in these spaces and why he feels compelled to do so.

Ferguson notes that Hurston characterizes Janie's husbands through familiar folkloric motifs within African American culture, and Tea Cake is an embodiment of the Black folk hero, Stackolee (Stagolee, Stacker Lee).[31] Tea Cake is loved as a central thread in the fabric of the community but is also antiestablishment and is known to disregard the strictures of conventionality. Tea Cake also resists the social, sexual, and gender mores of his day through a "freedom of spirit" that he shares with Janie.[32] Tea Cake includes Janie and invites her to share in these experiences with him both as an act of love and as the continuation of his capacity for troubling the conventions of normality upon which Black rural society was built. It is possible that Tea Cake wanted her to likewise experience the freedom of defying social norms, even if that defiance was neither exhaustive nor total. My point in emphasizing Janie's participation in these realms is not to suggest that Tea Cake purposefully alters or changes the gendered dynamics of the society of their time. Rather, perhaps in Tea Cake's invitation he enables Janie to rupture macro versions of the cultural glass ceiling that shaped the world in which Janie lived or that dictated women's social, economic, or political mobility. In this way, Tea Cake's relational practice prompts a defiance toward the bounds of male-dominated worlds, albeit in a limited fashion.

The relational and reciprocal undertones of Tea Cake's embrace of Janie as a subject are indicated through his acceptance of, and insistence on, her ability to participate in the same spheres of activity as the men in Eatonville. Consider their first conversation. Tea Cake inquires as to why Janie is not at the local baseball game, as "everybody else is dere" (95). This is an interesting contrast to note because it seems to indicate that Tea Cake *expects* Janie to be immersed within the life and activities of the townspeople. Comparatively, the same scenario, if it had taken place in Janie's previous marriage, may have ended with Starks's insistence on Janie's remaining relegated to the activities of the store on the day of the game and thus out of public recognition. The store, within which Janie was mere ornamentation and once a symbol of Joe's power and influence, was also a socioeconomic symbol—providing imagined lines of demarcation dictating class and caste. Tea Cake does not levy any sex role proclamation—he indicates an interest in *Janie as Janie*.

Tea Cake also recognizes Janie's intelligence, which he deftly attaches to an ability to participate in activities typically dominated by men. There are glimpses of this in the example of Tea Cake's instruction in checkers and Janie's learning to shoot guns. What I centralize specifically are the implications of Tea Cake's *extension of confidence* in Janie's ability to participate in these so-called masculine spheres. Doing so indicates Tea Cake's reception of Janie as a thinking, acting subject. When Janie reflects on her first checkers lessons from Tea Cake, the extent of her realization that someone took time to recognize her ability and potential passion for the game becomes obvious: "Somebody wanted her to play. Somebody thought it *natural* [emphasis added] for her to play." Janie almost appears surprised at the prospect of a man expressing confidence in her ability to play checkers, a game that "de men folks treasures round heah." Tea Cake's insistence on Janie joining him in the game is arguably rooted in a desire for companionship, but his acknowledgment of her intelligence is a subtle but additional feature of his acceptance of Janie as subject.

Whereas Starks "useter tell [Janie she] never would learn," a view no doubt rooted in his belief that "somebody got to think for women and chilluns and chickens and cows," Tea Cake defies this view. As Tea Cake notes, Janie "got good meat" on her head and further, as if to indicate the seriousness of this assertion vote of confidence in Janie's skill, promises to return and teach her more strategies and movements of the game. Within this context, playing checkers was a communal pastime that provided a certain pleasurable respite from the hustle and bustle of rural, agrarian life in Florida. For Janie, however, it became a way to realize another facet of her intelligence and autonomy that was largely quelled in her previous marriages. While most of the men of the era embraced gender frameworks that subordinated women and downgraded their abilities, Tea Cake posited Janie's intelligence as a given. Tea Cake emerges in this regard as arguably the first man in Janie's life who does not see her as "lesser" or as defined by the conventional standards of gendered behavior, identity, and relationships. In doing so, he can see within Janie not simply a formidable opponent in checkers but an intelligent, capable person who could learn and participate in the mundane and quotidian dimensions of everyday life—thereby betraying the societal and gendered constraints associated with female and male agency.

We can also observe the same features of Tea Cake's reception of Janie's full subjectivity as revealed through his expectation that Janie can engage in physical activities and work commonly ascribed to men. In contrast to Starks's placing Janie on a pedestal—insisting that she was a "bell-cow" who was to stand above lower-class Black women—Tea Cake betrays these categories by pressing Janie to find a purpose and function within the communal fabric of the work worlds of the rural folk life, thereby troubling the Victorian gender roles to which women of her time were often relegated. As Janie comments to Pheoby comparing Starks's treatment with Tea Cake's, "Jody classed me off. Ah didn't. Naw, Pheoby, Tea Cake ain't draggin me off nowhere Ah don't want tuh go. Ah always did want tuh git round uh whole heap, but Jody wouldn't 'low me tuh. When Ah wasn't in de store he wanted me tuh jes sit wid folded hands and sit dere. And Ah'd sit dere wid de walls creepin' up on me and squeezin' all de life outa me" (112). There is, thus, a literal mobility—a fluidity of movement that Janie experiences with Tea Cake that was unknown in her previous marriages. Tea Cake's acceptance of Janie as her own person within previous off-limits cultural and gendered spaces is evident when considering his giving Janie gun training and inviting her to work with him "on de muck" (128). All these actions indicate an acceptance of Janie as an equal partner and companion who can engage in the very same communal activities as himself.

After arriving on the muck (the Florida Everglades), Tea Cake opines that Janie must learn to shoot for the purposes of hunting. Tea Cake's pragmatic rationale underscoring his opinion regarding Janie acquiring this skill indicates an acceptance of her engaging in activities that are not only traditionally "masculine" but furthermore particularly critical in the agrarian pursuits upon which the life of the community depended. Over time, Janie "got to be a better shot than Tea Cake." Tea Cake, in providing an opportunity for Janie to put her skills on display, also enabled the townspeople, who may have shared rigid gender expectations for male and female activity, to possibly rethink conventional gender politics. Tea Cake does not change or eradicate the artificial boundaries of masculine spheres by having Janie participate. Yet it is possible that a consequence of Tea Cake's inclusiveness is the defiance of gendered expectations for how men and women interact in the quotidian spaces of everyday life.

Tea Cake's genuine desire for partnership, in both masculine spaces and beyond, is also driven by a desire for Janie to express herself openly and honestly, which, I submit, troubles any reading of Tea Cake's inclusion of Janie in masculine spaces as cursory. On this matter, I draw on Tracy Bealer's insights regarding Tea Cake's dialogical seriousness when communicating with Janie. With Janie's doubts and insecurities about the status of the relationship and Tea Cake's sincerity apparent, "Tea Cake teaches her to speak again by demanding that she clearly and honestly admit her feelings for him."[33] When Janie questions whether Tea Cake desires her company to a picnic and suggests that she wouldn't mind another woman going in her place, Tea Cake replies, "Naw, it ain't all right wid you. If it was you wouldn't be sayin' dat. Have de nerve tuh say whut you mean." Here, Tea Cake is clearly accepting and demanding nothing less than the expression of Janie's voice—her affections and desires. Tea Cake insightfully recognizes Janie's insecurity but refuses to let her withdraw. He demands that Janie speak those feelings and fears into their relationship. True partnership, based on this exchange, is built upon the expression of two personalities—two voices, in which both maintain a reciprocal integrity that does not deny but encourages the voice of the other.

And while it is possible that Tea Cake's desire for Janie's companionship was driven by a mix of vested interests and motivations, including loneliness, possible anxieties about infidelities, and concerns about her safety, what is unmistakable, however, is Tea Cake's love for Janie and his desire to have her present with him. Janie, accepting Tea Cake's love and his relational practice of mutual labor and partnership, notes, "Ah laks it. It's mo' nicer than settin' round dese quarters all day. Clerkin' in dat store wuz hard, but heah, we ain't got nothin' tuh do but do our work and come home and love" (133). Tea Cake's inclusive partnership—his recognition of Janie as lover, partner, and confidant—is a compelling reason behind Janie's decision to work with him. It was "mo' nicer" to be respected and valued as a contributor to communal life and the home rather than be pushed into a rigidly constructed paradigm of sex role restriction and classist lines of demarcation.

There is, however, an overlap regarding the unfavorable characteristics that Janie experienced in the previous marriages. Tea Cake's eventual violence and jealousy toward Janie provide a stark contrast to the other parts of his character because "he is so unlike Logan and Joe, yet sporadically performs the same dominative masculinity they do"; however, he still embodies and practices a love for Janie that proves to be liberatory, even as this love does not guarantee complete liberation from the social hierarchy of their community.[34] Tea Cake must be distinguished from Killicks and Starks because, "rather than revolting or stifling her, Tea Cake loves Janie by and through her equal participation in play and pleasure"—normalizing and validating Janie's desire for mutual interaction within herself and as experienced within the community, a desire denied in her previous marriages.[35] Still, ultimately Tea Cake exhibited a mixed bag of characteristics—some positive, many negative, and accounting for both is necessary in any critical evaluation of him as a representation or guide for reflection on Black male identity.

Tea Cake appropriates violence as a means of controlling Janie; however, what complicates this further is Janie's willingness to continue to accept and embrace these character flaws. Shawn Miller touches on some of these complications by outlining the problems that emerge from a strict feminist reading of *Their Eyes*—centered on Janie's quest for love and wholeness from object to subject in the face of oppression. Miller also notes that Janie "masters conventional [patriarchal] marriage" through creatively "negotiating oppression predicated on gender."[36] Janie's "go along to get along" ethos geared toward realizing her own autonomy presents another complicated and contradictory feature of the relationship—what Miller refers to as a "covert feminism." For instance, after a particularly violent night of gambling with two hundred dollars of Janie's money, after which Tea Cake returns home bloodied with his winnings, Tea Cake illustrates his acceptance of patriarchal arrangements in the sharing and distribution of money, on which Janie cosigns. I quote this scene at length:

> They counted it together—three hundred and twenty-two dollars.... [Tea Cake] made her take the two hundred and put it back in the secret place. Then Janie told him about the other money she had in the bank:
> "Put dat two hundred back wid de rest, Janie. Mah dice. Ah no need no assistance tuh help me feed mah woman. From now on, you gointuh eat whatever mah money can buy yuh and wear de same. When Ah ain't got nothin' you don't git nothin.'"
> [Janie replies,] "Dat's all right wid me."
> He was getting drowsy, but he pinched her leg playfully because *he was glad she took things the way he wanted her to* [emphasis added].

Janie eschews direct resistance to the unfavorable qualities that Tea Cake embodies but also seems to appeal to some of the patriarchal aspects of these qualities—in effect bolstering his role as imperfect but benevolent patriarch.[37]

Tea Cake's markedly less stringent co-optation of Janie's subjectivity within the marriage can possibly offset the other aspects of the marriage that proved not as progressive or fulfilling, indicating the extent to which Tea Cake proves to be a highly contradictory character—capable of both progressive and regressive behaviors. The analysis of Tea Cake must continually uphold a realistic appraisal of what his example can and cannot teach us. Returning to Miller, it may be that Janie's first marriages to Killicks and Starks enabled her to realize the futility of trying to unmake conventional (patriarchal) marriage and thus, with Tea Cake, she learned to appropriate this conventionality to achieve her own interests.[38] There is also a sense in which Katie Cannon's interpretation of the life of Zora Neale Hurston and Hurston's writings supplements Miller's reading. Cannon discusses "unctuousness as virtue"—an ethical posture predicated upon a realistic appraisal of survival within the impossible possibility of "perfectionism in the face of the structures of oppression."[39] This unctuousness, or survival ethics, promotes the survival of the continual struggle of the day-to-day but also appreciates and, when necessary, appropriates "the interplay of contradictory opposites" in order to carve out a sense of wholeness within a restrictive environment for Black women. In other words, unctuousness as virtue recognizes the absurdity of oppressive circumstances and promotes a cool disposition until an opportune time to make an advance and correct one's circumstances. Taken from this perspective, Janie's compliance with Tea Cake's flaws and failures through indirect means may shed some light on this feature of their relationship and why she remained in the marriage.

It would be unreasonable to expect Tea Cake to exhibit complete enlightenment on gender and sex roles, for he is located "within the traditional ideology of marriage prevalent in rural twentieth-century America."[40] Far from condoning or downplaying Tea Cake's patriarchal tendencies, this insight prompts an effort to remain realistic in drawing upon a deeply contradictory character for insights about manhood. Tea Cake as well as other male characters whom Janie encounters are imperfect, have clay feet, and therefore cannot be reasonably expected to embody ideals or sensibilities that run counter to the societal, literary, and sexual contexts of the period in which they (and Hurston) lived. Despite this, we may still appeal to the contradictory dimensions of Tea Cake's personality to reject those aspects of his personality that are harmful but preserve those qualities that are worth embodying and practicing within healthier expressions of male identity. There is, therefore, a pragmatic approach needed in consideration of how best to interpret and learn from Tea Cake's example—some of his attributes are worthwhile and admirable, while others should be dismissed. On one hand, some of what Tea Cake presents is obviously anti-relational and deviates from establishing and maintaining wholesome and reciprocal relationships: he exhibits a penchant for violent aggression against women and men, and he articulates at times a conception of men as the natural "head" within marriages and relationships. However inconsistently, he still demonstrates the capacity to embody and practice other features worth preserving—namely, he accepts Janie's humanity and provides occasion for her to express herself in ways that many men in that era thought unimportant.

Neither Tea Cake's flaws nor his positive attributes regarding masculinity are exhaustive; he is a shifting, transitional character. While these facets of his identity as a man evolve and regress, there is still ample evidence that he acknowledges Janie's full personhood and subjectivity. The objective is not to assert that Tea Cake is Janie's liberator. Positioning Tea Cake in this vein of thought would serve only to reinforce the patriarchal frames of reference and relationality. Tea Cake's overall development, while incomplete and leaving much to be interpreted regarding the full extent of his transformation and regression, still illustrates his capacity to recognize the humanity of women as well as model anti-relational praxis, and both attributes are useful in reflecting upon wholesome expressions of male identity formation for Black men.

Frank Money's Care(ful) Ethics

Toni Morrison's novel *Home* elaborates on gender identity and relationality by positioning trauma as a shaper of familial relationships, personal growth, and, in the protagonist's case, Black manhood. *Home* has several layers and thematic motifs that revise and reshape African American gender roles, notably insights into the complexities of participating in community, the role of "othermothers" in the cultivation of health and well-being, and redemption from traumas related to raced and gendered pain. Within *Home*, Katrina Harack notes, "Morrison reveals the power of facing traumatic memory, the healing ability of community, and the destruction of traditional gender roles."[41] *Home* centers the story of a war veteran, Frank "Smart" Money, who is returning home to take care of and rescue his sister, Cee, who has suffered sexual violence and experimentation at the hands of a doctor with a predilection for eugenic theories on race, thereby practicing what Derek Hicks refers to as a campaign of debasement upon the Black female body.[42] Frank's participation in the healing of his sister is a means through which he also wrestles with, and heals, the demons of his own past, including problematic family ties, psychological breakdowns resulting from his experiences in the Korean War, and childhood exposure to racial violence.

It is not the prospect of Frank's heroism that piques my interpretive interests but rather Morrison's portrayal of caregiving and the extension of self on behalf of others as the base of Frank's self-understanding and identity. Frank's participation in the care and healing of his sister illustrates the gift of *himself*—an embodiment of relational selfhood. Frank's example is marked primarily by a sacrificial quality. By "sacrifice," it is not my intent to imply a kenotic reading of Frank's actions. Any kenotic reading would be problematic because it raises the possibility of sacralizing the totality of Frank's actions, rendering him a savior figure. Kenotic interpretations of Frank here would also delegitimize Cee's agency and personal responsibility in her own self-care, driven by the women of the Lotus community in Georgia where Cee is recuperating. Rather, Frank's sacrifice is indicated in *his* choice to live into a relational identity, one that Morrison portrays through self-giving and caregiving. What Frank willingly gives up, from the standpoint of sacrifice, is a life contoured by a singular focus, shifting instead to an identity grounded in a caregiving relationship. In observing and taking a back seat to the power and insights of Black woman community and culture as it relates to Cee's health and healing, Frank re-creates and reconstructs new personal meaning through relationship that is marked by concern and regard for health. Morrison's centering of Black women's healing culture into the dynamic between Frank and Cee raises another significant point for consideration and opens space for womanist religious and ethical insights.

In an analysis and critique of American health care in *Breaking the Fine Rain of Death*, Emilie Townes advocates a communal framing of caregiving, healing, and restoration for spiritual and medical maladies. In positing health and healing as a social production and social responsibility, notes Townes, "cultural-empowerment" models emphasize an approach embedded through the *shared* work of the community and caregivers to restore well-being, empower the most vulnerable, and disentangle the societal and environmental pitfalls that negatively impact the life options of racialized, minoritized, and impoverished communities.[43] Morrison's description of the act of caregiving surrounding Cee, and in which Frank participates, is a powerful example of womanist care ethics. It is toward the ties between these features of caregiving, Frank's role, and the impact upon his notion of manhood in *Home* that I now turn.

Frank is a World War II veteran returning home to Georgia after receiving word of his sister's medical emergencies and subsequent illnesses due to the brutal experimentation of a racist doctor: "The letter said, 'She be dead.' Meaning she's alive but sick, very sick, and obviously there was no one to help her" (34). With deceased parents and despondent and uncaring grandparents, Frank embraces the burden of Cee's care and offers himself for her sake, which in doing so demands that Frank suspend any notion of his preconceived or assumed self-vested identity.[44] Morrison's prose captures Frank's internal feelings on his role as caregiver and how it is central to his newfound identity: "Maybe his life had been preserved for Cee . . . a selflessness without gain or emotional profit. Even before she [Cee] could walk he'd taken care of her" (35). While Morrison describes this feature as selfless, I read Frank's thoughts on his caregiving as an expansion of the meaning of him(self) as relationally tethered to the care and healing of others. The direction of his life and being in this way opens up a new horizon of visibility—the gift of himself on behalf of Cee. Frank embraces a reciprocal and empathic ontological connection that further reaffirms the relational turn in his self-understanding and identity; as he notes, "She was the first person I ever took responsibility for. Deep down inside her lived my secret picture of myself" (104).

After rescuing Cee from the doctor's imprisonment and bringing her home, Frank's role as caregiver almost immediately takes a back seat to the more pronounced and active caregiving of the community of Black women in the town. Practiced in the creative blending of healing herbs, and the alchemy of natural and spiritual remedies, these women "handled sickness as though it were an affront, an illegal, invading braggart who needed whipping" (121). The communal approach to Cee's care and healing deploys both esoteric and organic tools. After Frank's arrival, the women bar his presence, suggesting a regressive energy that would delay healing: "They believed his maleness would worsen her condition. She told him the women took turns nursing Cee and each had a different recipe for her cure. What they all agreed upon was his absence from her bedside" (119). This absence was likely called for, in the women's minds, due to Frank's palpable spirit of despair. This is illustrated through Frank's initial doubt in the presence of one woman, Miss Ethel: "Don't you let her die. . . . You hear me?" (119). Frank is subsequently expelled from their activities and commune, for his "evil mind-set," and is instructed to stay away until called for, thereby providing space for the flourishing of hope central to healing. Morrison's attention to Frank's expulsion and what they deem his psychospiritual weakness is interesting, especially when paralleled with Townes's indictment of the presence of despair in healing communities. Despair, says Townes, signals that "we have no confidence, no expectation, no yearning for a tangible justice or an immeasurable love."[45] In the absence of a sense of purpose and the lack of a future with any real meaning, nihilistic mentalities are the segue "toward our own annihilation."[46]

The women's caregiving also parallels womanism's separatist imperative. Alice Walker noted that womanists are "periodically separatist," for reasons of health and well-being, indicating an agentive self-segregation in preference for women's community, culture, and nurturing. Cee's caregiving intervention fully enfleshes this principle. This point in the novel is a striking turning point because it reveals an instance in which Frank is compelled to rethink the nature of his embrace of relational self-constitution and caregiving by deferring to Black women's communal authority, as they are now the primary initiators of Cee's healing, away from the throes of male-oriented and male-led culture. As Morrison notes of the women's community and Cee's continued progress, "Surrounded by their comings and goings, listening to their talk, their songs, following their instructions, Cee had nothing to do but pay them the attention she had never given them before. . . . There was no excess in their gardens because they shared everything. There was no trash or garbage in their homes because they had a use for everything. They took responsibility for their lives and for whatever, whoever else needed them" (122–123). When Frank was allowed to return to visit Cee, he is struck by not only her healthful appearance but also the strength of her sense of agency and self-possession. Miss Ethel captures Cee's newfound sentiment powerfully: "See what I mean? Look to yourself. You free. Nothing and nobody is obliged to save you but you. Seed your own land. You young and a woman and there's serious limitation in both, but you a person too. Don't let [anyone] decide who you are. That's slavery. Somewhere inside you is that free person I'm talking about. Locate her" (126). Through the women's tutelage, care, and unique practice of truth telling, they were able to heal and deliver to Frank "a Cee who would never again need his hand over her eyes or his arms to stop her murmuring bones" (128). While Morrison's focus toward the latter part of the novel is clearly fixed upon the restorative powers of women's community in the health and healing of others, it is not shortsighted to consider additionally how this experience may have impacted Frank's understanding of women's autonomy and agency. As Harack observes, *Home* deploys a gender calculus that rejects models of "individualism along with white, hegemonic, male ideologies of progress [and male proactivity], and instead celebrates the communal, productive, healing power of women and men who have faced the past, celebrate the present, and look forward to a future that is not rigidly defined by existing race and gender ideologies."[47]

As Morrison observes, "Frank alone valued her. While his devotion shielded her, it did not strengthen her. Should it have? Why was that his job and not her own?" (129). It is possible that Frank's previous associations of manhood with the kind of protectionism noted here come from a deeper, internal source. As with all gender identity formation, we cannot look at the development of a person without considering familial background and foundational contextual experience as a shaper of one's selfhood. As children, Frank and Cee bore witness to the aftermath of a Black man's lynching. *Home* begins with the trauma of this shared memory between the two and provides context for a significant feature of their childhood environment and the impact it had on their realities. Morrison therefore indicates the role that childhood traumas play in gender identity development, and this is an interpretive nuance that must be held in tension. Given Frank's early exposure to particularly brutal racialized violence, it is perhaps natural that he, as an adult, connects masculinity with power, but also with a capacity to defend and protect those dear to him.

Frank's protectionism is problematized—his "secret picture of himself" that he saw in her as her protector is deconstructed, with Cee taking its place. Frank reveals some internal conflicts regarding progressive views of women as autonomous and independent.[48] Sometimes, caregiving is not only directly applied, in terms of "hands on" engagement. Rather, as Townes observed, there is a network-based and communal approach to care ethics that involves multiple persons and entities. Because this is coalitional and collaborative caregiving, it is at times prudent for those providing care to know when to cede authority, and in some cases expertise, to others in the process. In this sense, caregiving, as Frank learned, expanded far beyond the "direct" protectionism and sense of responsibility he singularly practiced and took early on. By adopting and learning from the communal approach to health and healing from Miss Ethel and the commune of Black women in Lotus, Frank's relationality and approach to caregiving was likewise pressed to evolve as well.

Cee's healing, Frank's self-understanding, and the community of Black women illustrate some manners in which Frank begins to embody relational selfhood as a reflection of care ethics. His initial appearance illustrates his embrace of protectionism as a generative quality underscoring familial connection and belonging. This is a strong relational disposition because it hinges upon the profundity of self-giving and the self as gift on behalf of the well-being of others. In offering this portrayal, Morrison voices a powerful expression of Black manhood that deconstructs other distorted images dispensed in academic and social spaces. In a public lecture, Morrison described the opening pages of *Home* as an intro about manhood and notes that Frank went through varied locales and experiences to find his own, but it was when he learned to link love for others, namely his sister, to his identity as a man that he was able to embrace a fuller sense of himself—one that he "encouraged and found when he went home and took care of someone."[49]

Frank's relational identity, and arguably his identity as a Black man, was impacted through his experience of learning to adopt Black women's healing culture and community. Frank's exposure to the communal approach to caregiving among Black women proved to be instructive. Because the community of women disallowed his participation in their caregiving, he was compelled to disabuse himself of the idea of him(self) as Cee's protector and allow the healing community of Black women in his hometown to take the lead. Here, recognizing one's limits, realizing that there are occasions when singular agency alone is ill suited for larger cultural and societal prospects of communal health and well-being, provides space for a realistic appraisal of giving and helping others. Frank was able to see that sometimes deference and ceding presumed authority for the sake of others is a necessary feature of caregiving. The trajectory of Frank's relational identity therefore not only entailed the giving of himself but also ended up being an instructive experience in that he learned the value of recognizing limits and vulnerabilities in the face of challenges and ordeals larger than his capacities to care for his sister. Care ethics are not meant to be solitary, for the strategies of caregiving often "depend on the community and the caregiver working together as partners"—accountability and responsibility, thus, are personal *and* communal.[50] This was a valuable lesson for Frank, as he learned the value of care ethics in which burdens and responsibilities for the other are shared, thereby strengthening the communal resources and energies devoted to health and well-being. Here, individualized identity formation is bracketed and supplanted with a greater self-constitution that is realized through the act of considering and working toward the well-being of others.

Conclusion

In addition to my focus on the powerful lessons and insightful commentary regarding the illustration and affirmation of wholesome Black manhood within womanists' fiction and imagination, this chapter also sheds some light on the larger cultural debates pertaining to the representation of Black men as well as grapples with the *meaning* of Black manhood therein. On this score, Victor Anderson's framing of the variegated multiplicity of African American experience, which I will return to in the epilogue, aids my constructive thinking on the deeper complexity of Black men's personhood and identity. Following the work of theologian Edward Farley, Anderson notes that identity constructs such as race and gender all function as "deep symbols"—the "rooted categories of social meaning within our increasing, changing, and developing stock of knowledge."[51] These symbols constitute meaning for human life, but are increasingly on unstable terrain, are fluid in scope, and can be molded, adapted, and repurposed. Extending the notion of deep symbol further to include the construction and reconfiguration of Black manhood and the portrayal of Black men in womanist writings and in other spaces reveals another level of critical importance that many Black men attach to their representations. In other words, Black manhood, and the representation thereof, is a matter of abiding, life-altering concern. As a deep symbol, with powerful constitutive meaning, if popular constructions of Black manhood impactful upon Black men's sense of self are found wanting, then it is prudent to look to other spaces and within their own creative processes of discernment, to develop alternative frames of self-identity more in keeping with the realization of their highest subjectivity. In this chapter I have illustrated that the Black women writers who have deeply influenced womanists are excellent conversation partners and visionary meaning makers as it relates to the call for humanizing portrayals of Black male lives.

In *The Sexual Mountain and Black Women Writers*, Calvin Hernton discussed his hope for the prospect of Black men "being educated" by women's literature—prompting both rage and reticence about the embrace of various constructions of sexist behavior that are harmful for themselves, their communities, and Black women. In drawing upon the writings of Black women here, it is my view that such perspectives are instructive and, whether they are a source of contention in Black cultural spaces or not, still deserve greater scrutiny and recognition. Black men, as Gloria Wade-Gayles notes in the foreword to Hernton's book, may be aroused in anger in response to womanist writers like Walker, but *more* critical is the consequence that these writers serve as catalysts for self-critique and self-reflection about the quandaries and navigation of Black manhood, even if this process begins from a defensive posture.[52]

As Ishmael Reed makes clear in his recollections surrounding the pop culture firestorm surrounding the publication and production of *The Color Purple*, the presumption of Black male pathology as a matter of course in the portrayal of Black men was the tipping point for many African American men's reactions to Walker's literary and cultural stardom. Additionally, that the most passionate defenders of Walker's writings and the portrayals of Black men therein seemed to be White feminists left Reed and many other Black men feeling betrayed and that they were the subject of a vast ideological and representational conspiracy—all while illustrating the deeply political and contested sites of meaning applied to popular discourses on Black men as topics at the intersections of race and gender.[53] That Reed and other critics tie Walker and other Black feminist and womanist writers to a systematic and culturally driven praxis of Black male bashing reveals the extent to which perceptions of Black manhood, in academic, popular culture, and political spheres, is contested terrain. In these spaces and beyond, according to these critics, there is tacit acceptance of Black men's brutality and pathology as gospel truth.

While I remain sensitive to and mindful of the debate among Black men regarding their depiction within the larger corpus of Black women's writings, as well as within cultural and political discourses and in film and media, I propose here that womanist writings do not play a role in driving anti-Black male regimes. Throughout this chapter I have held in tension my desire to engage womanist-identified literature as an instructive discourse, with the often-contested political landscape of gender theorization and gender politics centering on Black males. To return to Walker's framing, womanism privileges the *survival of whole people, male and female*. With this ideological and tropological anchor in mind, when one considers the full scope of Albert, "Tea Cake," and Frank Money, the problematic and positive features of their identities as presented in each novel are not, to my mind, a moratorium on the pathology of Black men. Rather, they illustrate the ambiguities and contradictions at play in Black men's existence and lifeworlds. However, there is also an underlay of hope in the envisioning of alternative Black manhood constructs.

It is often charged that depictions and generalized perceptions of Black men and boys are singularly constructed in popular culture and in gender theories on masculinity as defective, suspect, and dangerous.[54] Through the perspective of Black male studies discourses, Tommy Curry and other theorists have effectively argued for interpretations of Black male life that reject anti-Black misandry and gendered racism, in order to dismantle reductionist and oversimplified understandings of Black men and their identities as only pathological and only patriarchal. These perspectives are important because they advocate for discursive and ethnological approaches that correct the "pathologizing of Black men and boys as theoretical advance and proposes the empirically informed accounts of Black male life . . . as the basis to condemn and object to Black male death."[55] These perspectives humanize Black male lives through centering social and empirical studies examining how Black men and boys understand their roles and identities against the backdrop of the cultural and social regimes that plague their capacity to flourish and thrive.

In looking to Walker, Hurston, and Morrison's fictional exploration of gender politics and Black manhood as examples of relational identity formation and as sites of contradiction and ambiguity, however, a case can be made for the usefulness of womanist-identified literature in humanizing Black men, warts and all—as a juxtaposition with the insights and humanistic endeavors central to Black male studies. Thus, a complementary rather than antagonistic relationship between womanism and Black-male-oriented scholarship is possible. Womanist writings, in contrast to demonizing Black men, present fuller explorations of Black male humanity and complexity, which, after all, is a more realistic and grounded approach rather than relying upon the extremes of either total pathology or total perfection.

3

James Baldwin, the Black Church, and Queering the Masculinist Oeuvre

The American ideal, then, of sexuality appears to be rooted in the American ideal of masculinity. This ideal has created cowboys and Indians, good guys and bad guys, punks and studs, tough guys and softies, butch and faggot, black and white.
—Baldwin, "Freaks and the American Ideal of Manhood"

If the concept of God has any validity or any use, it can only be to make us larger, freer, and more loving.
—Baldwin, *Fire Next Time*

In the first epigraph above, James Baldwin commented upon the false binaries of gendered identity and behavioral scripts—all of which are grounded in rather myopic understandings of sexuality and manhood. In the case of Black men, as the larger corpus of Baldwin's writings has commented upon, the process of embracing and living into one's full sexual identity is fraught with the idealizations and norms of a society that renders oneself and other Black men nightmarish tropes constructed by the White racialized psyche. Baldwin, given his identity as an out, gay male, was doubly and triply burdened with external tropes related to his presumed sexual deviancy: "On every street corner, I was called a faggot. This meant that I was despised, and, however horrible this is, it is clear."[1] Baldwin's relationship with some of his contemporaries was also hampered by homophobic sentiments. James Campbell's biography details Baldwin's soured literary relationship with Richard Wright, who was "disgusted" by Baldwin's homosexuality, and furthermore castigated the tone and thematic focus of his first novel, *Go Tell It on the Mountain*, for its "unmanly weeping" and overly "sensitive sentences."[2]

Scholarly commentary on the depth and complexity of Black male experience and identity has often looked to Black men's literature as a space for the reimagining and reconfiguration of Black men's subjectivity, agency, and telos in American society and abroad.[3] In referencing Black male subjectivity, I specifically refer to the capacity for Black men to redirect the trajectory of their own histories and futures—thereby transcending the limiting and limited "orthodox notions of male power and dominance."[4] The quest for expansive understandings of Black humanity and personhood speaks to the foci that inspired James Baldwin's writing, heightened his creative rendering of American race relations, and awakened his artistic vision. As Baldwin observes, "Writing was an act of love . . . an attempt—not to get the world's attention—[but] . . . to be loved. It was a way to save myself and to save my family. It came out of despair . . . it seemed the only way to another world."[5] Part of the alternative vision that Baldwin sought to re-create and reimagine into a new reality, involves the construction of alternate discursive worlds in which he, as a Black gay man, had space to truly *be*—beyond the confines and strictures of the racial, sexual, religious, and gendered mores of his time.

This chapter accents what I refer to as the *masculinist* posture in James Baldwin's writing. I place this literary interpretation into conversation with Black queer religious thought to critique Black church culture, which, as Baldwin illustrates, prompted a profound religious crisis in his own sensibilities. By "masculinist," I adopt Keith Clark's interpretation of Black-male-oriented literature. Clark utilizes an interdisciplinary analysis of Black male literary representation to uncover complex configurations of Black masculinity and subjectivity that are hidden or dismissed in favor of popular (and unnuanced) race and gender tropes.[6] As Clark makes clear, masculinism is an interpretive maneuver, based in literary methodology, that "extrapolate[s] the intersection between subjectivity and masculinity, exploring how male writers have negotiated and critiqued constructions of gender" and, namely, illustrates how the Black male literary subject is situated.[7] Baldwin's *Go Tell It on the Mountain* (1953) and *If Beale Street Could Talk* (1974)[8] work within a masculinist literary frame of reference, given that the portraitures of Black males throughout each embody open and fluid relational identities premised upon complex renderings of subjectivity that are *not* "circumscribed by a type of hypermasculine ethos" so often linked to the demonization of Black men.[9] Masculinism, therefore, is not linked to what theologian James Nelson describes as the distorted "sexual dualisms" that reify the patriarchal order.[10] Baldwin's masculinist writing resists the restrictive enframement of Black males by creating male characters that grow into and embody manhood in ways that amplify their humanity, complexity, voice, emotional depth, and capacity for wholesome relationships.

There is also a bent toward Black religiosity and the power of Black church culture that remains prominent in Baldwin's literary imagination. Michael Lynch opined that Baldwin is a "theological writer," evident through his constant wrestling with the meaning of God as well as his appropriation of Black Christian moral precepts to articulate his vision of the world.[11] Other critics of Baldwin have rightly focused on the role of religion in Baldwin's thinking and personal philosophical dispositions. Baldwin himself once declared in an interview with anthropologist Margaret Mead, "The whole question . . . of religion has always really obsessed me." Baldwin's fascination with and grounding in Black Christian thought, culture, and expression can be linked to his own rather traumatic induction into the faith through his family and, in particular, the abuses suffered at the hands of his stepfather, which is expounded upon in *Mountain*. In *Beale Street*, with Baldwin's take on the restrictive and judgmental excess of Black Christian fundamentalism, Baldwin extends his critique on the relational and interpersonal dysfunctions inaugurated by toxic Black church culture and the impact upon the Rivers and Hunt families.

In revisiting some of the implications of Baldwin's critical insight(s) toward Black religious life, and to centralize his voice as a gay man, I also find it necessary to read Baldwin within the context of Black *queer* religious thought. My turn to Black queer thought is responsive to Roger Sneed's push for a "black queer hermeneutics of retrieval"—an effort to foreground gay and lesbian experiences in Black religious scholarship. Sneed critiques Black liberation theologies and religious criticism for de-amplifying the voices of gay and lesbian perspectives, including ignoring Black gay men's literature.[12] In locating Baldwin within the masculinist tradition *and* as a source for Black religious reflection, I endeavor to read Baldwin within the context of a larger discursive and creative space in which Black manhood and Black male experience are reconceptualized beyond the myopic raced, gendered, and sexual enframements and binaries nurtured by the church. This read thereby reveals ties to queer religious scholarship and uncovers a critique of African American church culture and theological traditions that contribute to the gendered traumas and religious crises that impact gay, lesbian, and transgender persons.

Fellow novelist Norman Mailer once impressed upon Baldwin a noted desire to understand the nature of power. Baldwin responded: "I know how power works, *it has worked on me* [italics mine], and if I didn't know how power worked, I would be dead."[13] Part of this power, I submit, is the power of identity construction and self-making. If it is true, as Baldwin has reminded us, that the "nigger" is a figment of the White racial imagination, or specifically, the White racial nightmare stemming from an inability to confront the horrors of reality, to escape the racial and gender identity prison must include the embrace of a creative and robust selfhood that denies the rigidity of raced and gendered constellations driven by the machinery of White supremacy *and* patriarchal excess. This is what Baldwin refers to as the "achievement of identity."[14] The capacity to fashion one's identity, in the vein of Baldwin, is a mechanism of empowerment. In recovering Baldwin's voice and bringing it to bear upon the construction of Black manhood, I am spotlighting the capacity and power that Black men have to articulate complex understandings of themselves as subjects and agents in the fashioning of their own identities.

In an essay, "The Black Boy Looks at the White Boy," Baldwin commented upon the unfinished quality of Black manhood—the result of a racial gaze and racial power that delimits the fullness and scope of Black personhood: "To become a Negro man . . . one had to make oneself up as one went along. This had to be done in the not-at-all-metaphorical teeth of the world's determination to destroy you."[15] From a masculinist read of Baldwin's writings, the improvisational, self-making subjectivity of Black men is prominent, and in creating space for a fuller range of Black male experiences and personhood, Baldwin charts a course for the "achievement of identity"—thereby mitigating, or at best reversing, the tides of ontological displacement cast through the machinations of an American society that embraces the social and material deaths of Black people and that validates these deaths through dehumanization and deidentifying. These selected Baldwin novels provide an exploration of Black male experience and reveal how one can achieve a robust identity, despite the restrictions of the Black church and in the face of realities driven by family and communal conflict.

Manhood, Intimacy, and (Religious) Crisis in *Go Tell It on the Mountain*

As Baldwin's first published novel and arguably among his most acclaimed works, *Go Tell It on the Mountain*, is cited as a coming-of-age story with tinges of the autobiographical that mirror Baldwin's upbringing as a youth in Harlem.[16] By most biographical accounts, Baldwin's upbringing was marked by a sense of displacement within a family led by an abusive, self-hating, and religiously tyrannical stepfather. Baldwin's stepfather, David, "hated white people," and the capstone of his religious devotion was driven by a theodicy in which God's vengeance would be visited upon White society. The bitterness, racial hostility, and religiosity, however, were largely received by the Baldwin family as outright cruelty.[17] Like the paternal relationship experiences of the protagonist of *Mountain*, John Grimes, Baldwin's experience with his stepfather is best understood as the failure of "many a father and mother who gave to their children not bread but a stone" (124).[18] Baldwin sought self-esteem, guidance, and encouragement within his relationship with his stepfather, which never materialized. Struggles with his stepfather, linked to both the family's poverty and the restrictions of religious fanaticism, came to a head over the younger Baldwin's love of literature, his intelligence, and the expression of desires that lay beyond the immediate social circles confined to the Black church.

On this register, *Mountain* is a representation of Baldwin's struggle to find an identity grounded in an unrealized love from an emotionally absent and religiously abusive father. The emotional distance between Baldwin and the only father he ever "knew" reflects a biological and spiritual denial of birthright and symbolizes the racialized burden of African Americans who come of age in a society that neither wants nor values their presence.[19] My focus pivots upon Baldwin's portrayal of the quest for an unencumbered and liberated Black manhood centered upon the development of John, and as impacted through John's relationships with his stepfather, Gabriel, and friend, Elisha—all against the backdrop of the confessional, coercive, and conversion-brokering terrain of Black holiness culture in the urban north.

The fourteen-year-old John Grimes, like the younger James Baldwin, is caught at an identity crossroads squeezed by multiple backdrops: Black fundamentalist Christianity, the desire for legitimate familial belonging, burgeoning sexual maturity and self-discovery, and the allure of worldly fulfillment. This much is suggested in the opening narration: "Everyone had always said that John would be a preacher when he grew up, just like his father. It had been said so often that John, without ever thinking about it, had come to believe it himself. Not until the morning of his fourteenth birthday did he really begin to think about it, and by then it was already too late" (7). John's transition to manhood, therefore, is grounded in crisis. Personal and religious crisis in Baldwin's universe is the crisis of disunity and separation from kith and kin. It is a crisis of othered unbelonging. John seeks more from a life that is not tethered to either the theological rigidity or familial and social estrangement of his religious environment. John's crisis is encapsulated by the quandary of navigating an escape from the narrow confines of Gabriel's house and the strictures of his theology of dominance and damnation to (re)create his own identity by establishing fulfilling ties of relationship and belonging. Gabriel's house, a reflection of the local Black holiness church, represents more than an ideological and theological prison under which John struggles to flourish—it is a site of contestation, a warring of competing ideals for authentic personhood. From the autobiographical bent to Baldwin's portrayal of the dynamic between John and Gabriel, Baldwin once opined that writing *Mountain* helped him contextualize and dismantle the personal demons that impacted him and that destroyed his stepfather: "I had to understand the forces, the experience, the life that shaped him, before I could grow up myself."[20] Critics of *Mountain* have observed that the novel offers a strong focus on the interplay of the patriarchal excesses of the father and religion as central to John's transformation from boyhood to manhood. Trudier Harris argues that *Mountain* can be read "as a rite of exorcism against the tyranny of the father, especially when that familial figure uses the tyranny of the church to bolster his position."[21]

Gabriel's religious tyranny and its iron will over the household, however, reveals relational crisis—one that John must also dismantle and navigate. Interestingly, Gabriel's initial conversion from a wayward life of sin and toward his new role as a man of faith and leader within the church is not marked by either the pastoral or the priestly functions of religious leadership. Of Gabriel's conversion, Baldwin writes, "He wanted power—he wanted to know himself to be the Lord's anointed.... He wanted to be master, to speak with that *authority*" (97, emphasis added). This revelation spotlights the quality of the religious conversion experience shaping Gabriel's theological and personal maturation and that, likewise, impacts John's home environment. Gabriel's religious and salvific turn is marked by the desire for power and authority, and it is this very brand of authoritarian religious devotion that led both John Grimes and the young Baldwin to view religious faith in Black holiness culture as "the central promoter of emotional deadness and parental irresponsibility."[22]

In shifting to John Grimes's identity as a man, it is important to contextualize the relationships and personal discovery within Black church culture and its theologies. Clearly, the church plays a prominent role in Baldwin's *bildungsroman*, but specifically its placement in Grimes's development illustrates the extent to which religious space can serve both destructive and restorative ends in one's pursuit of fulfillment. John's process of self-discovery in the dismantling of Gabriel's authority and oppressive presence is grounded in the pursuit of robust manhood and a need for an extended intimacy and love beyond the confines of his religious community. I build upon these observations to focus on the relational quality of John's achievement of identity, both to highlight his quest for manhood and to make a sharp distinction to that of Gabriel. In contrast to the domineering and abusive features of Gabriel's masculinity, John's "deliverance" from his father's house and his destructive theology, which culminates in his conversion experience on the threshing floor of the church, is characterized by the fight and flight to embrace a manhood that endures through shared intimacy and love with others, something Gabriel neither embodies nor shares with John. The relational intimacy John grows to embrace through the conversion experience is linked to the influence, fraternality, and brotherhood of his friend Elisha.

Baldwinian intimacy, however, requires a nuanced interpretation, given the easy tethering to simplistic notions of sexual partnering.

Within the Harlem universe in which the young Grimes becomes a man, intimacy bespeaks shared ties in which the saving of others and being saved is a function of personal identity formation and praxis. John's quest for such an identity and intimacy, one in which he freely receives others and is received by others, constitutes a religious undertaking, as "religion's relationship to salvation is understood through how it opens itself spatially to those in need of saving . . . [intimacy] maintains the same power—to save."[23] In *Salvific Manhood: James Baldwin's Novelization of Male Intimacy*, Ernest Gibson argues that *Mountain*'s portrayal of John's search for identity is characterized by a desire for "space where he can be both vulnerable and strong in his manhood, where the shackles of society's perceptions loosen their hold on Black masculinity and intimacy."[24] While inclusive of romantic sexuality, Gibson renders intimacy as a kind of organic religiosity that is enfleshed and communally oriented. This modality of religious sentiment contrasts with the individualized conversion narratives that enjoy wide currency in evangelical Christian culture. Here, the salvation and well-being of others is privileged as a distinctive component of what it means to be relational—thereby expanding the strictly confessional, "soul-safeguarding" Christian theology endemic to John's religious orientation.

Intimacy and salvation are, therefore, linked and possibly interchangeable. Baldwin suggested a similar expansion of these features of Christian thought, adopting a relational underscoring of both: "Salvation is not precipitated by the terror of being consumed in hell [and] is not flight from the wrath of God. Salvation is not separation. It is the beginning of union with all that is, or has been or will be."[25] Baldwin's soteriology, prioritizing humanocentric union rather than the God-to-human dynamic, expands the relationality that comes to characterize John's religious maturation and furthermore grounds the nature of the masculine identity formation he learns to embrace with Elisha. With Elisha, John finds a compatriot who ushers him through his conversion experience and models a powerful relational intimacy, fraternal love, and manhood that ultimately indicts the domineering patriarchy and estrangement central to Gabriel's praxis of manhood and fatherhood.

The relationship between John and Elisha is often cited as a subtle nod to Baldwin's exploration of John's burgeoning homosexual identity. This much is hinted at in John's narrative following Elisha's judgment at the altar by the pastor for showing affection to another young woman in the congregation: "*Had* he sinned? Had he been tempted? And the girl beside him, whose white robes now seemed the merest, thinnest covering for the nakedness of breasts and insistent thighs—what was her face like when she was one with Elisha, with no singing, when they were not surrounded by the saints? He was afraid to think of it, yet he could think of nothing else" (13–14). Bryan Washington reads the dynamic between John and Elisha as a narrative that repackages the societal cues regarding the day's unspoken and unnamed taboos related to (un)sanctioned sexuality, namely outside the bounds of Christian marriage and heterosexuality. Washington attaches particular meaning to the wrestling match between Elisha and John—in which John found "wild delight" (52) in besting his slightly older friend, indicating that both "are wrestling with homosexual desire."[26] While analyzing the latent homosexual implications of John and Elisha's relationship is vital to understanding both Baldwin's sexuality as well as the sexual mores of his time, it is the relational complexity and intimacy of John and Eqlisha's platonic union that grounds my interpretive scope.

John's relationship with Elisha illustrates a "male-to-male love" that also unlocks a "new logic of salvation"—for Elisha literally, as John's brother in the faith, saves him from the confines of a life doomed by disunion, estrangement, and the need to dominate.[27] Moreover, it is Elisha who instructs John in the embrace of relationality as a feature of identity and self-making. While "it is the space-in-between John and Gabriel that shapes, colors, and breathes life" into the religious crisis that poisons their (lack of) relationship and alienates the Grimes home, John sees in Elisha "a younger antithesis of Gabriel, but also the image of Christian godliness," not marked by a moralistic vision and piety but including a praxis of faith in material life and brotherhood that is uplifting, edifying, and rooted in emotional depth and intimacy—thereby establishing a new model for the understanding of Black male identity. Earlier in the novel we find John "distracted by his new teacher, Elisha," and "admiring [his grace], and strength," "wondering if he would ever be holy as Elisha was holy" (9).

The liberative impact of John's relationship with Elisha is a striking contrast to Gabriel, who denied John familial belonging and love and routinely subjects him to ridicule and verbal abuse. These abuses were given an additional religious validation—in which John's phenotypical Blackness and personal appearance are amplified as moral and spiritual scourges unsuited for holiness. In one flashback, during the climactic conversion section of the book, John and Gabriel happen upon an inebriated woman:

> She was drunk, dirty, and very old, and her mouth was bigger than his mother's mouth, or his own; her mouth was loose and wet, and he had *never* seen anyone so black. His father was astonished to see her, and beside himself with anger; but John was glad. He clapped his hands and cried: "See! She's uglier than Mama! She's uglier than me!" "You mighty proud, ain't you," his father said, "to be the Devil's son?" (210)

Clarence Hardy cites Gabriel's treatment of John on this accord as a reflection of the tension regarding John's illegitimacy, a reminder of Gabriel's personal skeletons, and a feature of his racial self-loathing, in which Black bodies are largely cast as sinful, ugly, and reprobate.[28] I read John's maturation and development through his friendship with Elisha as the antidote to the anti-relational theology represented by his stepfather and the Church of the Fire Baptized. However, John Grimes's growth and embrace of a new identity is also the realization of a new manhood. As his aunt Elizabeth reflects on John's religious conversion experience on the threshing floor of the church, "she heard him cry; not the cry of the child, newborn, before the common light of the earth; but the cry of the *man-child*, bestial, before the light that comes down from Heaven" (202, emphasis added).

Baldwin's use of "man-child" as a description is interesting. A man-child, seemingly, is at a crossroads of maturity—marking an in-betweenness of childhood and adulthood, boyhood and manhood. If the man-child represents the liminal crossroads positionality that bridges the lacuna from boyhood to manhood, it is also, as Audre Lorde notes, a period of profound spiritual and emotional reckoning with the direction of one's identity and how this denouement also entails independence and agency: "And our sons must become men—such men as we hope our daughters, born and unborn, will be pleased to live among. Our sons will not grow into women. Their way is more difficult than that of our daughters, for they must move away from us, without us. Hopefully, our sons have what they have learned from us, and a howness to forge it into their own image."[29] Lorde's observations address the trials and challenges she reflected upon in the raising of her son as a Black lesbian mother, and she recognizes the trial-laden pathway(s) to manhood faced by Black males. In the case of John, what guides his growth and empowers his "howness" to grapple with the minefields of Black male identity is his struggle to realize and embody a powerful relationality grounded in fraternal embrace, love, and connection to others.

For Baldwin, authentic manhood is relational and connective. John comes of age, in toto, against the backdrop of multiple fronts: restrictive Black church culture, broken home life, and a toxic stepfather. Ultimately, however, despite the great lengths to which these features of his lifeworld negatively stunted his development, it is relational connection that saves him. The stony love of Gabriel "beat sin" (209) out of John and ruptured his personhood, diminished his capacity to experience love, and failed to model a holistic masculinity. It was the guidance and brotherhood of Elisha that unlocked a new theology of self. In this sense, as Gibson suggests, the Black manhood that Grimes grows to embrace through his connection to Elisha is salvific. The roots of transformed identity through deeper relationships reflect a saving endeavor because all "salvation connects, so that one sees oneself in others and others in oneself."[30] The logic of salvation operative in relational identity formation overturns estrangement, alienation, and disconnection. After John's conversion on the threshing floor of the church, Elisha is among the first to embrace him anew and inquires if he is now saved. Indicative of a newfound achievement of personhood and manhood grounded in the connectional theology of reconciliation to self and to neighbor, John replies: "Lord, I ain't no stranger now!" (219).

Fatherhood and Sonhood on Beale Street

Mountain served as Baldwin's foray into the quandaries and ambiguities that characterize Black men's pursuit of an embraced and *embracing* identity in the context of religious and familial dysfunction. Grimes's coming-of-age story not only offers a clear indictment of Gabriel but more broadly "criticizes the black church and Christianity by illustrating the tragedy of a perverted theology in most of the characters' lives and its construction of a false God."³¹ As I have maintained, the crux of the perversion and the true falsity of this religious orientation is anti-relation and disunity, which is manifest in the estrangement between John and Gabriel, and reconciled between John and Elisha. *If Beale Street Could Talk* (1974) reveals some of Baldwin's work on the themes of relationality and identity formation among Black men, again drawing upon the backdrop of and contrasts with fundamentalist Black church culture. In shifting to *Beale Street*, my focus is again on Black men and the constitutive power of relational self-perception and self-understanding, and in this light I examine Baldwin's construction of fatherhood and sonhood.

Beale Street is notable in Baldwin's larger corpus, with many critics taking note of his use of a female protagonist, Clementine "Tish" Rivers, as a literary device to explore multiple thematic foci, particularly Black female sexuality, intimacy, and sexual agency. Tish, who is pregnant, is in a passionate and loving relationship with Alozno "Fonny" Hunt, who is falsely accused of rape. While *Beale Street* pivots upon notions of Black women's agency as a significant feature of liberative Black love and Black relationships, the novel also centers Tish and Fonny's relationship, familial dynamics and care ethics explored within the context of the Rivers and Hunt families, and additional themes pertaining to racism and imprisonment. I pursue the religious and interpersonal exchange that transpires within the families, which is distilled through vestiges of Black church culture, and likewise reveal Baldwin's ongoing grappling with the contradictions of Christian faith and praxis when aligned with the pathologies of repressive sexual mores and precepts. Notably, I examine Baldwin's continued gravitation toward a radical religiosity premised upon relationality and connection, but I go further by applying this interpretive scope to the portrayal of fatherhood and sonhood.

Beale Street, as Christopher Hobson observes, is another in a long cadre of Baldwin's later novels in which religion and faith in God are not prominent features. Rather, *Beale Street* centers Black families that "are occasional churchgoers [and] the main religious opposition is not between God's unkept promises and human suffering, but between these characters' broadly tolerant, profane, yet still religiously observant lives and others' narrowminded and hypocritical 'sanctified' religion."³² In contrast to *Mountain*, it is the matriarchal paradigm in *Beale Street* that reveals the breakdown of relational self-understanding, illustrating a shift from male- to female-driven religiously inspired tyranny. The Hunt family is anchored by the mother, Mrs. Hunt, who hearkens to a deeply puritanical religious sensibility—one that is high on rigid moralism and doctrinaire codes of conduct related to piety, decorum, and sexuality, but low on connection, love, and felt presence. Mrs. Hunt's religiosity causes a palpable sexual estrangement from her husband and has alienated Fonny when he needed the entire family's warmth and care most. These conflicts are explored when the Hunt and Rivers families meet to discuss legal options for Fonny's false imprisonment.

Of Mrs. Hunt's religious fundamentalism and disconnected presence, Baldwin notes, "She was frightened: in spite of the power of the Holy Ghost. She entered smiling, not quite knowing at what, or at whom, being juggled, so to speak, between the scrutiny of the Holy Ghost and her unsteady recollection of her mirror" (61). Mrs. Hunt represents the austerity, distance, disrelation, and disunion that characterize Baldwin's critique of dysfunctional religiosity in some spaces of Black church culture. Whereas Baldwinian religion is grounded in love, organic connection, intimacy, and unity, Mrs. Hunt and her daughters' brand of Christianity functions through a lack of love and a lack of authentic presence. What is interesting about the Hunt family and their varying degrees of presence with Fonny is the intertwining with religious devotion, or, rather, the lack thereof. This becomes more obvious in Mrs. Hunt's exchange with Fonny's father, Frank, regarding how best to marshal the best legal resources for Fonny's defense.

In contrast to Mrs. Hunt and the sisters, Frank dismisses the rigidity of their Christian teachings and theological pronouncements. Mrs. Hunt relies upon prayer and appeals to God for support and defense, and her religious devotion alienates those who actively deviate from her rigid moral precepts. Not even the life of Tish and Fonny's unborn child was spared from her unforgiving theology: "I guess you call your lustful action love.... I don't. I always knew that you would be the destruction of my son. You have a demon in you—I always knew it. My God caused me to know it many a year ago. The Holy Ghost will cause that child to shrivel in your womb. But my son will be forgiven. My prayers will save him" (68). Frank, however, is incensed by the paradox of patripassianism and the suffering of his son. Frank is bewildered with the prospect of "how God expects a man to act when his son is in trouble." He continues, "*Your* God crucified *His* son and was probably glad to get rid of him, but I ain't like that" (65).

Frank's devotion, commitment, and love for the son therefore reverse and indict Mrs. Hunt's orthodox Christology—calling into question the very authenticity of the love of God for Christ the Son—dismantling the utility of the Christ event for salvation and wholeness. Fonny's sisters, Adrienne and Sheila, also practice dysfunctional and anti-relational religiosity, modeled after their mother's example. Tish calls attention to, for example, how she rarely sees his sisters visit him in jail—nor have they made any real effort to engage with the lawyer or raise concern in the broader community regarding Fonny's case. In response to this criticism, one sister, Adrienne, remained indifferent and "seemed to be resolving, in silence, that she would never again, allow herself to be trapped among people so unspeakably inferior to herself" (67). Mrs. Hunt's rigid embrace of "her" God—"her" religion—undermines both families' solidarity in gathering resources that impact her son's chances for freedom, and it is Frank, arguably the least religious and least reverent, who goes on to model a more holistic and organic understanding of relationality and connection.

It is not happenstance that Baldwin positions Frank, the most skeptical of religious faith and its restrictive theologies, as the one who models most powerfully the relational identity formation as a source of nurturing and care for his son. On one level, this move could be read as Baldwin again wrestling with the exploration of father figures who are present and engaged in the lives of their children and larger families. Yet while Frank is hardly faultless—he drinks heavily and in one scene subjects Mrs. Hunt to physical abuse—what is noteworthy is his modeling of manhood, which appears directly tied to his identity as a father. His fatherhood also functions as an indictment of what he considers to be the restrictive Christian theology contributing to his son's confinement and oppression rather than liberation. In contrast to the God of the biblical narrative, Frank imagines another way forward in Black fatherhood—one without appeal to divine authority but grounded instead in paternal presence and aid. Frank's self-understanding as both man and father is thus a direct rebuttal to the disunited relationality embodied in the religious devotion of Mrs. Hunt and her daughters.

Relatively speaking, the scenes between the Hunt and Rivers families are brief but are powerful examples of Baldwin's critique of the abusive religiosity of some spaces in Black church culture. Mrs. Hunt's theology is marked by a doctrinaire harshness that is divorced completely from relationality and care. But the destructive religious orientation she embodies quickens the death of familial belonging. The theme of religious crisis as disunity is again prominent—in which the breakdown of family is grounded in a lack of love and shared commitment to caring for others, which is decentered in favor of excessive reliance upon religious doctrine and dogmatic moralism. The dysfunction of Mrs. Hunt's anti-relational religious faith dismantles the prospects that could ensure more options for Fonny's release from prison, but it also serves a larger, more destructive end in that it alienates family cohesion and further ruptures the connection between mother and son.

Black Queer Religious Thought and Black Church Culture

As powerful commentaries on Black church culture, both *Mountain* and *Beale Street* prompt further conversation on the need for Black queer religious discourses as critical responses to the problematic and pathological features of fundamentalist religiosity in Black Christian spaces. On this point, I again invoke Baldwin's writing as a masculinist discourse—in which Black manhood and humanity are rendered in more complex and meaningful ways. In turning again to the representation of the complexity of Black male experience, queer scholarship is particularly useful. Queer discourses embrace the liminality and ambiguity of human identity—recognizing that unidimensional conceptualizations of human experience deny the full scope of lifeworlds. Some queer theorists cite Baldwin's writing as a complement to queer scholarship but that also issues challenges to the discourse itself. Queer theory, says Matt Brim, "names the enterprise devoted to the analytical and scholarly reimagining of . . . 'impossible' desires" explored in Baldwin's writing that is often pushed beyond the scope of gendered and religious legibility.[33] The legibility—or, rather, the recognizability—that was the pursuit of the Black men in Baldwin's writings embodies a queering impetus because it issues forth more unfixed manners of living into one's manhood. Black queer writers such as Baldwin, therefore, are important because they in effect claim their own voices and explore the meaning and significance of their own lives rather than leave this task to religious and cultural critics.[34]

Womanist scholar of religion Pamela Lightsey writes that as a religious and theological methodology, queering "is a deconstruction and reevaluation of gender perspectives that uses as its framework queer theory and its resources scripture, reason, tradition, and experience."[35] Black queer religious scholarship is apropos when reviewing Baldwin, given the problematic features of Black church culture as central to his creative exploration of Black life. Roger Sneed's work at the intersections of sexuality, liberation theology, Black religion, and cultural criticism illustrates the necessity of Black gay men's writings to unpack not only Black homosexuality but also Black and gay religious experience. Black queer writing, says Sneed, operates from a hermeneutic of retrieval, recovering "black queer experience from the periphery of black existence," but also "destabilize[s] stable, steady readings of black identity."[36] Queering Black literature and experience offers a rendering of Black existence, identity, and culture that "cannot be reduced to neat, distinct, and discrete categories."[37]

Queer thought is thus a liberative discourse that issues forth an acceptance and appreciation for the unresolvable, unfixed, and unpredictable tensions that characterize the full range of human experiences. This is an impetus well suited for Baldwin's literary masculinism and the exploration of Black men's lives. I align myself with Sneed's specific citation of the Black queer writers' hermeneutics of retrieval, as it both implicates Baldwin as a fixture in Black gay men's writings and, per Brim, places Baldwin squarely in the larger tradition of queer theory generally.[38] My focus centers upon Black queer religious thought as a response to the toxicity of Black church culture and the corresponding rigid theologies that restrain rather than replenish human experience and self-expression.

From the perspective of Black queer religious scholars and writers, we can grasp how the Black church is a source of oppression. Within the confines of the church and its theologies of restraint, which retard the full range of sexual identities, queer communities are rendered Other and are denied full acceptance and belonging. Black queer critiques of the Black church center on the themes of alienation, reconciliation, and revision—which all entail both the experience of gays and lesbians in these spaces and their efforts to find liberation.[39] Sneed cites the work of Horace Griffin and Victor Anderson as prominent examples of Black queer religious scholars whose work enlivens and makes more visible queer voices and sexual difference in Black theological discourses. Griffin's *Their Own Received Them Not: African Americans and Gays in Black Churches* is valuable for its foregrounding of gay and lesbian voices, making "public the often suppressed gay Christian narrative in black churches of victimization, ridicule, and rejection by a heterosexual majority."[40] Sneed celebrates Griffin's privileging of gay and lesbian experience but critiques Griffin's tendency to sanitize gay and lesbian sexuality by positioning Black queer monogamy as a *default* representation of the sexual diversity and difference he seeks to highlight—presumably as a tactic of sexual respectability politics meant to make gays and lesbians more palatable in Black Christian spaces.[41]

Victor Anderson's pragmatic theology seeks to displace rigid and reductionistic accounts of Black experience and theological conceptualizations of God as wholly responsive to White supremacy—the result of which is an "ontological blackness," the totalizing of phenotypical accounts of race and the flattening of the diversity of Black experiences. It is Anderson's refusal to relegate Black experience to one modality or narrative that is most attractive. In lieu of fixed narratives that present and represent Black lives in static manners, Anderson instead interprets Black life and religious experience as *grotesque*—a hermeneutical approach that eschews an easy synthesis of human experiences but rather leaves open "the feel of unresolved joys and laughter; open to the experiencing of the comedic and tragic in experience; open to the interplay of sameness and difference."[42] Anderson's theory of the grotesque overturns overtly linear qualities of Black religious experience and identity formation and opens space to likewise think through the tensions, ambiguities, contradictions, and contestations that fill African American churches and shape its relationship to gay and lesbian members. Ultimately, however, although Anderson's theology is valuable in its efforts to articulate difference in African American life, for Sneed there remains the question of how Anderson positions the function of gays in Black churches and what kind of ethics results from remaining committed to churches that espouse anti-gay theologies.[43]

Sneed also grounds his analysis of religious experience in the works of other Black gay writers such as Essex Hemphill and Randall Kenan. Similar to Baldwin, these writers also foreground the Black church, but these works illustrate vividly how the Black church, in contrast to the themes of Black liberation theology, is an oppressive institution rather than liberating.[44] In describing Kenan's novel, *A Visitation of Spirits*, alongside *Mountain*, for example, Sneed outlines how the Black church in both novels either eliminates or absorbs sexual difference and male homosexual desire. The sexual identity and masculinity of Kenan's central character cannot escape the rigid confines that dictate proper sexual orientation, and he succumbs to suicide. Baldwin's John Grimes experiences religious conversion, but the religious experience on the threshing floor is ultimately an acquiescence to the church's admonishments about homosexuality and issues no further challenge to the church's mission among gay and lesbian persons. The Black church in these writings offers no safe haven for gay and queer communities; rather, it presents them, and not the church, as in need of transformation and correction and furthermore proffers little recourse with which to resolve the social pressures levied upon their sexual identities.

Invitation to Openness: A Benediction

In a letter to his brother, David, James Baldwin observed that "innumerable human beings are being destroyed, in silence. We can't unlock the prison gates, but perhaps we can begin to break the silence."[45] Voice recovery, as Sneed's work illustrates, is a central component of his hermeneutic of Black queer retrieval in Black religious thought and in Black church studies. Foregrounding queer voices in religious and theological discourses offers one mechanism of breaking a silence that impacts a significant collective in the range of human sexual identities and experiences. This, however, is only part of the consequence. What happens when queer Black voices are unshackled? How might our religious spaces and fields of study shift because of this new(er) hermeneutical act of retrieval? How might our constructions of relationality and masculinity and their rootedness in problematic church cultures adapt and change?

I would suggest, partnering with further insights from Sneed, that queer thought prompts an invitation to *openness*. In his analysis of a church service scene in Langston Hughes's short story "Blessed Assurance," Sneed observes, "Once the voices of the silenced and marginalized are unleashed, they overwhelm the 'normative' heterosexuality represented by the traditional conservative services.... The unrestrained voices of the black queer disrupts and brings new vitality to the service to the point that the pastor can no longer contemplate the mundane ritual."[46] My point in emphasizing an openness to LGBTQ voices and religious perspectives is not to assign a heroic function to these communities. Nor do I dare suggest that these communities bear a salvific role in correcting social and interpersonal ills that find their way into religious spaces or in conflicts pertaining to gender. To do so would be an exercise in romanticization. Openness to queer voices reconceptualizes religious discourses and assists our efforts in the constructive work to reframe the nature of Black masculinity. Openness to other voices and other perspectives has the potential to "disrupt and bring new vitality" by introducing new registers of human be(ing) and exposure that are potentially liberating for both Black churches and Black men.

Sneed refers to this approach as an ethics of openness. Within the methodological contexts of Black cultural and religious criticism, this ethics "begins with a move away from traditional and rigid theological formulations and toward more expansive descriptions and critiques of human activity in the world."[47] While the import of Sneed's ethics is its relational impetus and its capacity to indict current systems and strictures that are oppressive within African American religious discourses, his broadened perspective on human space and place creates a necessary niche for queer people. Black queer religious scholars and writers foreground their lives, voices, and desires for fulfillment as part of an ongoing process of heightened visibility. As part of its reach, the visibility of queer lives and discourses offers a "mirror that reflects the experiences of African American gays and lesbians," and thereby the full diversity of Black experiences.[48] Their work is an act of creative defiance and soul sustaining that shuffles them(selves) loose from the bounds of obscurity and erasure engendered by a homophobic and queer-phobic church culture. Being shut out of the communality of the Black church and positioned as sexual others outside of the biblical paradigm for "proper" sexual partnering, the visibility of Black queer scholarship can be read as insurgency—an emphatic defense of queerness against the throes of heteronormativity.

Openness to queerness is to also be open to possibility—possibility that is inclusive of the "the whole of human behavior" and modes of identity formation.[49] This possibility also entails the possibility of embodying different mechanisms of identity formation and modes of being, including notions of manhood. José Esteban Muñoz notes that the emancipatory quality of queer thought is premised upon "the rejection of a here and now and an insistence on potentiality or concrete possibility for another world."[50] Muñoz's study centers upon the future of queer lives and endeavors to imagine "otherwise" worlds and queer *peoplehood* that stand beyond static enframements of place and space currently deemed closed and unalterable. Queer conceptual paradigms and norms—as well as those components of self-fashioning and self-identity most dear to us—hinge upon an openness to possibility and potentiality. Beyond rendering queer humanity visible and vibrant in its complexity and depth, queer thought also enables an accounting for broadening the scope and range of current understandings of Black manhood.

The masculinist themes in Baldwin's literature are marked by paradox. Queer Black men are situated alongside and in some cases are intertwined with "unqueer" men. But as Matt Brim reminds us, the paradoxical, queer quality of Baldwin's writing "refuses to efface the unqueer."[51] Rather, the queer and unqueer live together, marked by "unpredictable, unresolvable, and untenable relation[s]" among women and men.[52] The juxtaposition of the queer and unqueer in many ways already reflects the ecclesial arrangements of Black church spaces. As Victor Anderson observes, Black gays and lesbians are "Black Churches fathers and mothers, its sisters and brothers, uncles, aunts, and cousins ... we nurture Black youth as their teachers from pre-school till college."[53] In exploring framings of Black manhood in Baldwin, within the context of Black church culture, one is confronted by the push and pull of Black queer and unqueer experience and existence and, as such, encounters a model for transcending fixed representations of Black sexuality and gender.[54] It is in this sense that Baldwin's writing serves as a queering of Black masculinism and perhaps even the Black church. Whether in the description of John Grimes's homoerotic salvation, solace, and rebirth in Elisha's arms or through Frank Hunt's iconoclastic Christlike fatherhood over against the suffering of his son, Baldwin becomes both Black queer writer and Black queer critic by speaking into existence those realms of

Black life and sexuality that are "not wholly positive but also not wholly negative, and by presenting visions of difference."⁵⁵ It is these visions of difference in the lives of Black men that broaden the horizons of Black Christians and prompt an openness to the lives of queer communities. The full presence and unencumbered sexual expression of Black gay, lesbian, and trans communities "keep the Black Church itself sexually honest and . . . open the church to the worlds of sexual difference."⁵⁶

The transcendence of fixed representations of Black manhood and Black sexuality represents a long source of anxiety in African American communities. Phillip Brian Harper's study raises powerful critiques of both the crimes perpetuated against Black male identity and its relation to broader notions of African American peoplehood. Harper rejects group-think perceptions of authenticity and "realness" that leave no room for diverse conceptualizations of Blackness and in doing so undermines constructs of traditional masculinity and its import to Black identity.⁵⁷ The foregrounding of Black queer religious discourses and writings, with its strident insistence upon the visibility and centralized recasting of the lifeworlds of communities oft-ignored, is a welcome supplement to the project of reimagining Black male life and identity. If, as queer thought has revealed, one goal of recovering selfhood from the narratives and imposition of identities constructed by others is a newfound empowerment to tell one's own stories, then the reconfiguration of Black manhood in Baldwin's writing is positioned well within this same intellectual and cultural/critical spirit. Historically considered, and as the turn within Black male studies indicates, the unique and peculiar racialization and sexualization of Black males renders the prospect of transcendence an impossible burden. Tommy Curry clarifies this observation: "Black males are the depositories of negativity traditionally associated with Blackness that makes transcendence, socially, politically and conceptually" difficult.⁵⁸

Finding power to recast and retell our own subjectivity—thereby heightening Black male visibility and complexity on our own terms—becomes a means of liberation from the anxieties of impositioned objectivity. In the case of Black manhood, such a move necessitates proactive receptivity to the prospect of reimagining Black men. The embrace of *Black* masculinism is therefore not a one-off process, nor can it be grounded in an easy acceptance of recognizable, legible identity frames. Black masculinism in the vein of Baldwin and other queer writers expands and explodes the "chromatic black and white." It calls for the emergence and generation of a "communally rooted black male [subjectivity]."[59] The communal aspect of selfhood marshals the cultural and interpersonal resources for models that Black men and boys aspire to, that arise from their collective processes of discernment and reflection, and that embody an openness to others as a feature of one's own self-fashioning and self-construction. From the standpoint of communal openness, the achievement of Black male subjectivity is both self- and other-directed, illustrating that aspiring to Black masculinism is not an isolated, insular endeavor but has implications for one's place in connection to others. Sneed issues the following challenge pertaining to the perception and reception of queer persons in Black cultural criticism and religious thought:

> I am concerned that when discussing black queers, black religious critics have presented them as a problem to be fixed. If we as black religious scholars and if we as members of African American communities cannot *imagine* black life differently, and if we cannot view African Americans as individuals who may and do possess different commitments and different sexual orientations, we will forever be stuck within narratives of crisis and contamination, problem and plague.[60]

Embracing the agency that accompanies the telling and retelling of the narratives of our lives means employing new energies and new imaginative powers that call forth liberative and inclusive identity markers that eschew the limited and limiting excesses of racist and sexist gazes, along with patriarchy. Learning from queer writers and religious scholars, it is preferable to embrace this agency and our hard-fought visibility emphatically. If we will not or cannot develop our *own* modes of healthy and holistic masculinism, who will?

4

The Relational Turn in Black Male Theologies

Early expressions of Black liberation theology, notably in the work of James Cone and J. Deotis Roberts, among others, were marred by a gendered hermeneutic privileging the agency, perspectives, and mobility of African American Christian men. The 1966 statement issued by the National Council of Negro Churchmen on Black theology and Black power was particularly strong on the race question and the role of religious thought in combatting White supremacy in American society, but little was said about the equally critical realities of sexism and misogyny, not only as categorical social ills in broader society but as additional problems that splinter Black religious communities. Cone, in commenting on the inspiration for his classic and groundbreaking *Black Theology and Black Power*, noted that it was the Black Christianity of Martin Luther King Jr. and the radical affirmation of Black power in the political and religious imagination of Malcolm X that he synthesized in his creation of Black theology. While it is logical to imagine Cone reckoning with the complexities and problems of sexism and misogynoir in Black religious communities while writing in these early stages, an overt critique was largely absent from his work at the nascent stages of Black theological discourses as well as from other Black male scholars of religion generally.

In commenting on the legacy of Cone for Black men, Marvin Wickware observes that it is critical to contend "with the limits of Cone's work in relation to his struggle to fully appreciate the depth of the challenge presented to his theology by womanist critiques."[1] Love labor is central in Cone's liberation theology—that God embodies a divine love of Blackness, its culture, peoples, and life—but the earlier theological and cultural paradigms operative in Cone's theology fail to see the labor of love as affective *and gendered*. Love as affective work is grounded in birthing, developing, and nurturing human relationships—work that is unique to the role and place of Black women.[2] Wickware's turn to womanist theology to broaden the reach of Cone's paradigm helps situate what I now develop in this chapter as an expression of the content and form of *Black male theology*.

In making this distinction, a few clarifying observations are necessary. The introductory chapters of this book emphasized the importance of the aspirational and instructive impetus of womanist scholarship for reenvisioning Black manhood. That is, womanist thought has supplemented my critique and critical engagement related to the issue of Black men's identity and identity formation. This does not suggest that Black men *must* look to Black women's religious experiences or culture to address their own processes of personal discernment and fulfillment but is meant only to reinforce the responsiveness and self-reflexivity that the early Cone and other Black male religion scholars failed to embody in their work and to mitigate against the failure to find powerful interlocutors within womanist discourses. In framing the nature and scope of "Black male theology," I am driven not only by the humanizing project of Black male studies discourses but also by a desire to imagine a modality of religious reflection that centers Black male religious thought on the broadening of gender identity as a matter of ultimate concern and meaning. In Rudolph Byrd and Beverly Guy-Sheftall's edited volume, *Traps: African American Men on Gender and Sexuality*, Byrd, repurposing the creative spirit that underscored Alice Walker's coining of womanism, maps out a progressive masculinity "for Black men who are committed to the abolition of emasculating forms of masculinity; a mode of masculinity for Black men who are committed to the abolition of racism, sexism, homophobia, and other ideological traps."[3]

Many of these "traps," as I see them, coalesce around hierarchical arrangements of space, place, and identity—furthermore sedimented by racial, sexual, and gender-based constructions of human interaction and relating. Among the social, cultural, religious, and racial traps that stunt the growth and flourishing of Black men is the blind and often unwitting acceptance of conceptualizations of self and religious and theological commitments at odds with communal and individual well-being, wholeness, and fulfillment. Stemming from the challenges and critiques raised by womanist and Black feminist scholars of religion, Cone and other Black liberation theologians were therefore pressed to take more seriously the intellectual contributions and religious experiences of

Black women. In continuing this legacy of responsive and constructive theological discourse that engages womanism, there is space for a reconsideration of the sources, norms, and interpretive approaches that ground Black male theologies. The theological frame of this intellectual history needs to be refocused. To this point in the study I have been intentional in centering womanist and womanist-influenced religious discourses as important interlocutors in my ongoing construction and reconstruction of Black male identity formation. This chapter provides an alternative read on select perspectives considered constitutive for the philosophical and cultural underpinnings of Black religious thought that privilege Black men. In what follows, I review the religious writings and personal narratives of Howard Thurman and Martin Luther King Jr. in order to situate both of them as important representatives of the sources and norms that compose what I consider to be a necessary *relational turn* in Black male theologies and as formative as we continue to reconsider Black male identity formation.

In *Religion of the Field Negro* Vincent Lloyd argues that the Black theology project has been undermined by too much attention to, and reliance upon, secular discourses, thereby distorting its ties to the prophetic sense of urgency driven by a commitment to religious thought grounded in the liberation of Black lives. In doing Black theology, therefore, it is incumbent to provide a refractory consideration of the sources and norms of Black theological discourses for contemporary times. While Lloyd's primary focus is the interrogation of the complexities of secularization as a modality of Black theological critique, what I draw upon here is his push toward reframing the trajectory of Black theology vis-à-vis a reconsideration of its sources and norms.[4] Neither Thurman nor King's perspectives are novel features of Black religious thinking. Numerous volumes have devoted substantial study to the relevance of both as important sources for Black religious reflection, church studies, ecumenism, and civil and human rights.[5] It is also important to note that neither Thurman nor King's religious thinking or activism specifically addresses Black women's experience, but their insights nonetheless uphold the inherent dignity of all human communities, a point that womanist ethicist Katie Cannon highlights as illustrative of their utility for moral and ethical revisioning of the world.[6] These facts notwithstanding, my efforts to follow are meant to outline some of the distinctive elements of both Thurman and King's religious and theological contributions that illuminate and distill a relational conceptualization of Black male identity formation and practice.

Howard Thurman and the Mystic Chords of Unified Life

At last, a man's life is his very own *and* a man's life is never his, alone.
—Howard Thurman

In a 1927 address titled "Finding God," presented to the National Student Conference of the YMCA and YWCA, Howard Thurman discloses how the quest for God generates life cohesion—resulting in "an essential kinship of all the creations of all the people in the world," and in that genuine kinship "[one] can never be the kind of person [one] ought to be until everybody else is the kind of person that everyone else ought to be." His reflections on religious experience here serve as an early indication of his burgeoning religious thinking about the nature and trajectory of human personality and life, and particularly the relational spirituality at the heart of his theology of mysticism. Paul Harvey's religious biography of Thurman opines that thematically the overarching unity of all life is perhaps the defining foundation for Thurman's career, ministry, and religious thinking.[7] On this score, I'd also add the addendum that Thurman's conception of the unity of life bespeaks religious *and* racial ecumenism, in which notions of quintessential humanity enabled him to embrace a praxis of spiritual and social connection to the religious and racial stranger. The expectation and practice of this mode of relationality may have seemed utopian in early twentieth-century American race relations, and Thurman was no doubt reminded of this daily in his constant exposure to the indignities and slights that accompanied Black personhood. His 1924 essay, "College and Culture," published while a student at Rochester Theological Seminary, discussed the discrimination and racial microaggressions he and other Black students faced in predominately White institutions.

Rather than embracing racial hostility as a matter of course in response, Thurman advised, it was preferable to cultivate a "sympathetic understanding" of Whites born of "an attitude which says that a man of another race is essentially myself" and that "his needs and cravings and the drives which lie behind his actions are similar to mine in their essentials."[8] Thurman's racial philosophy is borne of a universal and shared sense of personhood unrestricted by race and class stratifications. Further, it is important to highlight how Thurman's religious thinking is multifaceted and rooted in multiple venues—regionally and philosophically. These realms include southern Black Christianity in the Waycross community of Daytona, Florida, of his youth, progressive social gospel Christianity, and the later cooperative interreligious ventures he undertook with his founding of the Church for the Fellowship of All Peoples in San Francisco in 1944. Acknowledging this, I specifically spotlight how Thurman's relational spirituality and theological orientation is directly linked to his mystical sensibilities and experiences. I begin by noting that Thurman's early life illustrated a unique proclivity for mysticism, which is reflected in his childhood experiences of the divine in the natural world.

Thurman's childhood years reveal a young man isolated from his peer group circles due to bullying and lacking immediate family male role models—typically finding solace in the embrace of his mother Alice (Ambrose) and grandmother Nancy, but particularly the latter. The man he assumed to be his biological father, Saul Thurman, died during his childhood.[9] In light of his outsider status within his social and cultural circles, young Thurman was compelled to seek out other spaces of self-worth and understanding. The splendor of nature and the sun and moon and stars provided such a respite, as "he found more companionship in nature than [he] did among people."[10] The Florida storms under the cover of night that enveloped Thurman, he once recalled, provided him refuge and "the numinous silence of sacrament."[11] Thurman often found refuge in the confines of nature to overcome and navigate the feelings of inadequacy imposed by a society that was unsparing in its racial, social, and gender-based rigidity. Thurman's early experiences finding God in the unbound spaces of the natural world enabled a feeling of oneness with the universe and provided his "rather lonely spirit with a sense of belonging that did not depend on human relationships."[12]

Those storms—and the broader natural world that was sustenance to Thurman's childlike mystical sensibilities—provided a personal and spiritual prophylactic in which he "was held by the storm's embrace," with the experience of the storms giving him "a certain overriding immunity against much of the pain [he] would have to deal with in the years ahead."[13] Thurman's outpouring of himself into the physical world evinced oneness and unity with nature in his early sensibilities and developing spirituality. Under the Florida palms, "Thurman could be alone with the sand, the sea, and the sky," and as he later observed, he sensed that all of nature and himself "were one lung through which all of life breathed."[14] Oneness with nature signifies a unified conceptualization of the telos and scope of his understanding of life—one in which the artificial barriers and arbitrary markers of alterity such as race or class could not fully collapse his spiritual vitality or essential being. Thurman's linking of mysticism with nature significantly shaped his concept of God, whom Thurman defined more in terms of eternal presence than an abject, etherealized subject of high theological doctrine. In naming the natural world as an enveloping and personalizing force that embraced him and with which he felt a sense of intimate belonging, Thurman's mystic connection to nature resulted in a higher consciousness in which the natural world revealed the hidden and subtle meanings of the divine mind and life. As he noted to an interviewer once, "[I] would go and sit with my back against the oak tree to talk to it about my problems.... I had a sense from my earliest memory of being a part of this whole rhythmic flow of life and my earliest religious experience. I would talk to God in that setting . . . this had more religious meaning for me than the things that happened in church."

The oneness with the natural world that Thurman describes provides a protective balm through which he was able to experience personal wholeness, but also provided a powerful material presence perhaps denied in the social networks of communal life. It seems appropriate, therefore, to highlight this early, developing sense of connection Thurman embodies, considering his later, maturing embrace of relational religious thinking and commitments. This early, organic sense of connection to nature was the inroad to an overarching sense of unity with humankind and became central to Thurman's self-identity and proved formative for his lifelong pursuit of racial, religious, and ecumenical inter-/intra-fellowship. Still, conceptually, mysticism conjures up a host of perceptions and assumptions, most of which suggest that the individual mystic is radically ascetic, ineradicably aloof, and divorced from the material world in a way that diminishes social and interpersonal contact. There is an assumption of an outright solitudinal bent to mysticism—an assumption that Thurman's case dismantles.

Theologian and ethicist Gary Dorrien links Thurman's mysticism to his first pastoral responsibilities at Mount Zion Baptist Church in Oberlin, Ohio, during which time he dabbled in contemplative prayer and meditation and sought to introduce his congregation to a modernized praxis and understanding of Christian faith that was more conversant with modern, secular, and interreligious dialogue. This period was said to bolster a "spiritual hunger" in Thurman, compelling him to "help people feel their spiritual unity in the love of God."[15] Thurman's concern with life's spiritual depth and connection to humankind's higher purpose was heartened by an introduction to Quaker spirituality, under the tutelage of Rufus Jones and the influence of Catholic mystic Meister Eckhart during a course of study while at Haverford College. With these guides, Thurman was able to distinguish his unique embodiment of mysticism.

Thurman's mysticism embraces a relationality that is central to the outward-focused and ethically consequential engagement with individual self and world. Coursework and mentoring under Rufus Jones at Haverford helped Thurman make the important contrast between *negation* and *affirmation* mysticism, with Thurman best described as the latter. In Jones's view, negation mystics were "solitary and determined souls who sought union with God, [and] absorption in his being."[16] The consequence of total absorption in God is the erasure of human self and being, and more importantly, the self is absolved of any reach (or relevance) toward the finite, material world of human relationships. Negation mysticism is founded upon a solitary life divorced from the social realm, rendering one impotent to be any earthly good or to contribute to societal transformation. Affirmation mystics, however, seek unity with God's will by prioritizing life that is built upon not simply "private inward bubblings, but in genuinely sharing in a wider spiritual order through which God is showing himself."[17] The construction of this vision of life unity requires outward participation with a larger social and spiritual order in which communality is the guiding impetus. That is, affirmation mysticism is born out in the world of experience and interaction, bespeaking a sense of moral, ethical, and *relational* obligation.

Though Thurman expressed bewilderment at Jones's lack of urgency in directing the ethical considerations of affirmative mystic thought toward African Americans and race relations, his influence on Thurman's linkage of mysticism to an ethic of socially responsible and transformative engagement cannot be denied.[18]

Thurman's religious thinking and his mysticism are inherently other-focused. By this, I simply mean that he upholds a view of human life as united, ineradicably social, interconnected, interpersonal, and reciprocal, and this is transmissible to his understanding of religious experience, matters of ultimacy, and meaning making in human social worlds. Such a view would run counter to both the kind of modern, neoliberal sensibilities that frame the human creature as meritocratic, rational actors unbound by structures and institutions as well as the individualized narratives of soteriology (salvation discourses) so common among evangelical Christians.[19] To be other-focused is the rule rather than the exception, and human life at its most authentic is found in the awakening of spiritual energies that reshape and refocus solitary life toward sociality. The embrace of a life that is other-focused forces a confrontation, and this confrontation, as Thurman reveals, is shaped by a question of prioritization and the refocusing of personal values. In a meditation on Jesus's temptation in the wilderness depicted in Matthew 4:1–11, Thurman comments on the parallel between Jesus's experience with questions of scarcity, need, and human survival:

> The quest in its practical bearing was this: How fundamentally important is bread, is feeding the hungry? It is true that man cannot live by bread alone. . . . But should this be his major concern? . . . Jesus reached an amazingly significant conclusion. Man must live on bread but not bread alone. There is more besides, and it is this that reveals the true stature of man. Man must have food, yes. But admitting this and seeing its practical significance in terms of actual survival, what then? He must let the bias of his life be on the side of those needs that cannot be adequately included in creature demands:
>
> > The problem for us is at once clear. I must not make the error of giving myself over to the meeting of these needs alone, but even as I recognize realistically the physical needs of men, I must let my bias be on the side of *their deeper concerns*; I must give priority to those of their desires and

yearnings that can never be met by a full stomach or by all the economic security available in the world.[20]

The focus upon needs and desires of humankind that are "deeper" than food or material sustenance reveals an impetus toward creaturely needs that reflect the realization of the higher ends of life, which hold in tension both biological drives and spiritual fulfillment.[21] Thurman's meditation above provides an appropriate segue in considering the nature of the outwardly focused mysticism that shaped his ministry, religious work, and writing. It was Thurman's reflection upon the ethics in the life of Jesus that best reveals the significant relational ethos manifest in Thurman's religious thought. On this point, it may be helpful to be more explicit in again restating that Thurman's mysticism, pivoting on the example of Jesus, is not simply outward-focused; it is *other-focused*. There is a humanizing and humane anchor point in this manner of social engagement and social transformation. On these ideas, Thurman's *Jesus and the Disinherited* assists many of my summary reflections on relational Black male identity formation. Paul Harvey notes that the basis for Thurman's work on Jesus privileges a hermeneutic positioning him as a political insurgent whose entire ministry is built upon "the marriage of religious being and nonviolent political action."[22] Per Thurman, the life of Jesus has direct implications for African Americans' pursuit of liberation through radical nonviolence. The lectures that grew out of these interests regarding socially engaged and other-focused mysticism were written and presented during the mid-1930s and the early 1940s and eventually served as the basis for *Jesus and the Disinherited*, which Thurman published in 1949.

The struggles Thurman faced in bringing the work to print centered upon the disconnects between his vision of the book and the editorial process. In fact, *Jesus and the Disinherited* was not Thurman's preferred choice for the title—instead desiring *The Religion of Jesus and the Disinherited*, which Thurman believed established a distinction and indictment pertaining to the organized Christianity and the ethical import and radicality of Jesus's ministry and preferential option for the dispossessed.[23] In the closing pages of the first chapter of *Jesus and the Disinherited*, Thurman identifies the "hounds of hell" that mark the penultimate obstacles to African American freedom and flourishing:

"Whenever [Jesus's] spirit appears, the oppressed gather fresh courage; for he announced the good news that fear, hypocrisy, and hatred, the three hounds of hell that track the trail of the disinherited, need have no dominion over them."[24]

Jesus and the Disinherited is about the relationship between Jesus's ministry and the life of the dispossessed and marginalized of society. While Thurman's specific focus privileges African Americans, the religion of Jesus and its relational quality stands as the most prominent feature that constructs Thurman's unity-based religious mysticism. As noted in the first sentence of the book, the religion of Jesus is most impactful upon the "people who stand with their backs against the wall."[25] That observation alone, while brief, suggests an initial relational exchange. The model of Jesus's ministry is profound for Thurman in that it hinges upon an embrace of the dismissed, disremembered, and dis-*membered* in American society. The disinherited and dispossessed have been denied belonging; they have been divorced from the universal brotherhood and sisterhood of humankind. Jesus, as an outsider in the social caste and class system of the Greco-Roman world, can relate to the experience of writ large social ostracization as characterized by the twentieth-century African American experience. Jesus modeled deep relational responsiveness for the marginalized because Jesus, too, like the disinherited Black masses, understood what it meant to "live day by day without [the] security" of humane belonging in a society that denied both refuge and recognition.[26] As psychologically and socially displaced people(s), Jesus and African Americans are linked in terms of shared experiences with the oppressive powers and principalities of racial and religious empire and, as would be argued later by Black theologians, shared ontological status as groups for whom God shared a particular understanding and preference.[27]

The other-focused quality of the life of Jesus that underscored Thurman's theo-ethical mystical vision also bodes well for reformulations of Black male identity formation. I posit that the rearrangement of the features of Black men's self-understanding and self-construction would greatly benefit from a consideration of Thurman's relational paradigm as housed within his mystic and religious sensibilities. The context of social life that often confronts Black male experience is founded upon the brutalization and demoralization "by the politics of disparity and disprivilege" that attends anti-Black misandry in American culture.[28] What we can learn from Thurman, however, is that despite the despairing circumstances that often contour the scope and direction of Black men's lives, and that invalidate those lives, we still nonetheless have life-giving resources and mechanisms of meaning making that remain within our grasp. One such approach on this register may include a shifting of our varied self-constitutions—a reconsideration of the scope and shape of both our personality and our role and place in the context of larger communal forces. That is, with Thurman we may confront forthrightly the notion of a masculine orientation that is relational in its other-focused sensibilities.

Alton B. Pollard notes that little attention has been paid to the extent to which African American males played significant roles in Thurman's development and maturation. As I noted in my brief biographical sketching of Thurman's early years in Florida, and as Thurman himself notes, his upbringing was largely matriarchal: "I have often wondered . . . how my orientation to life would have been had I grown up with brothers rather than sisters—or had my father lived longer. But from the beginning I was surrounded by women."[29] The nurturing community of women in his immediate family was clearly a critical component of Thurman's religious and spiritual development early on, and his own autobiographical recollections often speak to the importance of male teachers, professors, and religious thinkers who served in mentoring capacities. Very little, however, speaks to the role of Black men in terms of Thurman's gender identity as a Black male. Thurman once told an interviewer that a high school math teacher, J. A. "Pick" Grimes, was among "the first strong distinct sustained masculine influence on [his] life."[30]

The relative dearth of male figures in his early life is interesting on one hand because it challenges the notion that only men can usher boys into healthy adulthood and manhood. Thurman is clearly someone who benefitted from a caregiving and responsibility-based ethic modeled primarily by Black women, within both his immediate family and his educational settings, and his later growth can be attributed to powerful male figures among others who helped Thurman give his life greater focus, which his grandmother and mother helped further solidify. On the question of how to apply Thurman's religious sensibilities and their relational orientation toward the shifting of masculinity, it may be that Thurman's connection of human selfhood to an outward focus toward the world and larger social realities is born of his own internal process of discernment and reflection that was further supplemented and modeled by the care(ful) self-giving and self-extension of women and men in his communal context.

This brings us back to the prospect of Thurman's mysticism—namely its affirmational, other-focused impetus. Pollard's essay, "Magnificent Manhood: The Transcendent Witness of Howard Thurman," argues that central to Thurman's spiritual genius and mysticism was his ability to map out how people achieve their highest potential individually while also maintaining community and connection. The template—the model of human personality and self in community that Thurman provides, and one that I find useful for Black males—embodies a kind of self-surrender within the context of community. This self-surrender, perhaps ironically, is the relinquishing of the false consciousness of selfhood, one that is isolated and collapses into one's singularity. As noted in the opening quote from Thurman that begins this chapter, a "man's life is never his, alone." It is interesting that Thurman adopts the masculine in his observation on the unity and reach of individual lives as connected to others. While it is likely that Thurman, like most writers of the time, largely interpreted humanity in masculinized terms, I find his insights here an effective discursive forerunner of the male identity reenvisioning project central to this book.

In suggesting an about-face for Black male identity through this reinterpretive turn, facilitated through Howard Thurman's affirmational mysticism and ethics, I illustrate another source of religious and theological reflection that proffers the kind of affirmative reimagining of identity that will bolster Black male flourishing by considering a healthier approach to gender. The embrace of an outward-focused, other-centered framing of masculinity privileges a taken-for-grantedness as it relates to privileging the unity and connection central to male identity. Male life and notions of manhood thus repurposed take on a different significance because it is tied to the betterment, improvement, uplifting, and embrace of others. Conceptualizing male identity formation in this way renders manhood and masculinity as spaces of self-giving—thereby broadening the chords and ties of human connection. Thurman's invitation to embrace a self-surrendering ethic as normative in human affairs is a calling to a higher mode of human personality and meaning. Black manhood is mapped and modeled here after an intentional embrace of a unified and holistic identity that, in its outward focus toward others, is also intimately tied to an expansive concern with the well-being of others, making accountability and responsibility the constitutive ground and ethic.[31]

Unfinished Beloved Community and Communal Manhood

In *Where Do We Go from Here: Chaos or Community?*, Martin Luther King Jr. articulated an ecumenical vision of the "World House," in which "we have to live together—black and white, Easterner and Westerner, Gentile and Jew, Catholic and Protestant, Moslem and Hindu."[32] The communal implications of King's theology and religious thinking, which the above citation spotlights, have long been the subject of numerous titles.[33] While I revisit some of these and address more on this register in King scholarship, here I offer a new prospect for consideration by applying King's relational theology to my ongoing effort to reframe some of the conversations about Black male identity. I begin by locating this dimension of King's thinking primarily in his theology of the Beloved Community. Before doing so, however, it is necessary to properly contextualize King's religious thinking and its relational bent through consideration of his familial and cultural context.

Lewis Baldwin's attention to the cultural roots that underscore King's theological and political worldview is helpful on this point. Baldwin argues that "the Black experience and the Black Christian tradition were the most important sources in the shaping of King's life, thought, vision, and efforts to translate the ethical ideal of the beloved community into practical reality."[34] Taking Baldwin's interpretation seriously, I consider it valuable to begin by contextualizing the Beloved Community as a development in his theological and religious worldview modeled and embodied first by *southern* Black church culture. I make this interpretive intervention to emphasize the decisiveness of the Black church in King's philosophy and worldview. Among the many challenges that plague African Americans, King devoted much time to the following quandary: "How does one develop a self that preserves a sense of dignity and wholeness in the midst of a self-negating, racist society?"[35] The southern Black church afforded King psychic protection from the onslaughts of the anti-Black strictures of American culture and southern society. In a declaration paralleling Alain Locke's "New Negro" sensibility at the height of the Harlem Renaissance several decades earlier, King argued that the victories and forward progressivism tied to civil rights struggle enabled the reconfiguration of Black humanity. Per King, "the Negro . . . has come to feel that he is somebody . . . [the] new Negro has emerged with a new determination to achieve freedom and human dignity whatever the cost may be."[36] The succor of "somebodyness," conferred and sustained by the rhythms and cadences of the church, fed both Black bodies and Black souls. Within the Black church culture of King's religious habitus, somebodyness functions as an ontological and material safeguarding of oneself as being valuable, having dignity, and being worthy of respect. But to return to Baldwin to further accent this point, the somebodyness King observed and experienced in the Black church community also prompted a unique sense of belonging tied to the South, which further instilled within King an unshakeable confidence in his humanity and integrity.

The context for King's Baptist upbringing and the sustained connection therein was fed by a regionalized affinity and sense of belonging, which swelled further into an expanded conception of communal ties beyond his immediate family. The dignity of King's somebodyness and the somebodyness that he so desperately sought to make a reality in the African American psyche was therefore firmly rooted in a robust sense of peoplehood, borne of an organic communality in the Black Christian South, but that proved to have utility in his later thinking about achieving authentic integration in American society. This is a peoplehood that "involved an attachment to a particular home, kinship network . . . where there was a sense of identity, security, and belonging."[37] Experiences in this context helped King early on to develop a sense of agency in naming and knowing him(self). They also provided him the cultural and spiritual wherewithal to frame his initial gravitation toward the lifelong quest for human community and further animated his political and religious thinking on American race relations.[38]

In outlining the impact of southern Afro-Protestant Christianity on some of the early features of King's thought on human community and corresponding social arrangements, this is not to discount the profound impact that later encounters with evangelical liberalism, Boston personalism, the social gospel, and the nonviolent philosophy of Mahatma Gandhi would have on King's theology or political consciousness.[39] Rather, I faithfully illustrate how the Black church provided a *foundational* basis for King's worldview, which of course was further shaped by his intellectual formation at Morehouse College, then as a divinity and doctoral student at Crozer Theological Seminary and Boston University, respectively. These realms gave King an intellectual basis "to express his ideas about love, non-violence, the value of the human person, and the existence of a moral order in the universe," but it was the Black church and its deployment of an ineradicable confidence and personal dignity in King's selfhood that maintained the lion's share of influence on his theologies of race, relationality, and community.[40]

In an early statement on his calling to Christian ministry, King commented on an inner stirring that "expressed itself in a desire to serve humanity."[41] King's turn to ministry was more a reflection of his own process of discerning the substance and meaning of how he could be of value to others. King describes ministry largely in terms of a responsibility—one that compelled him to serve humankind.[42] Clearly, given this legacy, it is natural to assume that in part familial influence very likely played some role in King's embracing ministry as calling and vocation. What centers my thinking on this point is the relational or communal impetus that lay behind his inner conviction to serve others. The communal orientation, as Baldwin notes, is a recurring theme throughout the large corpus of his writings, published speeches, and sermons. The search for the Beloved Community represents in King's thinking a central component of his relational theology and his inner conviction that sparked his civil rights activism.[43]

King's vision of the Beloved Community, when situated within his overarching concern with making the hope of an integrated society a focal point of his religious and political work, is tied to a unique attachment to the quandary and quest tied to authentic relatedness over against the racist and racializing hierarchy of Jim and Jane Crow of the American South. The ideal of the Beloved Community in King's thought cannot be detached from a healthy regard of place and space. While the South did birth within King a regionalized sense of belonging nurtured by Black church culture, the paradox of this cultural oasis was not lost on him. King was aware of the "unity and nonunity" of southern culture stemming from its racial calculus. King found southern belonging within the context of the Black families and church families and in contrast experienced nonunity at the hands of the White South.[44] Despite the enmity and racial animus cultivated by centuries of racial hierarchies that shaped Black-White race relations, the clash of intercultural and interracial contact provided apt opportunities for relationships between racial and ethnic groups.

In an ironic twist on the assumed confines and restrictions of racial apartheid in America, there were still nonetheless slippages in the "cultural vortex that had made it possible for [Blacks and Whites] to influence each other's lives, thoughts, emotions, and destinies at almost every point."[45] Cross-racial contact between Blacks and Whites in the South allowed King to realize that racialized interdependence was already a reality. Despite being set apart and divorced from true communality marked by authentic knowing, the struggles Blacks and Whites "shared in a region stunted by poverty and racism helped define for King the very essence of place in a southern context and was in his view a possible foundation for creating genuine community."[46] What was lacking in race relations, King realized, was the impetus to live and love in a harmonious whole, reflecting a "deficit in human will,"[47] thereby exacerbating the estrangement and divisiveness of the racial apartheid system. The Beloved Community thus became the lynchpin in King's quest to realize the sought-after integration of society and to thwart the deficits that siphoned off Black from White—brother from sister.

The cultivation of the will to create and sustain the Beloved Community embodied the vision of human personality and societal coherence King privileged in his religious thought and activism.[48] In King's view, humans were at their most human when adopting a spirit of communality and cooperation with one's neighbors, and thereby shifting the scope from selfish provincialism to reciprocated responsibility toward others. He writes, "That seemingly elementary decision set in motion what we now know as civilization. At the heart of all that civilization has meant and developed is 'community'—the mutually cooperative and voluntary venture of man to assume a *semblance of responsibility* [italics mine] for his brother."[49] King's framing of theological anthropology within the context of Beloved Community can aptly be described as all persons sharing an interrelated responsibility for the other—a view rooted in the brotherhood and sisterhood of humankind under God. There is, in other words, a strident "indivisibility of human existence"; for we are all bound up together in an inescapable garment of human history in which "we are inevitably our brother's keeper because we are our brother's brother."[50] A religious and ethical imperative influences this vision. For King, the Beloved Community is a vision of human society in which the love of God is operative in the human heart and instills love and justice as the highest shapers of all human relationships. Within this mode of relationality, human communities can live in a harmonious, symbiotic whole and the dignity and inherent value of all life is affirmed.

Beloved Community represented a new *social* order in American society and beyond. This communal vision was tied to King's belief in the American Dream, which was also a feature of the grand democratic experiment—a vision "of all races, of all nationalities, and of all creeds can live together."[51] The optimism of King's communal ideal appealed to activists and freedom fighters who sought a new normal in American race relations and a reformed sense of peoplehood among racial and ethnic groups. For King, the hope of liberation and reconciliation became twin bedfellows in the communal exchange between Blacks and Whites. The "dream" of reconciliation within the Beloved Community in America, however, struck some Black theologians as naive and unrealistic. James Cone critiqued King on this point directly, opining that "Martin's goal of the beloved community with love at its center is fully identical with the Christian idea of the Kingdom of God; yet I think that he failed to see that whites were not as open to the ideal as he apparently assumed."[52]

King's vision of community and its inaugurating a new social order provides needed commentary on the broadening of the dream of an integrated society with the full inclusion of Blacks and other dispossessed and disinherited groups. If Cone's critique of King's vision of community was that it was an exercise in naivete on race, it was also yet a vision not extended to its most prophetic and revolutionary potential. It is notable that women are not featured or privileged in this communal vision in any substantive way. As Garth Baker-Fletcher notes, one of the fundamental weaknesses of King's views of human dignity as a feature of his communal philosophy "was his lack of awareness of the presupposition of male dominance," not only within his own thinking, but within the gendered assumptions of most men of his time.[53] The Beloved Community as an ideal in King's theological and ethical paradigm is incomplete. As it pertains to the inclusion of women, his profound insights about shifting our outlooks and expanding our notions of self as a feature of this revolutionary turn in human social behavior and life did not address the realities and impacts of sexism as dismantling features of full community. For this reason, at this point in my comments on King, I shift the discussion to offer more critique on the Beloved Community considering its failure to be inclusive of (Black) women and then extend my modification of King's vision as applicable to Black male identity formation.

There is to be sure a disconnect between the sexist underscoring of King's neglect of women and his vision of community—particularly considering the great hopes he attached to this vision as earmarking a new social order. This "new" social order, via the failure to address social and material conditions predicated upon sexism and misogyny, reflected the well-established trend of collapsing the specific slights and plights of women into male-oriented perspectives. As Katie Cannon observes, "As long as the white-male experience continues to be established as the ethical norm, *Black women, Black men*, and others will suffer unequivocal oppression."[54] The norm that guided King's notion of the Beloved Community was in theory that of Christian brotherhood and sisterhood, but it was largely the *masculinized* brotherhood of man that proved operative in the scope of the vision—diminishing, ignoring, and relegating the roles and place of women to the margins. Crystal deGregory and Lewis Baldwin have illustrated how King's inability to imagine a world beyond his own sexism was a significant factor that undermined the integrity of his moral and ethical envisioning. The relegation of the role of women to the margins into separate domains simply reified the public/private gender demarcation common in America during the fifties and sixties.

Regrettably, it never fully occurred to King that, despite his embrace of the philosophy of personalism, as well as the Christian concept of the *Imago Dei*, both of which held the affirmation and dignity of all humans, "sexism was as much a social evil as racism, classism, and colonialism, and that it too had to be resisted with unwavering determination and a fierce sense of urgency."[55] What is also interesting about King's personal view on gender roles is its ambivalence and, in some cases, contradictory character, considering his and most male clergy's gender politics in the Black church. Among King's contemporaries, it was agreed that he was sexist and had chauvinistic tendencies, but these attitudes on gender vacillated. To offer additional nuance on this point, it seems that King's chauvinism was particularly directed toward his view of gender roles in marriage, namely his own. Very early in his relationship with his wife, Coretta, King made it clear that "he wanted a wife who could adjust to black church culture in the American south, which meant submitting to the politics of gender identity, male authority, subordination of women, and separate gender roles."[56]

On other occasions, King would make public declarations on sex and gender that were strikingly progressive for the period. In a 1955 sermon, "The Crisis of the Modern Family," describing the social, cultural, and demographic shifts that have impacted American families, and proposing reconsideration of familial relationality as a remedy, King asserts, "The day has passed when the man can stand over the wife with an iron rod asserting his authority as 'boss.' This does not mean that women no longer respect masculinity . . . [but] it does mean that the day has passed when women will be trampled over and treated as some slave subject to the dictates of a despotic husband."[57] Progressive insights such as these also carried over into other areas of King's thinking; in contrast to his ministerial contemporaries, King supported the ordination of women in ministry and openly recognized the authority of female preachers.[58]

Despite these bright spots in King's forward-thinking perspectives on gender, he never seriously addressed patriarchy, sexism, or misogyny as central to civil rights, and this uncovered glaring blind spots in his moral vision of the Beloved Community. King's inability to see sexism as a legitimate manifestation of the same constellation of freedom struggles that included racism, poverty, and war also had the twin effect of blinding him to the unique gifts and talents women brought to the movement—gifts and talents that had the power to supplement the singularity of the movement's male-dominated approach.[59] There is, however, some evidence of King's willingness to embrace women's leadership in the larger movement, a point that cannot be glossed over, but that also prompts additional questions. Heralded for her organizational and workshop skills, expertise on voter education and registration, and the training of younger freedom fighters, King recruited Septima Clark to serve as director of education and teaching for the Southern Christian Leadership Conference.[60] Clark's later recollections of King also addressed this acceptance of women's leadership as a feature of King's gender politics not shared by other Black ministers:

> The thing that I think stands out a whole was the fact that women could never be accorded their rightful place even in the [S]outhern Christian Leadership Conference. I can't ever forget Ralph Abernathy saying, "Why is Mrs. Clark on the Executive Board?" And Dr. King saying, "Why, she designed a whole program." "Well, I just can't see why you got to have her on the Board!" They just didn't feel as if a woman, you know, had any sense. . . . I think that up to the time that Dr. King was nearing the end that he really felt that black women had a place in the movement and in the whole world. The men didn't, though! The men who worked with him didn't have that kind of idea.[61]

Clearly, King had the capacity to construct a coalitional political platform in his vision of community that was open to and inclusive of more robust understandings of women's roles and leadership. How much further would King's vision of Beloved Community have reached had he incorporated more fully the voices and talents of women? How do we account for the misguided lack of follow-through on what was surely evidence of the nascent kindling in King's views of gender parity that unfortunately never caught fire?

Noting all this, let us learn from King. What we can gain from King is a broader, more robust humanism—a humanism reflecting the relational paradigm central to the Beloved Community, but with an added emphasis on gender inclusivity and egalitarianism. As noted, King's vision of the Beloved Community was incomplete and splintered. A necessary addendum I propose in correcting this needed vision was embodied by another mother of the Black freedom movement, Fannie Lou Hamer. Says Hamer, "You know I work for the liberation of all people, because when I liberate myself, I'm liberating other people."[62] Hamer adopted a reciprocal vantage point that characterized her vision of community and freedom work—one more inclusive in her collaborative and coalitional vision and, ultimately, was a necessary interpretive turn unrealized within King's. As noted in Keisha N. Blain's volume on Hamer's life and contribution to the freedom movement, while Hamer maintained a healthy skepticism toward the larger (and White) women's liberation movement, this should not suggest that she or Black women were opposed to, or unschooled on, issues pertaining to women's rights.[63] Hamer regularly criticized the disrespect and humiliations faced by Black women that were largely ignored by White feminists. And while there is a feminist underscoring to Hamer's advocacy for more rights and opportunities for Black women, her vision of inclusivity and reciprocity that composed her understanding of community deviated from that of White feminists in one substantial way. Hamer "challenged what she viewed as white feminists' quest for liberation *from men*—a reaction to the era's focus on the need to free women from the confines and pressures associated with home and family."[64]

In a telling revelation tied to her suspicions about the women's liberation movement, Hamer addresses what I believe speaks clearly to the shortcomings of King's vision of community and relationality in its blindness on gender parity. Hamer centers the dynamics of her marriage and thereby extends it as a frame for communal liberation. Says Hamer, "I got a black husband ... that I don't want to be liberated from. But we are here to work side by side with this black man in trying to bring liberation to all people."[65] Hamer's words reveal a moral vision of community that is unburdened by the strictures of the gender hierarchy that weakened King's perspective of the Beloved Community. Hers was a vision rooted in mutual respect and the safeguarding of the integrity of others in the quest for full liberation. True liberation for *all* people, the goal of this revolutionary communal vision, by necessity requires bidirectional support and a network of mutual concern. Sectionalism, division, and hierarchies rooted in the marginalization and ostracizing of women ultimately serve only to reinforce yet another source of enmity and separation that deconstructs rather than upholds a full communal identity and disposition. As Hamer noted in a 1976 interview, "We respect each other. We're not here separately, we're here together ... to see what we can do to set this country straight."[66]

In modifying King's ideal of the Beloved Community for our current concerns for Black male identity in this way—in privileging a commitment to gender inclusivity concerning the plight and experience(s) of women—we can discern and disclose a new moral vision for ourselves. This moral vision grounds a communal impetus that both nourishes Black male theologies and cultivates Black male selfhood as interwoven with social and ethical obligation to the flourishing of others. Becoming communal selves thereby leans into the ideal that both King and Hamer's insights develop: authentic humanity is interrelated humanity. Echoing this ideal, with its moral and ethical implications, Katie Cannon notes that Black people "actualize their moral selves by realizing the indivisibility of human existence."[67] In like manner, wholesome constructions of Black male identity incorporate an interrelated notion of self as a matter of course in embracing the lifeworlds, experiences, and wisdoms of women as central to our own development, edification, and personal growth. Cheryl Townsend Gilkes advocates for a sociological perspective in which the indispensability of Black women in religious spaces is embraced as central to communal values and aspirations. For Gilkes, "taking seriously the social fact of gendered antagonism in religion means always addressing the patterns and processes that women and men construct as they go about the routine of doing sacred work."[68] In *shared* religious life and *shared* religious work among women and men, which I highlight as central to any vision of communal coherence, I see this intervention as needed not only within King's vision of community but also as a shaper of Black male identity. Arguably, developing an interrelated sense of our shared commitment to a more livable world and a more sustainable future both within and beyond our religious institutions must by default be inclusive of women without levying restrictive guidelines for their roles and functions. Should we embrace the challenge of repurposing our conceptualizations of manhood and masculinity in this manner, we are then confronted with the prospect of rediscovering and recovering a higher meaning and purpose for Black male identity beyond current cultural and social prescriptions that leave much to be desired.

Conclusion: The Realignment of Vision in Black Male Theologies

On the power and impact of mystical vision in human life, Howard Thurman notes in "Mysticism and Social Change" that there is a sense of community—"a unity not only with God but a unity with all of life, particularly human life."[69] These moments in the mystic's sight mark an event beyond an embodied ocular phenomenon; this category of vision channels moment(s) of moral and ethical revisioning and personal and self-oriented growth. As Thurman goes on to suggest, human vision, personality, and scope are properly aligned only "in a milieu of human relations."[70] Recognizing the need for a similar impulse in his quest to realize the Beloved Community during a period in human history stifled by racial strife and the looming threat(s) of geopolitical conflicts and genocidal wars, King likewise realized the necessity of "shifting our basic outlooks," to safeguard society from decline, disunity, eventual destruction.[71] In advocating for a relational turn in Black male theological discourses, I suggest, following Thurman and King, that an initial objective in this endeavor should involve a reevaluation of the sites and sights of the varied horizons that compose our world building and that shape the imaginative possibilities tied to our future(s) in the context of community. This means recalibrating the scope of self and collective understanding—revising how we *see* the connective ties that compose our identities.

An interrelated sense of human identity and gender identity, therefore, emerges as the *credo* in this hermeneutical intervention. The relational turn issues a challenge. It privileges the idea that Black men cannot afford to continue adopting a business-as-usual model of personal and interpersonal engagement and self-understanding and thus requires wrestling with imagining a better way forward. The embrace of a relational disposition is a necessary feature for healthier communities. Communal manhood, as central to a relational focus, also has the capacity to nourish the futurity of Black lifeworlds and staying power by distilling our collective commitment to dismantling the varied forms of intracommunal oppression that we visit upon one another through gendered violence, neglect, and rendering the experiences of our sisters invisible. Moreover, the relational turn is also founded upon the idea that theological discourses that center Black men must curate healthier and holistic constructions of masculinity as the primary point of departure. Such is a challenge because it effectively calls Black men to a higher aspirational vision of meaning making tied to the reconfiguration and refashioning of all the *failed* social scripts, religious and otherwise, that dictate the measure of manhood.

Gayraud Wilmore describes womanist theology and ethics as a recovery of "liberationist religious thought" so the "entire diaspora will be spiritually and materially enriched."[72] Mindful of what Wilmore cites as the recalibrative power and utility of womanist discourse, I should note that relational Black male theologies are also responsive to another challenge, which I address in the final chapter. This is the challenge of recovery work in Black male identity formation. In the introduction I referenced what Katie Cannon referred to as "soul work" embedded in womanist thought and praxis. Soul work is the work of humanizing. As Cannon knew, soul work is necessary because it properly distills a new consciousness and grammar of knowing as a constitutive feature of the assertion and safeguarding of one's humanity. In transitioning to the final chapter, I endeavor to offer an addendum to the notion of (re)covery as *Black men's soul work*—the process of uncovering the essential being of Black male identity.

5

On Black Male (Re)Covery

> To become a Negro man . . . one had to make oneself up as one went along.
> —James Baldwin, "The Black Boy Looks at the White Boy"

Musing on his conversations on race, writing, and America with fellow writer Norman Mailer, James Baldwin spoke of the unfinished quality of Black (male) existence in the bowels of White supremacy. As noted in the epigraph above, Baldwin surmised that, given the inevitability of American racism to destroy Black personhood and given the gentle indifference of the world to aid the identity construction of Whites as well, Black men were compelled to become adept in *recovering* the pieces of ruptured Black personhood to materialize the achievement of identity. What Baldwin suggests to Mailer, and which contours my thinking in this final chapter, pertains to the processual reclamation of Black male selfhood and identity. In the previous chapters, I attempted to trace and illustrate the wealth of discursive source materials available in Black religious thought and womanist and Black men's literature, formulating them as tools that assist the expansion and reconfiguring of the scope of Black male identity.

It has been my argument that privileging the relational orientation in these sources is a necessary intervention in Black men's self-making and self-constitution and assists our responsiveness to Black women's voices, religious experience, and empowerment. Attention to the nuances of Black religious thinking and cultural criticism in this way gives Black women's disavowal of the asphyxiating evils of patriarchal social worlds a second wind.[1] While a relational ethos has guided my writing throughout, I find it necessary at this juncture to provide more explicit context and theoretical depth for the praxis of relational identity formation in Black male life. What is at stake for Black men in adopting this aspirational vision of selfhood, and what are the consequences?

This chapter addresses Black male identity formation in terms of *renewal*. Renewal is marked by transition. To embrace renewal is ultimately to invite correction—a revision of the present state of things. Invoking the language of renewal provides an affirmational frame for self-formation and purpose as it relates to Black male identity. I define renewal in this sense, as "self-(re)covery." The renewal of self is recovery work. Renewal-as-self-(re)covery reinterprets, remolds, and reshapes sexist mechanisms of being and behavior that ground the person and the identity within community. As James Baldwin wisely knew, the independent, agentive, and self-making process of earning an identity is an achievement. For Black men, shaping and reframing identity is hard-fought and beset by multiple difficulties and traumas. Because Black men and boys struggle to sustain themselves in a society that has historically not met their basic needs for love, nurturing, belonging, or acceptance, the quest for wholesome and healthier identities is perilous. As John Edgar Wideman observes in commenting on the instability of the perception of Black male personhood, "One minute you're a person, the next moment somebody starts treating you as if you're not . . . [particularly] if you are a black man in America."[2] Due to the challenges that characterize Black male existence and that greatly complicate the journey from childhood to adulthood, it is imperative that Black males seek new resources and recourses for self-affirmation to enliven the coherence of their humanity.

Noting this, however, should not suggest that Black men are blameless, even as they struggle against the imposition of false subjectivities imposed by larger social structures in and beyond America. My observations here do not absolve Black men from propping up systems and structures of pathology that sometimes entrap them. What I am clarifying, rather, is that pathological excess and deficiencies of personal character are not our *only* story. The truncated, limited gaze of demonization levied upon Black male personhood cannot and does not have the final word. The (re)covery of Black males is a humanizing project that issues an alternative way of thinking about Black male identity. (Re)covery promotes a broader humanism for Black male self-understanding and development that resists *all* the modes of being that serve neither the ends of our liberation nor the empowerment of women. (Re)covery rejects all communal dispositions that retard or retreat from the ties of relational connection and shared obligations to others. (Re)covery encompasses an ongoing commitment to reclaim the primordial ground of relational selfhood. In the process of (re)covery, I propose a different orientation for Black men's various lifeworlds and futures, while imagining new horizons of possibility in Black male life options.

To distill the unique character of the primordial ground of selfhood central to (re)covery, I begin with an exploration of essential personhood in Africana anthropologies. These paradigms solidify the idea that authentic personhood and even gender identity can never be realized when disconnected from the realm of relationships. African-based interpretations of human nature and human personality will elucidate the nature of relational selfhood as the ground of essential (human) being. I complete the chapter with extended commentary on the nature of (re)covery as a *psychosocial* endeavor that aims to reclaim more holistic understandings of Black male identity. Drawing on insights from pastoral theology and counseling tailored to Black male well-being as well as gender studies, I map (re)covery as a collaborative spiritual praxis offering the possibility of realizing a better way forward in the healthy construction and ongoing revisioning of Black manhood.

Africana Relationality and Essential Being

Throughout this book, I have been mindful of the need to rely closely on formative resources that both resonate with my own social location as a Black male and reflect my intellectual and cultural grounding in the African diaspora. When James Cone initially wrote *Black Theology and Black Power* and *A Black Theology of Liberation*, he was critiqued by his peers for what seemed to be too great a reliance upon White and European theological and historical sources to shape his theological perspective. These critiques prompted Cone in his later works to ground his theological methodology and thematic approach to Black liberation, entirely from Black sources and norms, interwoven with and applied to Christian thought.[3] Pivoting on this observation, I begin by conceptualizing the nature of the human from the standpoint of Africana relational anthropologies, which also have some insights on gender identity formation. Given my overarching concerns with the gender identity experiences of Black males, it seems necessary to account for the ways in which many of our accepted gender paradigms may, in fact, not be true representations of relationality and gender constructs that emerge with our forebears in the continent of Africa. African notions of subjectivity are distinctive but, more importantly, for my purposes, are also illustrative of the centrality of community and social relations as constitutive of the human person and human personality. Attention to subject formation in these realms is useful for rethinking gender among Black males.

In her engagement with the relational implications of African gender theories, South African feminist philosopher Azille Coetzee notes that the hallmark of "African constructions of the subject and the world is the significance of community and relationality."[4] This observation advances an ontological and metaphysical notion of the arrangement of self and community in African contexts—one in which human selfhood is indistinguishable from the creation of social worlds inhabited by oneself and others. This point is perhaps most famously articulated by Kenyan Christian philosopher John Mbiti: "I am, because we are; and since we are therefore I am."[5] Mbiti's relational perspective, which is also informed by his theological convictions, is articulated through the *Ubuntu* concept endemic to African cultural contexts. As a central ethical ethos of African thought and life, *Ubuntu* suggests that all persons, each of us, are bound ineradicably to one another; "none of us comes into the world fully formed," because we are already dependent upon others, and they on us.[6]

While Mbiti does not explicitly cite the *Ubuntu* ethic in his classic *African Religions and Philosophy*, he does imply its influence in kinship, which carries over toward broad conceptualizations of familial ties and shared interdependency in social worlds. Kinship models govern essentially all socialites that mark human relationships, including plants, animals, and nonliving material. Kinship represents a relational ethos that normalizes "the behaviour, thinking and whole life of the individual in the society of which he is a member."[7] Kinship systems, in their societal reach, are inclusive of all people in any locality, meaning that "each individual is a brother or sister, father or mother, grandmother or grandfather, or cousin, or brother-in-law, uncle or aunt, or something else, to everybody else."[8] Because one has infinite numbers of extended familial ties wherever one finds oneself, the treatment of others is founded upon the ethical premise that no one inhabits social worlds with strangers. There are no strangers because all other persons are familial extensions of oneself. Self and community are marked by inexhaustive ties of belonging and mutuality, in a symbiotic, reciprocal whole. The *Ubuntu* ethical ideal, therefore, as reflected in African social ties and kinship, embodies a corporate, relational construction of selfhood. As part of a larger whole, individual women and men owe their existence to past and present societies; for it is the community collective that produces the individual.[9]

Self and community, from this perspective, are reciprocal—each is mutually reinforced by and nourished by the other, illustrating the interdependency of (human) being. Kwasi Wiredu further fleshes out the relational underscoring of African notions of community and self through a linguistic analysis of the primordial links between self, other, and social world in Akan (Ghanian) notions of being. He writes that "to be" verbs in Akan language patterns are incomplete, "requiring some specification of place, however indeterminate." (Be)ing never stands alone but rather requires a reference point or corresponding complement for its full flourishing.[10] Wiredu accentuates this point by citing Rwandan philosopher Alexis Kagame, who further expounds upon the existential and relational distinctiveness of African linguistic concepts. Kagame argued "that the existential verb 'to be' does not occur in the Bantu group of languages and pointed out that the Bantu analogue of 'to be' always prompts the question 'to be what where?'"—indicating again the relational positionality that characterizes the philosophical base of African constructions of anthropological and social categories.

Relational constructs and anthropologies in African philosophical discourses issue substantive challenges to Western assumptions about the universal categorization of individual subjectivity. Culturally embedded African philosophical and social commitments to *relational subjectivity* highlight notions of the human as defined by social relationships and communitarian frameworks. Relationality and reciprocity, and not the ethos and mythos of rugged individualism often seen as central to Western societies, condition human selfhood and (be)ing, and furthermore cultivate the necessary tools for cultural and communal survival. There are also gendered interpretations of personhood and subjectivity in Africana discourses. While personhood is captured through intersubjective encounter and connection, it is also true that persons *become persons* foundationally through connection to others. Oyèrónkẹ́ Oyěwùmí's insights on the matripotent impulse in African thought, the ontology of motherhood, and the resulting formation and cultivation of the human is particularly poignant.

It is appropriate to first contextualize Oyěwùmí's scholarship by highlighting her work on the decolonializing of gender regimes, notably as filtered through her regional and cultural (Yoruba) social location. *The Invention of Women: Making an African Sense of Western Gender Discourses* challenges Western constructions of womanhood as endemic to the cultural and linguistic context of Yoruba epistemological reference points. The "fundamental category 'woman'—which is foundational in Western gender discourses—simply did not exist in Yorubaland," or presumably in other African societies prior to colonial interference and impositions.[11] From the standpoint of Yoruba communities, it was not until the arrival of the colonial presence in these spaces that static gender hierarchies (and corresponding notions of femininity and masculinity) were imposed on Yoruba communities and other African civilizations. Rigid gender binaries between women and men were relatively absent in Africana societies prior to contact with the West: "The fact that western gender categories are presented as inherent in nature (of bodies) and operate on a dichotomous, binarily opposed male/female, man/woman duality in which the male is assumed to be superior and therefore the defining category, is particularly alien to many African cultures."[12] According to the dictates of Western cultural logics on gender, says Oyěwùmí, biological determinism is the modus operandi. This means that "social categories like 'woman' are based on body-type" alone, and this inevitably creates a society where the privileging of certain body organs and/or body types conditions social positionality.[13]

Language and the political processes that underscore translations pertaining to gender, to be sure, are critical here. Language and discourse function as participatory social institutions that reflect "patterns of social interactions, lines of status, interests, and obsessions."[14] In other words, language usage and language choices dictate social perceptions, which then influence social behaviors. (Woman)hood, when fixed through the strictures of Western modernity, reveals a disconnect in cross-cultural translations of gendered (or genderless) terms that have overdetermined the nature and terms of African subjectivity. Oyěwùmí is adamant on this point, noting that, particularly within the Yoruba context, language is gender-neutral—not ascribing social roles or subordinate status based on one being biologically male or female. Despite the significance of this feature of Yoruba language and its capacity to inform scholarship on gender, Oyěwùmí notes that contemporary scholars have failed to examine the meaning and implications of genderless linguistic constructs in African culture.[15] In the case of African women, Oyěwùmí criticizes the tendency in Western writing to de-agentify and victimize African womanhood. "There is no room to imagine African women who can help themselves, or *African cultures* poised to teach the world important lessons, including the benefits of matripotency."[16] In addressing the anthropological and relational themes within Yoruba notions of motherhood, which Oyěwùmí also addresses, I make good on her call by giving due consideration to the positive consequences of porous gender constructs in some African languages and dialects, and how these bear specifically upon conceptualizations of the relational ground of human personhood commencing in the mother's womb.

Per Oyěwùmí, Western-based gender and sexual mores are not natural features of African culture but instead, when issued as the norm and standard for communal, social, and individual habitus in African societies, represent what theologian Willie James Jennings refers to as "imperial adjustments" imposed over against African societies, cultures, and lifeworlds. The imposition of Western gender regimes, which were likely coupled with the fusion of empire and Christianity, underscoring the colonial project, enabled colonizers to arrange and control the place of native "objects" while rendering them permanent outsiders, subordinate to the raced and gendered significations of Europe.[17] The consequence of this is the disruption of Yoruba language; this is the divorce from its linguistic gendered openness and neutrality, which, given the impact of language on social institutions, has further consequences for communal arrangements. Racial and gender-based paradigms arising out of the West supplemented the imposition of a restrictive gaze that was then deployed to control, or explicitly to make *subordinately legible*, the object status of African people, particularly the African woman. One central refutation of Western ontologies of self, community, and gender, which spotlights the relational importance of progressive African notions of self as formed by community and self in community, coalesces around the ontology of motherhood. My particular focus centers on Oyěwùmí's tracing of the matripotent character of Yoruba social contexts, in which there is primordial distinctiveness associated with motherhood and child-rearing, which further has powerful consequences for relational personhood. Matripotency is of course in contradistinction to the "matriphobia," outlined famously by feminist writer Adrienne Rich and as reflected in the criticisms of feminist theorists.[18]

Yoruba spirituality, particularly divination systems, provide the backdrop for the matripotent impulse in relational selfhood. As Oyěwùmí observes in *What Gender Is Motherhood?*, the *Ifá* is a system of knowledge and divination process "that generates stories, myths, and narratives that profess to be God [sent], and which make assertions about anything and everything in Yoruba life."[19] Ifá diviners are persons with specialized knowledge and serve as intermediaries between the spiritual and material planes that provide spiritual insight into the lives, conflicts, and futures, individual and collective, of the Yoruba people. Diviners are powerful community fixtures whom Yoruba people seek, in that they make authoritative declarations regarding all "divine origins . . . regarding the essential being of every object and idea, from the beginning of time and extending into the limitless future."[20] Even among Ifá diviners, gender parity remains a common, accepted given. To accent this point, Oyěwùmí notes that the spiritual counsel of a diviner, the *babaláwo*, is not bound by gendered authority. To the contrary, because the *baba* in babaláwo is better equated with expertise and mastery, the term is used with equanimity for both male and female diviners who have been trained and vetted for inclusion into Ifá.[21] The gender parity of religious and social divination orders in Yoruba society was disrupted by multiple features, namely Western misunderstandings of Yoruba lifeways stemming from sexist interpretations of "male-only" spaces of religious authority.[22]

Ifá divination narratives, thus, build the Yoruba peoples' metaphysical, ontological, and social lifeworlds, and women and men Ifá diviners are powerful conduits of the Yoruba values that sustain and render coherent all social norms. This would include, also, Yoruba constructions of gender and personhood, which I argue pivot upon the matripotent impulse. In contrast to gender-based systems practiced in the West, in

Yoruba social worlds *seniority-based* systems normalized the nature of relationships rather than biology, anatomy, or genitalia. The central component of the seniority system was premised upon age, thereby establishing the primary mode of relationality that governed one's role, status, and place within a given community. But as Oyěwùmí further clarifies, social relationships grounded in seniority through age were also highly situational because social positions "shifted constantly in relation to those with whom they were interacting," illustrating the unfixed and nonessentialized character of Yoruba social categories.[23]

As this example suggests and reaffirms, the seniority principle established the terms for social intercourse and provided the necessary world sense that structured society. Seniority systems were/are "fluid and more egalitarian given that each person in society can be junior or senior," regardless of biological sex.[24] Among the most senior of social positionalities and sociospiritual categories is that of the mother, the Ìyá. Ìyá is typically, as Oyěwùmí notes, interpreted as a totally gendered concept denoting "woman," which, given our previous comments, betrays the seniority-based epistemological and social frame of Yoruba contexts and instead interjects "an epistemological shift from a nongendered worldsense to an increasingly gendered worldview."[25] Ìyá, as Oyěwùmí elaborates, expresses a matripotent vantage point of seniority, with spiritual and material power due to the procreative role of mothering/motherhood. The strength and generative import of Ìyá is most pronounced when considered in relation to their birth children. The matripotent ethos expresses the seniority system in that Ìyá is the venerated senior in relation to their children. Since all humans have an Ìyá, no one is greater, older, or more senior to Ìyá.[26]

As the matripotent principle, Ìyá is, to borrow from M. Shawn Copeland, the new anthropological subject, signifying the new terms and conditions for how human (be)ing and human becoming is occasioned.[27] The primary emphasis that grounds my analysis of the role and function of the Ìyá is the primordial relational orientation; Ìyá signifies the full relational character of human identity and how it is the primordial ground of being. The Ìyá-child dyad, notes Oyěwùmí, is of a particular symbolic and distinctive order, reversing the primacy given to being born into particular families. In the Yoruba tradition, children are "their Ìyá's children in the first instance, most fundamentally."[28] The fundamental, sociospiritual link between the child and Ìyá is based upon cosmology narratives in divination, which describe the process by which pre-earthly souls prostrate themselves before the respective deity to procure a good destiny in one's earthly existence.[29] Regarding the primordial quality of the Ìyá-child connection, Yoruba societies theologize birthing, rendering it a spiritual more than biological process.[30] Oyěwùmí further writes, "The Ìyá-child relationship, however, is constructed as longer, stronger, and deeper than any other. The relationship is perceived to be pre-earthly, pregestational, lifelong, and even persisting into the afterlife in its vitality."[31]

The social and spiritual significance of the Ìyá upon personhood is thus stated: Ìyá confers relational selfhood, which is the core of human being, personality, meaning, and purpose. To be human is to be in relationship, and to be in relationship is the marker of one's essential humanity. Birth connection to the Ìyá conditions the relational impetus of all life. One's very being—one's humanity and process of human becoming—is steeped in relationship. Human personality and being on this register are tied to a spiritual, psychic, social, and familial belongingness that constitutes both human life and social worlds. However, it would be problematic to assume that only the infant born to the Ìyá experiences anew the emergence of new selfhood. The Ìyá-child relationship not only is the primordial ground of human personhood but also illustrates co-constitutional and *reciprocal* relational formation as foundational for one's humanity. In this tradition, the Ìyá is also born when the child is born, for "at the moment of birth, two entities are born—a baby and an Ìyá."[32] The Ìyá experiences rebirth into new being even as she gives birth to the child. In this way, the Ìyá's bond to the child is reciprocally reinforcing, as the identities of both have generative spiritual power. Both are procreative. The Ìyá and child are co-procreators in the construction of new selfhood and relational selfhood. Both, in their bond with one another, nourish and cultivate a new identity for the other that models the basis for human life, sociality, and identity. Therefore, while the "Ìyá figure is representative of humanity—[the] archetypal human being from which all humans derive," even this heralded figure in Yoruba cosmology and theological anthropology is beholden to a sacred framework in which essential personhood is inevitably tied to the social worlds we inhabit with others.[33]

So why are these frameworks useful for the imaginative capacities of Black males to reimagine self-constitution and self-identity? While I dare not catastrophize the meaning of this endeavor, in my view the turn to relational self-formation as mapped within the above discourses is a matter of life or death. Death in this sense should be understood not as material or physical demise but rather *as social separation*, as estrangement. If being is conditioned and shaped through communal connection, what then can we surmise about personhood in the absence of concrete relational and social ties? From Oyěwùmí, we have seen that Africana personhood is rooted in embodied existence and interaction with other persons. Intersubjective encounters are the foundation for our social worlds and identity formation, and it is through social relations with others that we become persons. To deny relation as a constitutive feature of human personality is to deny the human telos, which is forged only with others. Following these insights, anti-relational mechanisms of being in male life—for example, notions of maleness that privilege hyperaggression, the subjugation of women, and sex-based degradation—amount to *spiritual death*. This is a death rooted in communitarian estrangement—an existential rudderlessness with no anchoring point because this version of selfhood is little more than a mirage that upholds a false consciousness. Anti-relational assertions of self are vacuous and lacking in substance—a furled shell of unrealized flourishing that is divorced from the higher quality of knowing and meaning that is always bound—always tied—to others.

Rejecting the social and communal boundedness central to personhood and human development signals the death of self via estrangement from others. Relational death is spiritual death in its disavowal of the interrelated foundation for human existence, being, and purpose. Perhaps what is needed, as Clenora Hudson-Weems suggests, is a reorientation of our value systems toward Africana communality—particularly emphasizing those values that privilege reciprocity and mutuality as central to our cultural, spiritual, and political survival.[34] In doing so, Black men can develop the communal wherewithal and resources to solve particular problems that plague the health of our communities and that burden the prospects of our material and spiritual well-being, and we will also have recourse to address those potential features of our identities that are tethered to the death and dysfunction of our sisters, our brothers, and our larger social worlds.

Africana thinking on relationality reminds us that developing a robust self-identity is inconceivable in solitude, separation, and estrangement. Because all persons are "inextricably bound together as equals" as a tool of survival, our way forward by necessity involves the presence of others.[35] We cannot hope—and cannot hope *to be*—absent brother, sister, and neighbor. The intersubjective, interconnected quality of life necessitates a continued restorative and constructive effort to develop self-identities that embrace the cultural and historical features specific to our experiences of the world that also emphasize the deeply relational orientations that characterize human existence. The reorientation of values and vision in Black male identity and life, to be sure, is reconstructive work. And while this reconstruction is a difficult process that tests our willingness to reorient the deeply held values and the accepted social norms that have conditioned our individual and collective framings of gender identity, it is a process that is nonetheless *ours* to undertake. What are we willing to risk in our pursuit of (re)covery, and how may we go about doing so?

(Re)covering (Re)covery

Beginning to (re)cover essential Black male selfhood and identity—as grounded in the inescapable ties of social relations—is imaginative and aspirational. But this process is also an exercise in hope. This is hope in *possibility*—a hope for what *could be*. My thinking on this point is influenced by the vision of Black manhood articulated in Mark Anthony Neal's *New Black Man*. Neal advocates the cultivation of post-civil-rights-era progressive Black male identity formation that is realistic about the staying power of traditional and performative aspects of Black masculinity and privileges the prospect of Black men embracing a feminist consciousness, even as we recognize that Black masculinity is nonlinear and still under construction. Per Neal, who accents this point further in his elaboration upon the New Black Man trope,

> It is crucial that readers understand that I am not the *New Black Man*, but rather that *New Black Man* is a metaphor for an imagined life, one that I fail to live up to every day of my life. *New Black Man* represents my efforts to create new tropes of black masculinity that challenge the most nega-

tive stereotypes associated with black masculinity, but more importantly, counter stringently sanitized images of black masculinity, largely created by blacks themselves in response to racist depictions of black men.[36]

The hope of (re)covery that I envision is not premised upon a fantastic, shape-shifting "fairytale masculinity that has no basis in the everyday reality of relationships and lived experiences" of Black men, but rather represents the hope of a new life in Black male existence.[37] Like Neal, part of my aim with self-(re)covery is concerned with curating discursive spaces and psychic resources that breathe life into "new tropes for situating formations of black masculinities in ways that are less constricting and more liberating for black men and black communities."[38]

To be responsive to Neal's call to challenge this anti-relational investment in destructive modes of self-understanding, I offer an addendum to Neal's point by advocating (re)covery as psychosocial spiritual praxis whereby Black men are enabled (and allowed) to see them(selves) anew through a self-affirmational lens that is more relational and connective. How might self-(re)covery serve as an exercise in sharpening Black males' self-image to establish more robust communal ties with others? How might we create spaces that prompt Black men to see beyond and reimagine the social enframements that distort their humanity precisely by curating a higher consciousness grounded in connection? One recourse on this point finds useful wisdom in Black-male-centered interventions in pastoral care and counseling, to which I now turn.

I must first clarify my meaning regarding (re)covery as a psychosocial *spiritual* praxis. In thinking through this nuance, I am weighing the problems and pitfalls of adopting terminologies that are culturally laden with misnomers that distort the central idea of what I am proposing here. Spirituality and self-help platforms are common features of the self-improvement industry and are accepted fixtures in our current social milieu. I am tentatively cautious tying spirituality to my framing of (re)covery—mainly because of the degree to which neoliberal and capitalistic ventures underscore the societal trends that dictate the *purpose* for self-improvement. As Jeremy Carrette and Richard King observe, contemporary notions of spirituality have often been co-opted as ambiguous, floating signifiers that function to establish particular market niches—thereby revealing an uneasy fusion of free-market, business-driven motivations and extractive predation through the manipulation of popular concepts in consumer culture.[39] More explicitly, this branding of spirituality operates from the idea that spirituality is grounded in human growth, well-being, and fulfillment not for its own sake but rather "to meet individual wants and needs socially, professionally, or financially."[40] The spiritualization of self-improvement, when defined along these terms, is largely seen as a measure of the intersections between consumption, productivity, and the need for self-modification as a means of procuring the compensatory fruits of particular labor. (Re)covery, in my formation, reverses the individualistic and self-aggrandizing impetus that is so often attached to consumer-based spiritualities and instead locates it within a relational paradigm that is responsive to human well-being and thriving.

On that note, in framing (re)covery as a spiritual endeavor I take my cues partly from Marla Frederick's ethnographic study of African American women's spirituality, *Between Sundays: Black Women and Everyday Struggles of Faith*. For Frederick, Black women's spirituality is interwoven fully in their quotidian political and economic realities and therefore is an embodied phenomenon borne out of the specificity of their lives. Theirs is a spirituality that "is about living through moments of struggle and moments of peace and ultimately acquiring a better life"— which is steeped within Black women's social worlds.[41] The adaptive, creative, and regenerative impetus that Frederick maps as characteristic of Black women's spirituality is lodged within the day-to-day spaces in which Black women form coalitional and collaborative resistance communities that enable them to establish and cultivate spaces of nurturance, education, and mentoring to create and sustain their livelihoods and communal well-being in the midst of struggle. Frederick notes that for the women in her study spirituality is grounded in a broad sense of the common good and is responsive to the particular needs and flourishing of Black women.[42] What Frederick points to in Black women's spiritual practices, and which I find useful in (re)covery, is the emphasis on collaborative knowing, discovery, and reflection as the means of stilling oneself in the trauma and chaos of the world around us, while also fashioning for oneself a new identity. In citing (re)covery as psychosocial spiritual work for Black males, I consider how insights from pastoral care and psychology further along and tease out the psychological, spiritual, and relational import thereof.

(Re)covery is a processual holistic and spiritual endeavor to realign Black male notions of self to its relational and connective moorings, through the specific disavowal of patriarchal frames for Black male identity formation. While we've noted in the Africana discourses above some of the primordial, cosmological, and metaphysical assumptions that underscore the quality of essential being/personhood, it is necessary to shift now to more practical concerns as they bear upon the question of how relational frameworks for male identity and masculinity address sexism and misogyny among men and boys. I frame sexism and misogyny here as harbingers of relational death, which traffic in unhealthy modes of sociality and deny the essential ties that are endemic to what it means to be human. Anti-relational in character, they dismantle rather than sustain healthy social ties to others, and authentic human meaning and fulfillment, which is found only within the world of social relations, is rendered impossible. Because I center Black males in this discourse, I also consider how patriarchal identity formation, alignment, and self-conception are personally harmful and death-dealing, necessitating the need for (re)covery.

(Re)covery entails the rejection of patriarchy and its varied psychic and social remnants in toto for Black male self-identity formation. It is disloyalty to mechanisms of manhood and masculinity dictated by dominance and hierarchical arrangements in our social worlds. The fodder of patriarchal masculinities is most aptly enacted through the deployment of sexism, misogynistic aggression, dominance, and violence as determinative in men's self-understanding and within the sphere of our intersubjective contacts and connections to others. It is the connective strand to others—with others—that makes (re)covery a vital aspect of spiritual fulfillment and healthier self-understanding. In commenting on the tools to cultivate a "Hope to Keep Going" framework for the pastoral care and counseling of African American males, pastoral theologian Nicholas Grier highlights *connection with people* and *connection with self* as essential to Black male flourishing and spirituality. Grier writes that spirituality is always grounded in "connection with something greater than oneself—a source which extends beyond the wisdom of any one individual."[43] Grier's elaboration accents the core of my understanding of the (re)covery of Black males from the constraints and death-dealing / relationship-destroying thorns of patriarchal identity.

Connection with people is the central joy of relational life. In keeping with all previous observations in Africana thought, the capacity to connect with others is our(selves') literal lifeline, whereby we establish belonging with others, our ancestors, and the larger Universe. The web-like quality of connection to people cultivates spaces and spiritual tools for our survival, liberation, healing, and flourishing as Black men.[44] Regarding psychic health and wholeness, connection to self enables a stronger awareness of one's ontological and existential significance—a proper self-knowledge and self-regard that functions as a psychological balm nurturing the demonizing and dehumanizing that often contours Black male existence in American society. Connection to oneself, which is critical to (re)covery, is recalibrative. It represents the effort to establish oneself more faithfully in healthier self-regard. By healthiness, I am suggesting that Black male selfhood can never be divorced from the ineradicable social ties of relationships, in which responsiveness to the well-being of others, particularly women, constitutes the intentional arc of our moral, social, and primordial concerns.

Among the social and discursive forces that have contributed to Black male pathology and dehumanization, which necessitates (re)covery, are the negative images and treatment levied on Black men, the lack of empathy and support for Black women, and the embrace of a moral ethic that dehumanizes gay, lesbian, trans, and queer people and sexualizes women.[45] These stressors, among so many others, contribute to the anxiety and psychological and psychosocial maladaptation of Black males, resulting in the destructive practices that impede quality of life as well as that of their women counterparts, to which communal agency, writes Grier, is the apt response. Communal agency is meant to be a supportive mechanism for change in Black male life, wherein Black males are no longer considered afterthoughts. On this score, communal agency means that we're called upon to "reflect, develop and maintain awareness, support, and engage in social justice activism to nurture the survival, liberation, healing, and flourishing of Black men."[46] This effort calls upon both the larger community and Black men to embrace community-based agential change as a mechanism of survival, followed by cultivating an "ability to resist oppressive ideologies, cultures, institutions, and relationships" diminish the prospect of healing.[47]

(Re)covery, in my view, is a welcome supplemental discursive and praxis-based shift in one's psyche and personal conduct that mirrors the proactive and communal stance that Grier suggests is necessary for Black male flourishing. While the community is still called upon as a nurturing, affirmational space for Black men, there is also an onus placed upon Black men to *be* active change agents in their capacities as faithful resisters to patriarchy. Connection to others, which is the marker of healthy self-regard, forms the basis for psychic and spiritual tools of (re)covery and rejects all remnants of patriarchal dividends and their practice in relational self-formation. In explicit terms, the standard is as follows when navigating the intersubjective quality of our lives and our conduct, personal behaviors, and/or civic pursuits: if it is not good for the flourishing of women, it cannot be good for either ourselves or communal coherence. Patriarchal social worlds promote broken ways of relating, and this results in the rupturing of a higher self-consciousness that not only damages the life options for women but is equally damaging to our own self-connection—our capacity to experience anew an identity that thrives in the thriving of women. Embracing patriarchy as essential to male identity formation promotes only estrangement and alienation—thereby bolstering our communal and social pathologies. The (re)covered Black male self, however, thrives in relational coherence and connection. This modality of selfhood is in alignment and harmony. (Re)covery entails the adamant refusal of patriarchy as an unwell mindset that is a harbinger of relational and spiritual death and therefore provides patriarchy and its anti-relational praxis no safe haven.

While (re)covery is intentional about the refusal of patriarchy, it is also important to emphasize the psychological affirmation and esteem that underscores this shift in perspective and growth. (Re)covery of relational self-understanding in male identity in this sense is restorative. It is restorative to the degree that the realignment of men's understanding of personhood is now based upon an essential humanity that replenishes its connective and relational strands to others. In a word, (re)covery is how we come to know ourselves and our(selves') import in our varied social worlds and how we experience psychic balance. Psychologist Thomas A. Parham refers to this aspect of self-knowledge and self-formation as the principle of harmony. Living into relational and personal harmony adopts communality "for one's source of sustenance and support."⁴⁸ Connection to others, and a commitment to others' well-being as a constitutive aspect of one's identity, is the rule and not the exception because human beings thrive when connection with others is central to how we understand selfhood.

(Re)covery is also about restoring balance—an equilibrium of interpersonal and psychic congruence. The (re)covered self, or the self that seeks (re)covery, thrives in the thriving of others, revels in the flourishing of women, and acts to maintain and support the parity in our varied social worlds by denying the estrangement of women and men through patriarchal masculinity and social structures. One becomes estranged, within this framing, "when a person acts in opposition to one's nature"—when "he or she loses his or her self-essence, as well as balance."⁴⁹ Within (re)covery—(re)covered male identities, (re)covered relationships—the values of harmony are embedded in that those spaces cultivate and provide the wherewithal to reimage Black male identity with balance and through lenses that promote more porous spaces of meaning and self-understanding that are detached from the rigidity of harmful gender norms. Working toward congruence within Black male identity enables and strengthens the capacity to resolve the disconnect engendered by misogynistic and sexist identities and embraces an organic, relational identity that values the humanity of others in ways that embrace and appreciate, in lieu of coerce and dominate.

While (re)covery is a call to embrace and realize new being for Black men, it is, however, just a call. As noted previously, (re)covery encompasses an aspirational vision. With all visionary efforts, there is, constantly, a need to refurbish one's sight. Living into liberated and (re)covered identities is a process. (Re)covery work is ongoing work. According to bell hooks, "No man who does not actively choose to work to change and challenge patriarchy escapes its impact."⁵⁰ In making this observation, hooks was commenting on the capacity for men's conscious, repetitious, and ongoing work to be disloyal to dominating, violent, and regressive patriarchal models for family life and even spousal arrangements. I find the emphasis here to be not only on the shift in attitude among men but moreover on the *sustained onus of accountability* that should underscore (re)covery. Part of my advocacy for proactive accountability in (re)covery is driven by a desire to see Black men be as steadfast in their antisexist religious and ethical paradigms as they are with antiracist platforms. If it is true that "wrenching ourselves free from the long nightmare of racism will require collective determination, countless individual acts of will," it is equally true that we must be just as vigilant and urgent in doing the constructive work of ridding ourselves of the soul-killing and self-killing parasites that emerge from patriarchal and misogynistic consciousness.[51]

In addition to seeking freedom from the restrictions of patriarchal, misogynistic, and hierarchical approaches to human relationships, (re)covery necessitates confrontation with the reality that relational self-renewal as the condition and foundation for Black male identity formation has no endpoint. What is the result of this extensive reflexive process of (re)covery? What I want to consider is that *there is no end*. And perhaps the lack of finality in this endeavor is an ideal that can spur us on toward new imaginative possibilities for self-identity. What if we consciously denied the prospect of final results in Black male self (re)covery? And what if the denial of end goals—the denial of a completely healed, (re)covered self—made us more vigilant, more watchful of the anti-relational, destructive remnants of patriarchal thinking and conduct? On being vigilant against patriarchy as an always already possible feature of male identity formation, I am reminded of the wisdom of the Black women care community in Morrison's *Home*: "Misery don't call ahead. That's why you have to stay awake—otherwise it just walks on in your door." Patriarchal masculinity and manhood is a form of misery against which we must remain watchful. But to remain watchful—to protect our necks from the stranglehold of sexism's reach and from its tethers—it is imperative that Black men adopt a spirit of corrective revisioning and envisioning that is sustained and continuous, recognizing that we all, each of us, may struggle with the allure of adopting patriarchal identities.

An ethic of nonfinality in Black male (re)covery holds with suspicion any notion that we can outrun the strands of sexism and misogyny as formative in our self-constitution. Finality suggests a finished state of things. Finality in (re)covery in this sense would mean that Black males have fully arrived—that we have reached our full potential and have evolved beyond sexism and misogyny. Aside from ignoring the pervasiveness of sexism and intraracial intimate partner violence in the Black community, which arguably are tied to environmental traumas and problematic gender constructs, the assumption of finality cedes no possibility of further growth or maturation. This is a proposition I cannot abide. Sexism and misogyny, as the ideological kith and kin of patriarchy, are ingrained in the cog and wheel of our social worlds and are reified in virtually all global gender frameworks, albeit with varying degrees of prominence. Susan Douglas touches upon some of my concerns on this point in *Enlightened Sexism*. Douglas argues that contemporary societies are misguided about the extent of women's empowerment, overstating the presumed systemic, cultural, and economic gains stemming from the women's liberation movement and their inroads into media and marketing. Because of popular culture's easy portrayals of fantasies of "woman power" as depicted within the specter of mass media, says Douglas, contemporary women and men have adopted a less vigilant, muted sense of urgency in addressing the intractability of sexism and misogyny—ultimately assuming that, societally, we've disabused ourselves of systems, structures, and mindsets that foster the sexist mistreatment and disenfranchisement of women.[52]

In like manner, by privileging nonfinality in Black male (re)covery, I seek not an easy retreat from the responsibility and accountability embedded in the restorative work of rejecting patriarchy. Moreover, I do not absolve myself or other Black males from thinking through our collective roles in either perpetuating or dismantling the harms visited upon the women in our lives and beyond. Rather, constant vigilance—adopting caution in our efforts toward a healthier self-regard—must be the rule and not the exception in the process of (re)covery from patriarchal thinking and praxis. In the perpetual struggle with patriarchy, sexism, and misogyny, which manifest in the disregard for women's health, thriving, and well-being, it is useful to (re)cover (re)covery. By this I mean that the process of freeing oneself from the throes of patriarchy is lifelong, replete with ebbs and flows, setbacks, disappointments, and backsliding. The reality of ongoing failure in realizing this relational ideal thus requires an ongoing commitment to the deconstruction of distorted notions of masculinity and manhood through sustained engagement with the experiences and insights of women, something I've modeled throughout this work.

In (re)covering (re)covery, we acknowledge that we've not embraced a true sense of self within community. We recognize that we are not what we should be. And despite the nonfinality of this process—in spite of the lack of full embodiment of a relational identity—we nonetheless press on with the aspirational hope of (re)covery. In our commitment to (re)covering (re)covery, we also hold ourselves accountable for our efforts to continue our reflexive work—that we are open to new insights, new lessons, wherever they may emerge. If we accept that there is no finality in the process of (re)covery, we accept that we will never "get it right" as it relates to sexism, misogyny, and other gendered social ills that hamper our communities and relationships. By embracing the always-but-coming, perpetually transitional process of (re)covering (re)covery, we accept the obligations regarding the need to continually keep ourselves "in check" because we realize we will always have a shortsighted, truncated grasp of what it takes to realize the relational identity we aspire to embody.

On a final note, I am pressed to address the participatory aspect of (re)covery. As (re)covery is participatory, and thus driven by the inclinations and processes of discernment unique to each individual Black man, it is ultimately an organic process that cannot be coerced or forced but coincides with the agency and choice of Black men to consider another way forward as we live into our identities. I can easily surmise that my suggestions here may lend to the perspective that Black males are irredeemably broken, somehow in perpetual need of "fixing," as if their very nature is suspect and deficient. This is a concern I spoke to in the introductory chapters. My purposes with the notion of (re)covery do not privilege a priori assumptions of Black males as ontological, racial, or gendered problems. To do so only recycles the history of anti-Black misandry *and* misogyny that divorces Black people from their personhood. It is not my objective to tie inherent pathology to Black manhood. I cannot be any more explicit on this point. I'm more concerned with the prospect of Black men's health and flourishing, which, I argue, must include sustained attention and intention toward reimagining the scope of our self-identity and how this is filtered through gender.

Black male (re)covery cannot function without their express participation and commitment; however, it is important to avoid the rigid and totalizing praxis that creates a fanatical utopian vision of participation that ostracizes those who may deviate from or reject the nature of this vision. By this, I simply mean that the values of relationality and self-(re)covery incorporate a heightened vision of the dynamic between self-formation, self-identity, and community. Black men may or may not see the value of this internal and psychic work. This fact does not deny our collective role or opportunity to imagine new spaces for identity formation in Black male futures. For the Black man, my reflections here are meant to simply offer an invitation: to participate in the possibility of preserving the integrity of all relationships through an acceptance of the responsibility of ongoing (re)covery. Further, this invitation also remains grounded in recognition of the value and integrity and wholeness of relation to others. We literally find our(selves) within relation, and we begin the process of healing from anti-relational frameworks by reuniting and reconciling ourselves to others. While (re)covery places primary responsibility on the shoulders of Black men, it still indicates a concern for others, as (re)covery has the potential to impact women and our larger community. Self-(re)covery serves a relational function in that it is a means by which the healing of self and self in relationship within community becomes a possibility. It is on the fulcrum of this possibility that the meaning and scope of Black male identity formation is given renewed focus.

Epilogue

Black Masculinity Otherwise

In this book I have tried to reimagine a new way forward for Black males in the realization of new identities unmoored by the pitfalls of patriarchy and misogyny. Juxtaposed with my disdain for the ongoing problems pertaining to sexism, misogyny, and the failures in Black religious thought to be more explicit in its disavowal thereof, I am also angry at some of the reasons that necessitate humanizing projects centering Black males at all. I spoke to this anger in the introduction, arising from personal experiences as a doctoral student, and stemming from what I deem the cultural currency of anti-Black misandry in some sectors of the Black community and in academe. Black male studies powerfully interrogated the misandrist bent within academic theory, given the overall silence toward Black males as subjects worthy of study beyond the realm of defect, pathology, or patriarchal excess. On another level, Black male studies spotlights disturbing trends of cultural approval sanctioning the disgust, disdain, and distrust toward Black men and boys. While criticized for defensiveness, Earl Hutchinson pointed out that scapegoating Black males as a cover for society's racial ills is a favorite pastime in American racial politics and race relations.[1] Sadly, however, this pastime still seems well entrenched and in good health, both within and beyond Black communities. Why, for example, is it fashionable, and cheered on even, to refer to Black males as "bullet bags," considering the vulnerabilities of all Black bodies in the militarized American police state?[2] Why is there open and running commentary on the benefits of Black male infants being aborted—a cause that has disturbing ties to modern eugenics and the work of Margaret Sanger?[3] Such discourses as these, which are rife in the Twittersphere (or, now, X-sphere) and disseminated by a host of social media curators, should not be discounted due to their digital imprint. This fact does not, in my view, lessen the severity of their psychological and sociocultural impact.

In the first chapter, I referenced Emilie Townes's work on the identity displacement suffered by Black women and girls—necessitating theo-ethical countermemory endeavors as powerful mediums of self-reclamation. This mode of (self-)defense exemplifies a deeply instructive practice from womanists that I've tried to model and suggest as transformative for Black males. Safeguarding Black male integrity, humanity, and dignity creates a basis for moving beyond what Maurice Wallace refers to as the *monocularity*, or a singular, monolithic vision applied to Black male lives, bodies, and identities.[4] What I ultimately affirm, thus, is the call to change and refocus these narratives—to assert that the caricatures and identity impositions of others upon the Black male cannot have the final determinative "say" in identity formation. I propose another alternative. Let us take ownership in this matter. Let us *re-see ourselves* differently. Imagine for a moment what it may be like to come of age within a context in which it is overtly claimed, and subtlety intimated, that your very being is that of deficit. Furthermore, imagine what kind of impact such messages and scripts may have on your self-image—your psyche, your consciousness. The psychic and spiritual rupturing that adjoins identity displacement is an embedded feature of African and African American experiences within the context of anti-Blackness, which stems from the colonial wounds of enslavement and from the contested site of Western categories of meaning and racialized hierarchy in the taxonomy of human community. In beginning this epilogue with comments on the nature of a consciousness under siege—a consciousness potentially retarded by the intracommunal, discursive, and systemic overdeterminations of Black humanity—I center my final thoughts on the open and porous quality of Black male identity formation—as disentangled from patriarchy *and* divorced from the toxic gendered and raced scripts that posit the deficiency of Black male (in)humanity and (non)personhood.

To embrace an agentive, proactive bent in the fashioning and construction of one's identity allows for greater empowerment, purpose, and meaning. I believe, with Patricia Hill Collins, that within the psyche-scape of renewed consciousness, there is a space of freedom. In the awareness of and insistence upon the fullness of selfhood, freedom is realized. Restoring consciousness prompts all discerning persons, women and men, to "forge an identity larger than the one society would force upon them," and "that very consciousness is potent."[5] Collins fleshes this out through the prospect of self-naming and self-definition as central to Black feminist thought and praxis. Drawing upon Black women's literature as source materials for Black feminist theory, Collins interprets the role of self-definition as central to Black and other minoritized women's resistance strategies against patriarchy and the general devaluing and silencing of women's voice. To be clear, there is very much a this-worldly impetus that accompanies self-definition in the heightening of consciousness. This is due to the societal constraints that work against the flourishing of one's being—materially and ontologically. Whether from the standpoint of the ostracization of Black bodies stemming from slavery and American racial apartheid or based upon what Emilie Townes called the ideological funhouse mirror of distortion, innuendo, and caricatures that have dictated Black (in)humanity, there are clearly a trove of racialized tropes and cultural scripts that are predatory to Black selfhood.

This reality notwithstanding, the potency of identity (re)formation lies in its imaginative nonfixity. If there is freedom in restored consciousness, this freedom is found in the possibilities—the realm of what is imaginable, what is hoped for, what is aspired to. Possibility is a sustained thread underscoring the scope of this book, which has centered Black males and gender identity. Notions of possibility are powerful because of the implications of unboundedness. Possibility speaks to nonborders. Possibility is transitionally porous. Conceptualizing Black male identity formation and meaning within the space of openness and possibility might, moreover, proffer a new way to approach both a discursive and an ontic space of insurgency. What results from conceiving Black male identity, masculinity, gender formation, from an *otherwise* posture—a space of potentialized yet undefined and limitless agentive openness?

If we recall from James Baldwin the effort Black males must exert to fulfill the achievement of identity, it is critical to again foreground the dangers. These are the pitfalls, ideological and otherwise, that beset the identitarian pathways of Black male reckoning with the reclamation of selfhood. The notion of (re)covery from the final chapter, I realize, may strike some as an unsuitable rejoinder—that it is too open-ended and abstracted. However, in conceiving of (re)covery as a process with no finality, I point to the power of imaginative openness to dismantle our devotion to constructions of Black male identity and iterations of manhood that imprison the capacity to live and thrive into registers of being that are liberating and relationship-oriented. To return briefly to insights from Victor Anderson's *Beyond Ontological Blackness*, the open and porous nature of Black male identity formation I envision on this score is a rejection of *ontological Black masculinity*. Anderson's critique of Black theology highlighted its reliance upon and indebtedness to Black political histories of radical opposition to Whiteness and White racism—effectively raising anti-Black White racism to the level of ultimate concern for Black liberation.[6] Anderson laments onto-Black theology because it collapses the fluidity and diversity of African American cultural life and production, which is not, by default, tied to struggle and crisis narratives involving White supremacy. These theological frames ultimately catastrophize the narrative surrounding Black agency and identity, thereby diminishing the creative, the beautiful, and the sublime modes of meaning making and world making in African / African American existence.

Anderson's insights about the consequences of devotion to rigid conceptualizations of Black identity in the fields of Black religious studies and theology offer a point well suited to my endeavors here to construct Black male identity formation in nonfixed, open, otherwise categories. To reject ontological Black masculinity is to deny and call into question ideas about Black males wedded to rigid, delimiting enframements and that deny their capacity for cultural creativity and agency as evolving, complex people, rather than bound by raced and gendered pathologies. On these restrictive enframements, we must extend our perceptive and critical lenses not only to the larger social context of gender identity formation and the ubiquity of harmful race and gender scripts, but ultimately, back toward ourselves and our conduct therein. Jaunting from the culpability and consequences of our loyalty to patriarchy is an easy but ill-advised descent toward diminished connection with ourselves and others, notably, in the latter case, as we turn from our moral and ethical obligation to others in realizing full communal liberation. We, too, play our own respective roles in imbibing the momentary gratification tied to gender hierarchies that, however slight, bolster privilege, power, and dominance over women.

Embracing the remnants of patriarchal relationality and selfhood is to also embrace the delimiting and delimited enframements that serve not the ends of Black male liberation or buttress the flourishing of our sisters, wives, mothers, or children. If we are serious about self and communal liberation and thriving, we must adopt a critical posture toward the cultural remnants featured in Black male life that both help us and harm us. The aims of a critical posture in the retrieval of liberating proclivities in Black male life and identity formation require a robust description of the "patterns of social life that intend human fulfillment" and a criticism of "cultural activities that undermine human fulfillment."[7] This approach echoes what Kelly Brown Douglas describes as the need for bifocal hermeneutics in addressing the cultural maladies that negatively impinge upon Black communities but that are also *sustained and nourished* therein.[8]

To be sure, however, even this bifocal approach requires balance and nuance. We need not engage in or accept perspectives that demonstrate an overzealousness in demonizing the untoward facets of male culture(s) in Black communities.[9] Rather, the better approach is to encourage and cultivate a spirit of both self-critique *and* imaginative openness among Black males as they pursue their varied life options and self-fulfillment. This means, practically, taking a serious look at the allure and alienating tendencies of gender identity constructs and norms that we cultivate and how they contribute to or digress from our collective liberation, flourishing, and survival. Anti-relational modes of identity formation, which are tied to the forces of patriarchy and misogyny, represent soul-killing, death-dealing, and community-estranging mechanisms of self-constitution in Black male lives and identity that need discarded. But where are we going? What grounds self and communal (re)covery? As noted before, there is no fixed endpoint on the horizon—only open bounds, only possibilities in exorcizing and exercising the terms of Black male self-identity.

Roger Sneed's work at the intersections of African American religious and cultural criticism and Black gay men's and queer literature, which I referenced in our engagement with Baldwin in the third chapter, prompts his turn to an ethics of openness that I draw upon here to round out the emergence of otherwise possibilities in the construction of Black male identity. Open possibilities of self-understanding and self-disclosure, Sneed writes, are not assured to provide us flattering glimpses of either the ideal or the real in our coveted self-image; rather, possibilities proffer the space for "self-reflection, examination, and correction."[10] Sneed's move toward the ethics of openness in Black religious and theological discourses is a constructive ethical endeavor that seeks to sustain more robust interpretations of human activity in the world.[11] The critique of this ethical posture can be applied to the ongoing evaluation of patriarchal identity formation and declaring its futility for realizing liberation for women and men. The demand for an expansive understanding of human activity also requires a robust understanding of the ebbs and flows of human identity. As noted throughout this book, Black males should not be rendered the sum of their untoward and problematic behaviors tied to flawed gender norms. We can and should examine and correct the problems that stem from sexist and misogynistic self-regard, but we are by no means locked into those problems as constitutive of Black male being. Embracing a realistic appraisal of the evolving quality of human experience and the complexity of self-formation is necessary to avoid the fixing of Black males and notions of Black masculinity and manhood as writ-large deficient and pathological. The humanistic impetus of this openness, namely privileging human activity and meaning in manners that promote flourishing, fulfillment, and individual and collective liberation, is the feature that segues to the discursive value of an otherwise conceptualization of Black male identity.

Much has been noted about sight, seeing, and visions. This book began with a desire to formulate visions of Black manhood that one could aspire to. If seeing differently is a feature of renewed Black male consciousness—renewed Black male identity—one's vision is likewise implicated in the process. But the direction of the vision remains locked within the realm of possibility. In our drive to restore, (re)cover, and *see* Black male identity anew, our imaginative powers must be expanded— this expansion is open-ended. It is otherwise. Seeing differently—seeing Black male selfhood differently—hinges upon opening windows to new worlds. These are worlds and meanings that are otherwise—unrealized, but possible within the scope of imagination, as the "imagination is necessary for thinking and breathing into the capacities of infinite alternatives" for self and self-construction.[12] Ashon Crawley's fusion of theo-poetics and Black study elaborates upon an otherwise sight toward Black male identity. In *Blackpentecostal Breath: The Aesthetics of Possibility*, Crawley distills an insurgent, radical impetus from Black religious culture that disregards the imposition and "is-ness" of inhumanity and injustice that frame the conditions of Black life. Rejecting the premises thereof, Crawley adopts the openness of otherwise possibilities in Black life and thought. Otherwise possibilities give birth to an awareness—a new consciousness that disrupts the systems and categories of meaning constructed as the norm. Otherwise thought breaks "with the known, the normative, the violent world of western thought and material condition."[13] The impositions of Western thinking, including its gender norms and gender subjectivities, have staying power and exert considerable power and influence in the lifeworlds and identity formation of Black people. But there is otherwise.

An otherwise response to the coherence and ubiquity of Western paradigms, molded after the lifeworlds, soundscapes, artistry, creativity, and religiosity of the African diaspora, generates an ideological, ontological, and discursive rupturing. Otherwise thinking and knowing, writes Crawley, "[charge] us to do something, to perform, to produce otherwise than what we have. We are charged to end, to produce abolition against, the episteme that produced for us current iterations of categorical designations of racial hierarchies, class stratifications, gender binaries, mind-body splits."[14] Otherwise possibilities, therefore, represent a new grammar of knowing and Black being. The embrace of otherwise positionality allows one to see sights and dream dreams previously unknown and unconsidered, which shifts one's focus and activity in the material world. Crawley frames this powerful concept as a reprieve of Black study—the intellectual and cultural project of accenting and illuminating the gift and weightiness of Black life, thereby inaugurating a project of retrieval from the ideological and disciplinary strongholds of Western discourses. I find, however, great value in applying the disruptive capacity of otherwise possibilities toward rethinking Black male identity through the expansion of imagination and vision.

Can Black males live into otherwise possibilities? Can our visions of manhood be mapped in this manner? An otherwise frame would suggest that there are multiple visions for Black males. Seeing Black male identity otherwise would mean opening and broadening our conscious self-regard to "the fact of alternative infinites to what is." That is, within this mapping, there exist open frames for identity construction that explode the bounds of current practices that account for what is deemed socially acceptable and complete about the markers of Black manhood. Otherwise Black male identity is unfixed—indicative of a broader human register of meaning for the possibilities of Black manhoods and boyhoods. This means that Black men and boys are unbound in their respective pursuits of meaning, purpose, and fulfillment. Self, when perpetually bound to new heights and sights of personhood, is therefore unshackled by present registers and ideological tethers that are found to be wanting or that do not privilege individual or relational well-being.

So, what could this vision mean—what do the otherwise self and world building tell us constructively about seeing Black males in practical terms? The production of a different grammar of knowing self and self in community is one consequence of otherwise possibility for Black male identity. Responding to the world imaginatively through the prospect of a new one, we therefore contest the givens and norms that have guided our prior enframements—namely the gendered norms for masculinity and manhood. Breaking with the accepted gender moralities pertaining to male identity of the present episteme means saying no. Otherwise Black male identity seeks abolition from modes of masculinity and the afterlives of masculinity dictated by desire to inhabit and possess the worlds and bodies of women manipulated by the whims of patriarchal dominance. Seeing Black men anew in this way reconstitutes the nature of human relationships but doesn't offer complete resolve for them. For Black men, I believe openness to other worlds, particularly those of women, within and beyond their scope of knowing, is beneficial to broadening of our humanity and our ability to prioritize a communal, relational disposition. Making the lives and worlds of women central to our sight allows us to generate futures that are coalitional and collaborative rather than a reflection of our own gaze. These new visions thereby provide the wherewithal to imagine "alternatives to what is as a means to disrupt the current configurations of power and inequity" between women and men.[15]

Given the representational fixity of Black males I've noted, adopting an otherwise posture gives us power to reclaim our own world makings—our own world meanings and self-identity therein—in registers that are unbound to ideological, disciplinary, or cultural scripts that diminish the integrity of Black male identity and humanity. The stakes of self-naming and self-definition are high, echoing Audre Lorde's powerful insight: "If I didn't define myself for myself, I'd be crunched into other people's fantasies and eaten alive." In Barry Jenkins's coming-of-age film *Moonlight* (2016), the father figure, Juan, has a conversation with the childhood version of the main character of the film, Chiron, in which he details experiences of his life in both America and Cuba. After highlighting different experiences of race and place in both locales, Juan notes, "At some point you gotta decide for yourself who you gon' be. Can't let nobody make that decision for you." Positioning Black male identity from an otherwise lens provides the proper, that is, *agential* and open-ended, scope for Black male meaning making and identity construction. What Juan was in effect saying to Chiron was to chart his own pathways of meaning—to define his own being independent of the limitations imposed by the conditions of a less-than-ideal, inhospitable world and despite the machinations of others. And so it is with Black males here and now. As we seek abolition from the harmful remnants of patriarchy, we must also divest ourselves from the equally harmful cadre of tropes and images that suggest our perpetual pathology. The gift of sight enmeshed with otherwise possibilities encourages disbelief in the narratives, untruths, and innuendos that distort the truths of our existence, experiences, and emotional depth. This position is no doubt defensive, but it is a defense of a different character—not out of a sense of shame, but (self-)defense. Seeing beyond the narratives that are anti-Black male in scope—to see the potentiality in Black men and boys to reconstruct their own worlds and meanings—is to say "HELL NO" to gender regimes that dismantle our humanity, poison our self-image, and rupture our capacity to imagine more livable futures with others. Dissecting the reductive ideological prison house of Black male identities will provide, as I have endeavored here, an opportunity to (re)imagine and (re)cover another way in the framing of manhood and masculinity.

Throughout this book, I have outlined a relational hermeneutic that casts forth a lens for rethinking and seeing anew Black male identity formation. Black religious thinking, in womanist and theological discourses, and literary discourses that center Black men provide powerful interlocutors for these reflections and occasion alternative visions of Black males that reveal the depths of their complexity and humanity and, moreover, point to embodiments of manhood that turn away from anti-relational, antisocial remnants of patriarchal excess. Along with

Alice Walker, I desire Black men to live liberated lives. I do desire that Black men learn to reflect upon the implications and consequences of their sexism and misogyny. I also hope that scholars in Black religion work to be more explicit and interrogative in their critiques of the nuances of sexuality and gender. Moreover, I hope my meager reflections here contribute to scholarship that is unafraid to see—to imagine—the value and worth of Black males as worthy subjects of study, beyond notions of defect, but rather in the fullness and complexity that characterizes all human life.

In the (re)covery of Black male identity—in learning to see our(selves) anew, to see ourselves otherwise—I must recall some of the wisdoms of Alice Walker in her reflections on Zora Neale Hurston. We must never be willing to "throw away our geniuses," but if by chance they are discarded, it is our responsibility—our calling—to reclaim and embrace them again and again. My call to (re)cover and see Black males anew is my effort to give due diligence to this insightful womanist wisdom. I embrace the fact of Black male genius. I embrace the wholeness and survival of Black males. I embrace the value of Black male life. I embrace the wider horizons and scopes of vision of Black males in new registers of meaning. I embrace the (re)covering of (re)covery in Black male lives. And I embrace the continued work of cultivating and sustaining healthier expressions of Black male culture that are driven by the agentive possibilities of imaginative power. While the lives and lessons and experiences of Black men and boys are often deemed cursory, if not outright disregarded, I take pride in this work, which repurposes the scope, meaning, and significance of Black male identity—not just for Black males in the present but also as embodied by those Black male lives that are not yet to be.

ACKNOWLEDGMENTS

I can scarcely believe I'm in a position to write and publish a book—especially a book that centers topics so near and dear to my being. Yet, here we are. It is often said that your writing reveals not only your thoughts—your writing reveals you. In reading this book, you are reading me. But as you turn these pages to read me, you are also reading the experiences and wonderful communities that have nurtured my scholarly voice, awakened the clarity of my musings, and unlocked the imaginative possibilities that swell within the recesses of my mind. I now tarry with those communities in solemn, but appreciative reflection.

I am nothing without my immediate family, for whom I offer thanks to God who has granted me the gift of their presence as I wrestled with these ideas during doctoral work and through to the completion of this book. To my parents, Rev. Dr. Derrick and Sharron Hills—there are no words to fully capture my thanks for your presence and support. Dad, you gave me my manhood and showed me what wholesome paternal presence is all about. Mom, you embody a quiet, dignified spirit of strength that womanists laud for all Black women and girl's empowerment. Thank you, Mom, for also showing me what virtuous womanhood and motherhood means to the soul of the Black male child. It was your strength early on in insisting "I'm not just a minister's wife; I'm Sharron" that awakened within my childlike sensibilities what Hortense Spillers calls the power of the Black maternal. For the gift of cultivated openness to the worlds and words of Black women, I thank you. To my sister Brittany, I pray this book is enriching and a welcome respite from your steadfast creativity and hard work. Thank you for your good humor, sisterly wisdom, and for not judging me too harshly for being too absent. Perhaps now I can take a breather. I love you all, and I appreciate you.

Many of the ideas in this book began while I was a doctoral student at Rice University. My time in Houston provided a wellspring of resources, people, and communities that gave me life and light as I wrote. Drs. Stacey Floyd-Thomas, Anthony Pinn, Nicole Waligora-Davis, and Elias Bongmba have all been deeply supportive for virtually all my intellectual and professional pursuits—always encouraging me to ask the hard questions, but never accept the easy answers. Most notably, my doctoral advisor, Anthony Pinn, has been my model and inspiration ever since I dared pursue a PhD. Dr. Pinn, you are the consummate professional, and represent the highest caliber of scholarly productivity and excellence. Your example is one I am forever chasing to emulate. During my time at Rice, I also had the good fortune to have peers who pushed me further to develop my ideas and voice, and inaugurated moments of levity and good cheer that stilled me during moments of doubt. I highlight Drs. Christopher Driscoll, Jonathan Chism, Biko Gray, and Jason Jeffries for their camaraderie. It is wonderful to see you all on the other side and doing well in academia.

I also thank former colleagues in the Department of Philosophy and Religious Studies at Morgan State University, which provided the ground for my first foray into the increasingly precarious world of the tenure-track job market. During the later years at Morgan, I began the early chapter drafts and secured the book contract from New York University Press. I also thank my current academic home, the Department of Religious Studies at Grinnell College. As I've said continuously, Grinnell has been good medicine. It is unspeakable joy to walk into your "job" and to have it not feel like work. To my department colleagues, Drs. Henry Rietz, Elias Saba, Tim Dobe, Caleb Elfenbein, and Dixuan Chen—thank you for your generosity and your warmth in bringing me into this chapel of pedagogical and scholarly excellence situated in the rolling cornfields of Iowa.

To the many brilliant brothers in Black male studies who've inspired me over the years and pushed me to wrestle with the political implications of my work—I am forever in your debt. Drs. Tommy Curry, T. Hasan Johnson, Ryon Cobb, and Ron Neal—thank you for your continued support, prodding, and insightful read into my thoughts, worries, and concerns regarding the interplay of cultural criticism, Black men, and gender politics.

As noted, I am shocked to have the opportunity to publish a book. I am not shocked, however, that the glowing reputation of Jennifer Hammer, my editor at NYU, lived up to the hype. Submitting my proposal and getting valuable feedback was a breeze, due in no short order to

Jennifer's professionalism and timely responses. Thank you for this wonderful opportunity.

I've had the good fortune, both as a grad student and now as a professor, to be well-supported and well-funded for my research. Throughout my graduate school experience, the Fund for Theological Education (now the Forum for Theological Exploration) and the General Board of Higher Education and Ministry of the United Methodist Church awarded doctoral fellowships that made my coursework experience very low-stress, which is not common at all for graduate work. These resources were a godsend to me. I was able to complete my dissertation due to a fellowship awarded from the Louisville Institute. This book was also supported by a First Book Grant, also awarded from the Louisville Institute. I will forever be grateful for the winter seminars hosted by Louisville Presbyterian Theological Seminary; I met friends and colleagues there who've remained strong support networks as I do my work. Finally, I extend the deepest thanks to Phillip Goff and all the associated staff with the Center for the Study of Religion and American Culture. During 2020–2022 I was selected for the Young Scholars in American Religion program at the height of the COVID-19 pandemic. During the seminar workshops, my cohort proved deeply engaged with book chapters I submitted for critique and were a wellspring of critical insights that helped me further elucidate my ideas. For cultivating such a wonderful space for reflection away from the hustle and bustle of academic semester blues, I extend thanks especially to my mentors, Drs. Jonathan Walton and Penny Edgell.

Life throws you curveballs. In those moments, you must roll with the punches and continue navigating the wilderness. Life also throws you gifts in the form of people. These are people who remind you of what's important and vital. These are people who remind you of the best parts of yourself. These are the people who remind you that life is a gift. Embracing the gift of life is overwhelming, but you feel pure gratitude daily when you're able to do so fully and authentically. There is one such person who, in her own way, became a lifeline when I was stumbling in the dark, grasping at the wind, and seeking a path. Neither of us expected to find each other along the way. Yet, here we are. Thank you for inviting me into your world. Thank you for grasping my hand to assure me all would be well. Thank you for loving me *softly*. Jennifer Naus, it was always you.

NOTES

INTRODUCTION

1. Yukich and Edgell, *Religion Is Raced*.
2. Pinn, *Varieties of African American Religious Experiences*.
3. Touna, *Strategic Acts in the Study of Identity*, 7.
4. Smith et al., "'You Make Me Wanna Holler and Throw Up Both My Hands!'"; Curry, "Killing Boogeymen"; Griffin and Cummins, "'It's a Struggle.'"
5. Butler, *Giving an Account of Oneself*.
6. Stacey M. Floyd-Thomas, "Introduction: Writing for Our Lives: Womanism as an Epistemological Revolution," in Floyd-Thomas, *Deeper Shades of Purple*, 3.
7. Lloyd, "Masculinity, Race, and Fatherhood."
8. Curry, *Man-Not*, 6.
9. Butler, *Gender Trouble*, 6–9.
10. Butler, 10, 15.
11. See Neal, *Looking for Leroy*, and Wallace, *Constructing the Black Masculine*.
12. Staples, *Black Masculinity*, 7. See also MacKinnon, *Toward a Feminist Theory of the State*. MacKinnon's feminist dominance theory essentially posits the idea that womanhood is a class defined by their sole subordinated status in a patriarchal world. The consequence of this view is that patriarchal excess, the oppression of women, and misogynistic violence are universalized as masculine categories, with the assumption that all men writ large, regardless of race and class, wield unlimited power over women.
13. Townes, *Womanist Ethics*.
14. Curry, *Man-Not*, 170.
15. Evans, *Burden of Black Religion*, 7.
16. Stevie Wonder, "Misrepresented People," track 2 on *Bamboozled*, Motown Records, 2000, compact disc.
17. Curry, *Man-Not*, 6.
18. Hernton, *Sexual Mountain*, 45.
19. Reed, *Writin' Is Fightin'*, 145–146.
20. Carby, *Race Men*, 3–5.
21. Harris, "On *The Color Purple*," 155.
22. The cultural dynamic Harris describes surrounding the cultural importance of Alice Walker has tempered some aspects of my interpretive moves in this book and has shaped my understanding of the "optics" of being a Black male scholar focusing on womanist religious thought and scholarship from a critical standpoint.

23 Harris, "On *The Color Purple*," 157.
24 Reed, *Writin' Is Fightin'*, 150.
25 Harris, "On *The Color Purple*," 158.
26 Ware, *African American Theology*, 28.
27 See Anderson, "Abominations of a Million Men."
28 Walker, *In Search of Our Mothers' Gardens*.
29 To be sure, many of these critiques were specifically targeting Black feminists. Robert Staples's article "The Myth of Black Macho: A Response to Angry Black Feminists" is a good representation of the contested space between Black male critics and Black feminists.
30 Floyd-Thomas, "Katie's Canon."
31 Curry, *Man-Not*, 228.
32 Curry, "Decolonizing the Intersection," 150.
33 Hills, "'Admirable or Ridiculous?,'" 15.
34 Curry, *Man-Not*, 19.
35 Curry, 229.
36 Curry, 197–228.
37 Emilie M. Townes, "The Womanist Dancing Mind: Speaking to the Expansiveness of Womanist Discourse," in Floyd-Thomas, *Deeper Shades of Purple*, 245.
38 Anderson, *Creative Exchange*; Anderson, *Beyond Ontological Blackness*; Anderson, "Relational Concept of Race."

1. CHARTING RELATIONALITY IN BLACK RELIGIOUS THOUGHT

1 Trimiew, *Voices of the Silenced*, 98. Trimiew traces his conceptions of responsibility to H. Richard Niebuhr's *Responsible Self*.
2 Staples, *Black Masculinity*, 2.
3 Myers, "African American Males Speak."
4 Essed, *Understanding Everyday Racism*; Hartfield et al., "Gendered Racism Is a Key."
5 Staples, *Black Masculinity*, 11.
6 Goff, Di Leone, and Kahn, "Racism Leads to Pushups"; Hunter and Sellers, "Feminist Attitudes among African American Women and Men."
7 McClintock-Fulkerson, *Changing the Subject*, 7.
8 Tracy, *Plurality and Ambiguity*, 96.
9 Emilie M. Townes, "The Womanist Dancing Mind: Speaking to the Expansiveness of Womanist Discourse," in Floyd-Thomas, *Deeper Shades of Purple*, 245.
10 Townes, 247.
11 Cannon, *Katie's Canon*, 132.
12 Anthony Pinn, "What's the Theological Equivalent of a Mannish Boy? Learning a Lesson from Womanist Scholarship—A Humanist Response," in Floyd-Thomas, *Deeper Shades of Purple*, 275–281. See also Pinn, *Embodiment and the New Shape of Black Theological Thought*, chap. 3.
13 Cannon, *Katie's Canon*, 132.

14 Cannon, 132.
15 Baker-Fletcher and Baker-Fletcher, *My Sister, My Brother*, 16–17.
16 Alice Walker, "Coming Apart (1979)" in Phillips, *Womanist Reader*, 7.
17 Walker, 7.
18 Walker, *In Search of Our Mother's Gardens*, xi.
19 Katie Cannon, "Mapping Methodological Directions for Womanist Scholarship," in Rivera and Saracino, *Enfleshing Theology*, 35, 37.
20 Kelly Brown Douglas, "To Reflect the Image of God: A Womanist Perspective on Right Relationship," in Sanders, *Living the Intersection*, 67–77.
21 Floyd-Thomas, *Mining the Motherlode*.
22 Floyd-Thomas, 9.
23 Floyd-Thomas, 51. See also Townes, *Womanist Ethics*.
24 Cheryl Townsend Gilkes, "The Loves and Troubles of African American Women's Bodies: The Womanist Challenge to Cultural Humiliation and Community Ambivalence," in Cannon, Townes, and Sims, *Womanist Theological Ethics*, 95.
25 Rivera and Saracino, *Enfleshing Theology*.
26 Volf, *Exclusion and Embrace*, 169.
27 Copeland, *Enfleshing Freedom*, 90.
28 Hills, "Admirable or Ridiculous?"
29 Copeland, *Enfleshing Freedom*, 57, 84.
30 Eboni Marshall Turman, "Today a Black [Wo]man Was Lynched: A Womanist Christology of Sandra Bland," in Rivera and Saracino, *Enfleshing Theology*, 29.
31 Copeland, *Enfleshing Freedom*, 126.
32 Stephen G. Ray Jr., "Black Lives Matter as Enfleshed Theology," in Rivera and Saracino, *Enfleshing Theology*, 83–94.
33 Hull, Scott, and Smith, *All the Women Are White*, xvii.
34 Copeland, *Enfleshing Freedom*, 107.
35 Copeland, 127.
36 Copeland, 125.
37 Copeland, 63.
38 Copeland, 65.
39 Copeland, 164n25. See also Schillebeeckx, *Jesus*.
40 Copeland, *Enfleshing Freedom*, 92.
41 Copeland, 94.
42 I specifically have in mind religious philosopher Martin Buber, who supplements Copeland's relational framework by arranging the nature of reciprocity of human social life at the primordial level. In Buber's view, "I-Thou" subjectivities take precedent in the world of human relations because the "other" is recognized as coterminous with dignity, humanity, and worth of the self-constitution of another self's alterity, or distinctive separateness.
43 Copeland, 94.
44 Shults, *Reforming Theological Anthropology*, 30.
45 Montgomery, Oord, and Winslow, *Relational Theology*, 2.

46 Process religious thought and theological frameworks have multiple representative voices, but for interested readers seeking foundational texts about its early formulations, see Alfred North Whitehead's *Process and Reality* and Charles Hartshorne's *The Divine Relativity* and *Omnipotence and Other Theological Mistakes*.
47 Baker-Fletcher, *Dancing with God*, ix.
48 Baker-Fletcher, 5.
49 Volf, *Exclusion and Embrace*, 181.
50 Pally, *Commonwealth and Covenant*, 217.
51 Baker-Fletcher, *Dancing with God*, xi.
52 Baker-Fletcher, 18.
53 Thurman, *Jesus and the Disinherited*, 76.
54 Pally, *Commonwealth and Covenant*, 5.
55 Baker-Fletcher, *Xodus*, 5.
56 Baker-Fletcher, 6.
57 Baker-Fletcher, 24–25.
58 Baker-Fletcher, 37.
59 Baker-Fletcher, 37.
60 Baker-Fletcher, 37.
61 Baker-Fletcher, 37.
62 Baker-Fletcher, 39.
63 Baker-Fletcher, 38–39.
64 Hunter and Davis, "Constructing Gender." Strikingly, this study also found that attributes related to power, specifically the power to control others, including women, was rated as least important among Black men, though men of lower social status and income tended to emphasize it more than middle- and upper-class men.
65 Kane, "Racial and Ethnic Variations."
66 Emilie M. Townes, "Ethics as an Art of Doing the Work Our Souls Must Have," in Cannon, Townes, and Sims, *Womanist Theological Ethics*, 41.
67 Baker-Fletcher, *Xodus*, 38.
68 Baker-Fletcher, 38.
69 Baker-Fletcher, 39.
70 Baker-Fletcher, 41.
71 Baker-Fletcher, 40.
72 See Sanders, *Queer Lessons for Churches on the Straight and Narrow*, and Griffin, *Their Own Received Them Not*.
73 Egbuna, "Black Men, We Must Be Better"; Janee, "Who's Going to Ride or Die for Black Women and Girls?"
74 Baker-Fletcher, *Xodus*, 41.
75 Baker-Fletcher, "Xodus or X-Scape?," in *Black Religion after the Million Man March*, 28.
76 Cannon, *Black Womanist Ethics*, 6–7.

77 Floyd-Thomas, "That We May Dare to Suffer."
78 Hopkins, *Shoes That Fit Our Feet*, 2.
79 Hopkins, 51.
80 Hopkins, 51.
81 Hopkins, 60. Hopkins considers, among others, *Beloved, Sula, Tar Baby*, and *The Bluest Eye*.
82 Hopkins, 63.
83 Hopkins, 63–64.
84 Hopkins, 63.
85 Emilie Townes, "They Came Because of the Wailing," in Floyd-Thomas, *Deeper Shades of Purple*, 251.
86 Hopkins, *Shoes That Fit Our Feet*, 65.
87 Hopkins, 218.
88 Hopkins, 67.
89 Westfield, *Dear Sisters*, 7.
90 Marla F. Frederick, *Between Sundays*.
91 Baldwin, *Notes of a Native Son*, 24–25.
92 Townes, *Womanist Ethics*, 30.
93 Townes, "Vanishing into Limbo. Part II: Black Men as Endangered Species . . . Not," in Hopkins and Thomas, *Walk Together Children*, 102.
94 Lorde, *Sister Outsiders*, 137.
95 Townes, "Vanishing into Limbo," 86.

2. BLACK MANHOOD IN THE WRITINGS OF ALICE WALKER, ZORA NEALE HURSTON, AND TONI MORRISON

1 Wallace, *Constructing the Black Masculine*, 5.
2 Wallace, 25.
3 Wallace, 33.
4 See Majors and Billson, *Cool Pose*; Smith, Hung, and Franklin, "Racial Battle Fatigue"; Harper, *Are We Not Men?*
5 Summers, *Manliness and Its Discontents*.
6 Walker, *Color Purple*; Hurston, *Their Eyes Were Watching God*; Morrison, *Home*. All citations and direct quotes referenced in this chapter are based upon these editions.
7 Watkins, "Contested Memories," 272.
8 Townes, "Ethics as an Art of Doing the Work Our Souls Must Have," in Cannon, Townes, and Sims, *Womanist Theological Ethics*, 36.
9 Collins, "What's in a Name?," 10.
10 See Cannon, *Katie's Canon*, chap. 7; Spencer, "Value of Lived Experience"; Dandridge, "Male Critics/Black Women's Novels."
11 Cannon, *Black Womanist Ethics*.
12 Curry, *Man-Not*, 230.
13 James Baldwin, "To Crush a Serpent," in Baldwin, *Cross of Redemption*, 164–165.

14 Particularly raced and sexualized bodies.
15 Baldwin, "To Crush a Serpent," 164.
16 El Kornegay, *Queering of Black Theology*, 14.
17 Baldwin, "To Crush a Serpent," 164.
18 Day, *Unfinished Business*, 98.
19 Douglas, "To Reflect the Image of God," in Sanders, *Living the Intersection*, 73.
20 That I use the language of humanization to describe Harpo is my effort to allude to his expansion of his own humanity and identity through his extension of care toward Albert. It is the very extension of self—the placing of another within the field of one's scope of human relations—that indicates the enlargement of human personality.
21 Arvidson, *Sphere of Attention*, 150.
22 Arvidson, 150.
23 Arvidson, 169.
24 Arvidson, 150.
25 Neal, *New Black Man*, 21–28.
26 Hemenway, *Zora Neale Hurston*, xii, emphasis added.
27 Miller, "'Some Other Way to Try.'"
28 Miller, 75.
29 Neal, "Finding Tea Cake."
30 Ferguson, "Folkloric Men and Female Growth," 185.
31 Ferguson, 185.
32 Ferguson, 192–193.
33 Bealer, "'The Kiss of Memory,'" 320.
34 Bealer, 312.
35 Bealer, 320.
36 Miller, "'Some Other Way to Try,'" 84.
37 Miller, 86.
38 Miller, 92.
39 Cannon, *Black Womanist Ethics*, 104.
40 Miller, "'Some Other Way to Try,'" 92.
41 Harack, "Shifting Masculinities and Evolving Feminine Power," 372.
42 Hicks, *Reclaiming Spirit*.
43 Townes, *Breaking the Fine Rain of Death*, 151–157.
44 My interpretation of caregiving and the themes of self-extension is also modestly influenced by Jean-Luc Marion's phenomenology of "the gift" and givenness as expressions of relational exchange. See Marion, *Being Given*.
45 Townes, *Breaking the Fine Rain of Death*, 182.
46 Townes, 182.
47 Harack, "Shifting Masculinities and Evolving Feminine Power," 372.
48 Harack, 374.
49 Morrison, "Home."
50 Townes, *Breaking the Fine Rain of Death*, 156.

51 Anderson, "Relational Concept of Race," 30. See also Farley, *Deep Symbols*.
52 Hernton, *Sexual Mountain*, xxiii.
53 Reed, *Writin' Is Fightin'*, 152.
54 Curry, *Man-Not*, 20.
55 Curry, 228.

3. JAMES BALDWIN, THE BLACK CHURCH, AND QUEERING THE MASCULINIST OEUVRE

1 Baldwin, "Freaks and the American Ideal of Manhood," in *Baldwin: Collected Essays*, 821.
2 Campbell, *Talking at the Gates*, 75.
3 Leak, *Racial Myths and Masculinity*, 133.
4 Clark, *Black Manhood*, 3.
5 Leeming, *James Baldwin*, 21.
6 Clark, *Black Manhood*, 2.
7 Clark, 13.
8 All citations from the novels draw upon the following editions: *Go Tell It on the Mountain* (New York: Everyman's Library, 2016) and *If Beale Street Could Talk* (New York: Vintage, 2006).
9 Clark, *Black Manhood*, 5.
10 Nelson, *Body Theology*, 26.
11 Michael K. Lynch, "A Glimpse of the Hidden God," in Harris, *New Essays*, 33–34.
12 Sneed, *Representations of Homosexuality*, 84–85.
13 Baldwin, "The Black Boy Looks at the White Boy," in *Baldwin: Collected Essays*, 279.
14 Baldwin, 279.
15 Baldwin, 279.
16 Hereafter referred to as "*Mountain.*"
17 Leeming, *James Baldwin*, 8.
18 Lynch, "Glimpse of the Hidden God," 42.
19 Leeming, *James Baldwin*, 3.
20 Trudier Harris, "Introduction," in Harris, *New Essays*, 2.
21 Harris, 9.
22 Hardy, *James Baldwin's God*, 25.
23 Gibson, *Salvific Manhood*, 50.
24 Gibson, 3.
25 James Baldwin, "To Crush a Serpent," in Baldwin, *Cross of Redemption*, 164.
26 Bryan R. Washington, "Wrestling with 'The Love That Dare Not Speak Its Name': John, Elisha, and the 'Master,'" in Harris, *New Essays*, 91.
27 Gibson, *Salvific Manhood*, 27, 45.
28 Hardy, *James Baldwin's God*, 31.
29 Lorde, *Sister Outsiders*, 73.
30 Baldwin, "To Crush a Serpent," 165.

31 Lynch, "Glimpse of the Hidden God, 36.
32 Hobson, *James Baldwin and the Heavenly City*, 6.
33 Matt Brim, *James Baldwin and the Queer Imagination*, 1.
34 Sneed, *Representations of Homosexuality*, 109.
35 Lightsey, *Our Lives Matter*, 27.
36 Sneed, *Representations of Homosexuality*, 111.
37 Sneed, 112.
38 Brim, *James Baldwin and the Queer Imagination*, 6.
39 Sneed, *Representations of Homosexuality*, 152.
40 Griffin, *Their Own Received Them Not*, xiii.
41 Sneed, *Representations of Homosexuality*, 94–95.
42 Anderson, *Creative Exchange*, 11.
43 Sneed, *Representations of Homosexuality*, 105.
44 Sneed, 139.
45 Yeboah, "Why the West Could Not Hear Beale Street," 11.
46 Sneed, *Representations of Homosexuality*, 134.
47 Sneed, 179.
48 Sneed, 175.
49 Lightsey, *Our Lives Matter*, 34.
50 Muñoz, *Cruising Utopia*, 1.
51 Brim, *James Baldwin and the Queer Imagination*, 5.
52 Brim, 6.
53 Victor Anderson, "The Black Church and the Curious Body of the Black Homosexual," in Pinn and Hopkins, *Loving the Body*, 310.
54 Sneed, *Representations of Homosexuality*, 187.
55 Sneed, 187.
56 Anderson, "Black Church and the Curious Body," 310.
57 Harper, *Are We Not Men?*
58 Curry, "Michael Brown and the Need for a Genre Study."
59 Clark, *Black Manhood*, 128.
60 Sneed, *Representations of Homosexuality*, 189, emphasis added.

4. The Relational Turn in Black Male Theologies

1 Wickware, "Labour of Black Love," 3.
2 Wickware, 4.
3 Byrd and Guy-Sheftall, *Traps*, 2.
4 Lloyd, *Religion of the Field Negro*.
5 Cone, *Martin, Malcolm, and America*; Erskine, *King among the Theologians*; Dixie and Eisenstadt, *Visions of a Better World*; Neal, *Howard Thurman's Philosophical Mysticism*.
6 Cannon, *Black Womanist Ethics*, 174.
7 Harvey, *Howard Thurman and the Disinherited*, 33.
8 Harvey, 34.

9. Harvey, 9–10.
10. Eisenstadt, *Against the Hounds of Hell*, 35.
11. Eisenstadt, 36.
12. Eisenstadt, 35.
13. Eisenstadt, 36.
14. Eisenstadt, 36.
15. Dorrien, *Making of American Liberal Theology*, 560.
16. Eisenstadt, *Against the Hounds of Hell*, 114.
17. Eisenstadt, 114.
18. Eisenstadt, 115.
19. On the question of neoliberal values as an interpretive lens for human behavior and its impact on vulnerable communities along racial and gender-based lines, see the introduction to Keri Day's *Unfinished Business*.
20. Howard Thurman, "What Shall I Do with My Life?," in Fluker and Tumber, *Strange Freedom*, 31, emphasis added.
21. Thurman, 31.
22. Harvey, *Howard Thurman and the Disinherited*, 92.
23. Eisenstadt, *Against the Hounds of Hell*, 264.
24. Thurman, *Jesus and the Disinherited*, 19.
25. Thurman, xix.
26. Thurman, 23.
27. James Cone argues that God is Black in *God of the Oppressed* (1975). Blackness, in Cone's usage, expands beyond a mere racial category and suggests instead an experiential dimension of God's self-revelation in Jesus. God shares in and is sensitive to racialized Blackness, notably through Jesus's own suffering within the context of an oppressive society that disregarded his humanity and integrity. Black liberation theologians like Cone argue that Jesus's life resonates with the racially marginalized in the present, particularly African Americans. Pertaining to shared understanding of racialized, state-sanctioned violence, Cone extends this argument in *The Cross and the Lynching Tree* (2011).
28. Alton B. Pollard III, "Magnificent Manhood: The Transcendent Witness of Howard Thurman," in Boyd, Longwood, and Muesse, *Redeeming Men*, 222.
29. Thurman, *With Head and Heart*, 253.
30. Eisenstadt, *Against the Hounds of Hell*, 53.
31. Pollard, "Magnificent Manhood," 228.
32. King, *Where Do We Go from Here: Chaos or Community?*, 167.
33. Cone, *Martin, Malcolm, and America*; Baldwin, *There Is a Balm in Gilead* and *To Make the Wounded Whole*; Smith and Zepp, *Search for the Beloved Community*; Erskine, *King among the Theologians*; Ivory, *Toward a Theology of Radical Involvement*.
34. Baldwin, *There Is a Balm in Gilead*, 2.
35. Baker-Fletcher, *Somebodyness*, xi.
36. Martin Luther King Jr., "The Case Against Tokenism," in Washington, *Testament of Hope*, 108. Regarding Alain Locke, see his edited volume, *The New Negro* (1925),

for its collection of Harlem Renaissance-era writers on the topic of Black self-affirmation.
37 Baldwin, *There Is a Balm in Gilead*, 35.
38 Baldwin, 23.
39 See Smith and Zepp, *Search for the Beloved Community*. Interestingly, Baldwin critiques Smith and Zepp's volume for overstating and unduly centralizing the value and reach of the White intellectual and theological sources that supplemented King's religious and racial philosophies.
40 Cone, "Martin Luther King, Jr.," 411.
41 Martin Luther King Jr., "My Call to Ministry" (August 7, 1959), in *Papers of Martin Luther King, Jr.*, 368.
42 Baldwin, *There Is a Balm in Gilead*, 280.
43 Smith and Zepp, *Search for the Beloved Community*, 141–145.
44 Baldwin, *There Is a Balm in Gilead*, 43.
45 Baldwin, 44.
46 Baldwin, 44.
47 King, *Where Do We Go from Here: Chaos or Community?*, 177.
48 Smith and Zepp, *Search for the Beloved Community*, 129.
49 King, "The Ethical Demand for Integration," in Washington, *Testament of Hope*, 122.
50 Smith and Zepp, *Search for the Beloved Community*, 133; King, *Where Do We Go from Here: Chaos or Community?*, 181.
51 Smith and Zepp, *Search for the Beloved Community*, 139.
52 Baldwin, *To Make the Wounded Whole*, 73.
53 Baker-Fletcher, *Somebodyness*, 172.
54 Cannon, *Black Womanist Ethics*, 3, emphasis added.
55 Crystal A. deGregory and Lewis V. Baldwin, "Sexism in the World House and the Global Vision of Martin Luther King, Jr.," in Crawford and Baldwin, *Reclaiming the Great World House*, 108.
56 DeGregory and Baldwin, 110.
57 King, "The Crisis of the Modern Family," in *Papers of Martin Luther King, Jr.*, 212.
58 DeGregory and Baldwin, "Sexism in the World House," 112.
59 See chap. 17 in Paula Giddings's *When and Where I Enter*. Giddings recounts how Black women organizers for welfare rights confronted and criticized King for his leadership on the Poor People's Campaign. Notably, King failed to acknowledge their consistent and antecedent work on urban poverty and ignored their expertise and knowledge on pertinent policy platforms.
60 Grace Jordan McFadden, "Septima P. Clark and the Struggle for Human Rights," in Weisenfeld and Newman, *This Far by Faith*, 306.
61 McFadden, 307–308.
62 Lewis V. Baldwin, "Toward a Broader Humanism: Malcolm, Martin, and the Search for Beloved Community," in Baldwin and Al-Hadid, *Between Cross and Crescent*, 315.
63 Blain, *Until I Am Free*.

64 Blain, 67–68, emphasis added.
65 Blain, 68.
66 Blain, 69.
67 Cannon, *Black Womanist Ethics*, 170.
68 Gilkes, *If It Wasn't for the Women*, 6.
69 Howard Thurman, "Mysticism and Social Change," in Fluker and Tumber, *Strange Freedom*, 116.
70 Thurman, 116.
71 King, *Where Do We Go from Here: Chaos or Community?*, 170.
72 Wilmore, *Pragmatic Spirituality*, 64.

5. ON BLACK MALE (RE)COVERY

1 Teresa Fry Brown, "Avoiding Asphyxiation: A Womanist Perspective on Intrapersonal and Interpersonal Transformation," in Townes, *Embracing the Spirit*.
2 John Edgar Wideman, "The Night I Was Nobody," in Belton, *Speak My Name*, 25. See also Majors and Billson, *Cool Pose*.
3 See Cecil Cone's *The Identity Crisis in Black Theology*. James Cone's *God of the Oppressed* was an effort to respond to the criticisms of *The Identity Crisis in Black Theology*.
4 Coetzee, "Feminism Is African," 4.
5 Mbiti, *African Religions and Philosophy*, 108–109.
6 Gathogo, "John Mbiti's Ubuntu Theology," 4.
7 Mbiti, *African Religions and Philosophy*, 104.
8 Mbiti, 104.
9 Mbiti, 108.
10 Wiredu, "Toward Decolonizing African Philosophy and Religion," 24.
11 Oyěwùmí, *Invention of Women*, ix.
12 Oyěwùmí, "Conceptualizing Gender," 4.
13 Oyěwùmí, *Invention of Women*, x.
14 Oyěwùmí, "Translation of Cultures," 76.
15 Oyěwùmí, 78–79.
16 Oyěwùmí, *What Gender Is Motherhood?*, 215, emphasis added.
17 Jennings, *Christian Imagination*.
18 Oyěwùmí, *What Gender Is Motherhood?*, 213. See also Rich, *Of Woman Born*, and Hallstein, *White Feminists and Contemporary Maternity*.
19 Oyěwùmí, *What Gender Is Motherhood?*, 12.
20 Oyěwùmí, 20.
21 Oyěwùmí.
22 Oyěwùmí, 17–19.
23 Oyěwùmí, *Invention of Women*, xiii.
24 Oyěwùmí, *What Gender Is Motherhood?*, 10.
25 Oyěwùmí, 58.
26 Oyěwùmí.

27 See Copeland, *Enfleshing Freedom*. Copeland adopts a womanist and Catholic hermeneutic that posits the bodily and racial experiences of Black women as mirroring the body of Jesus—thereby privileging the bodies of the marginalized and oppressed as living sacraments that can shape more holistic and liberatory theological reflection. It would appear that the Ìyá functions similarly as it relates to the prominence ascribed to African procreation/mothering. However, Oyěwùmí does operate from the same theological or religious commitment in emphasizing the matripotent line of thought.
28 Oyěwùmí, *What Gender Is Motherhood?*, 60.
29 Oyěwùmí, 59.
30 Oyěwùmí, 61.
31 Oyěwùmí, 61.
32 Oyěwùmí, 61.
33 Oyěwùmí, 62.
34 Hudson-Weems, *Africana Womanist Literary Theory*, 88–89.
35 Hudson-Weems, 94.
36 Neal, *New Black Man*, xx–xxi.
37 Anthony, *Searching for the New Black Man*, 16.
38 Henry, *Searching for the New Black Man*, 16.
39 Carrette and King, *Selling Spirituality*.
40 Frederick, *Between Sundays*, 11.
41 Frederick, 14.
42 Frederick, 12.
43 Grier, *Care for the Mental and Spiritual Health of Black Men*, 97.
44 Grier, 104.
45 Grier, 130.
46 Grier, 137.
47 Grier, 138.
48 Parham, White, and Ajamu, *Psychology of Blacks*, 95.
49 Parham, White, and Ajamu, 96.
50 Hooks, *Will to Change*, 59.
51 Wideman, "The Night I Was Nobody," 27.
52 Douglas, *Enlightened Sexism*.

EPILOGUE

1 Hutchinson, *Assassination of the Black Male Image*.
2 Brown, "What Is a Bullet Bag?"
3 Glaister, "Abort All Black Babies and Cut Crime."
4 Wallace, *Constructing the Black Masculine*, 20.
5 Collins, *Black Feminist Thought*, 125.
6 Anderson, *Beyond Ontological Blackness*, 91–92.
7 Anderson, 17.
8 Douglas, *Black Christ*, 115.

9 One such example of this demonization in recent online public memory is demonstrated in the social media backlash to Damon Young's Very Smart Brothas op-ed article "Straight Black Men Are the White People of Black People." Young's critique of the "intraracial privileges" that Black men wield over women writ large, while an insightful observation, struck many as tone deaf to the historical, economic, and social disenfranchisement that shapes Black male existence as well as an overgeneralized pillorying of Black male gender politics.
10 Sneed, *Representations of Homosexuality*, 175.
11 Sneed, 179.
12 Crawley, *Blackpentecostal Breath*, 3.
13 Crawley, 5.
14 Crawley, 1.
15 Crawley, 3.

BIBLIOGRAPHY

Anderson, Victor. "Abominations of a Million Men: Reflection on a Silent Majority." In *Black Religion after the Million Man March: Voices on the Future*, edited by Garth Kasimu Baker-Fletcher, 19–26. Maryknoll, NY: Orbis Books, 1998.
——. *Beyond Ontological Blackness: An Essay on African American Religious and Cultural Criticism*. New York: Continuum, 1999.
——. *Creative Exchange: A Constructive Theology of African American Religious Experience*. Minneapolis: Fortress Press, 2008.
——. "A Relational Concept of Race in African American Religious Thought." *Nova Religio: The Journal of Alternative and Emergent Religions* 7, no. 1 (2003): 28–43.
Anthony, Ronda C. *Searching for the New Black Man: Black Masculinity and Women's Bodies*. Jackson: University Press of Mississippi, 2014.
Arvidson, P. Sven. *The Sphere of Attention: Context and Margin*. Dordrecht: Springer, 2006.
Baker-Fletcher, Garth. *Black Religion after the Million Man March: Voices on the Future*. Maryknoll, NY: Orbis Books, 1998.
——, ed. *Somebodyness: Martin Luther King, Jr. and the Theory of Dignity*. Minneapolis: Fortress Press, 1993.
——. *Xodus: An African American Male Journey*. Minneapolis: Fortress Press, 1996.
Baker-Fletcher, Karen. *Dancing with God: The Trinity from a Womanist Perspective*. Atlanta: Chalice Press, 2003.
Baker-Fletcher, Karen, and Garth Baker-Fletcher. *My Sister, My Brother: Womanist and Xodus God-Talk*. Maryknoll, NY: Orbis Books, 1997.
Baldwin, Clive. *Anxious Men: Masculinity in American Fiction of the Mid-Twentieth Century*. Edinburgh: Edinburgh University Press, 2020.
Baldwin, James. *The Cross of Redemption: Uncollected Writings*. Edited by Randall Kenan. New York: Pantheon Books, 2010.
——. *The Fire Next Time*. New York: Vintage, 1993.
——. *Go Tell It on the Mountain*. New York: Everyman's Library, 2016.
——. *If Beale Street Could Talk*. Repr. ed. New York: Vintage, 2006.
——. *James Baldwin: Collected Essays*. Edited by Toni Morrison. New York: Library of America, 1998.
——. *Nobody Knows My Name: More Notes of a Native Son*. 1st Vintage international ed. New York: Vintage, 1993.
——. *Notes of a Native Son*. Boston: Beacon, 1957.
Baldwin, Lewis V. *There Is a Balm in Gilead: The Cultural Roots of Martin Luther King Jr.* Minneapolis: Fortress Press, 1991.

———. *To Make the Wounded Whole: The Cultural Legacy of Martin Luther King Jr.* Minneapolis: Fortress Press, 1992.

Baldwin, Lewis V., and Amiri Yasin Al-Hadid. *Between Cross and Crescent: Christian and Muslim Perspectives on Malcolm and Martin.* Gainesville: University Press of Florida, 2002.

Bealer, Tracy L. "'The Kiss of Memory': The Problem of Love in Hurston's *Their Eyes Were Watching God*." *African American Review* 43, no. 2/3 (2009): 311–327.

Belton, Don, ed. *Speak My Name: Black Men on Masculinity and the American Dream.* Boston: Beacon, 1995.

Bergson, Henri. *The Two Sources of Morality and Religion.* New ed. Notre Dame: University of Notre Dame Press, 1977.

Blain, Keisha N. *Until I Am Free: Fannie Lou Hamer's Enduring Message to America.* Boston: Beacon, 2021.

Boyd, Stephen B., W. Merle Longwood, and Mark W. Muesse, eds. *Redeeming Men: Religion and Masculinities.* Louisville, KY: Westminster John Knox, 1996.

Brim, Matt. *James Baldwin and the Queer Imagination.* Ann Arbor: University of Michigan Press, 2014.

Brown, Ann. "What Is a Bullet Bag? Inside the New Liberal Smear Against Black Men." *Moguldom Nation*, September 13, 2021. https://moguldom.com.

Butler, Judith. *Gender Trouble: Feminism and the Subversion of Identity.* New York: Routledge, 1999.

———. *Giving an Account of Oneself.* New York: Fordham University Press, 2005.

Byrd, Rudolph P., and Beverly Guy-Sheftall, eds. *Traps: African American Men on Gender and Sexuality.* Bloomington: Indiana University Press, 2001.

Campbell, James. *Talking at the Gates: A Life of James Baldwin.* Berkeley: University of California Press, 2021.

Cannon, Katie G. *Black Womanist Ethics.* Eugene, OR: Wipf and Stock, 1988.

———. *Katie's Canon: Womanism and the Soul of the Black Community.* New York: Continuum, 1998.

Cannon, Katie G., Emilie Townes, and Angela D. Sims, eds. *Womanist Theological Ethics.* Louisville, KY: Westminster John Knox, 2011.

Carby, Hazel. *Race Men.* Cambridge, MA: Harvard University Press, 1998.

Carrette, Jeremy, and Richard King. *Selling Spirituality: The Silent Takeover of Religion.* New York: Routledge, 2005.

Carter, J. Kameron. *Race: A Theological Account.* New York: Oxford University Press, 2008.

Clark, Keith. *Black Manhood in James Baldwin, Ernest J. Gaines, and August Wilson.* Urbana: University of Illinois Press, 2004.

Coetzee, Azille. "Feminism Is African, and Other Implications of Reading Oyeronke Oyewumi as a Relational Thinker." *Gender and Women's Studies* 1, no. 1 (2018): 1–16.

Collins, Patricia Hill. *Black Feminist Thought: Knowledge, Consciousness, and the Politics of Empowerment.* New York: Routledge, 2009.

———. "What's in a Name? Womanism, Black Feminism, and Beyond." *Black Scholar* 26, no. 1 (1996): 9–17.

Cone, Cecil. *The Identity Crisis in Black Theology*. Nashville, TN: AME Church, 1975.
Cone, James H. *Black Theology and Black Power*. Repr. ed. Maryknoll, NY: Orbis Books, 1997.
———. *A Black Theology of Liberation*. 40th anniv. ed. Maryknoll, NY: Orbis Books, 2010.
———. *The Cross and the Lynching Tree*. Maryknoll, NY: Orbis Books, 2011.
———. *God of the Oppressed*. Rev. sub. ed. Maryknoll, NY: Orbis Books, 1997.
———. "Martin Luther King, Jr., Black Theology–Black Church." *Theology Today* 40, no. 4 (January 1984): 411.
———. *Martin, Malcolm, and America: A Dream or Nightmare*. Maryknoll, NY: Orbis Books, 1991.
Cone, James H., and Gayraud S. Wilmore, eds. *Black Theology: A Documentary History*. Maryknoll, NY: Orbis Books, 1992.
Connell, R. W. *Masculinities*. 2nd ed. Berkeley: University of California Press, 2005.
Copeland, M. Shawn. *Enfleshing Freedom: Body, Race, and Being*. Minneapolis: Fortress Press, 2009.
Crawford, Vicki L., and Lewis Baldwin, eds. *Reclaiming the Great World House: The Global Vision of Martin Luther King Jr.* Athens: University of Georgia Press, 2019.
Crawley, Ashon T. *Blackpentecostal Breath: The Aesthetics of Possibility*. New York: Fordham, 2016.
Curry, Tommy. "Decolonizing the Intersection: Black Male Studies as a Critique of Intersectionality's Indebtedness to Subculture of Violence Theory." In *Critical Psychology Praxis: Psychosocial Non-alignment to Modernity/Coloniality*, edited by Robert K. Beshara, 132–154. New York: Routledge, 2021.
———. "Killing Boogeymen: Phallicism and the Misandric Characterizations of Black Males in Theory." *Res Philosophica* 95, no. 2 (2018): 235–272.
———. *The Man-Not: Race, Class, Genre, and the Dilemmas of Black Manhood*. Philadelphia: Temple University Press, 2017.
———. "Michael Brown and the Need for a Genre Study of Black Male Death and Dying." *Theory & Event* 17, no. 3 (2014).
Dandridge, Rita B. "Male Critics/Black Women's Novels." *CLA Journal* 23, no. 1 (1979): 1–11.
Davis, Angela Y. *Women, Race, & Class*. 1st Vintage ed. New York: Vintage, 1983.
Day, Keri. *Unfinished Business: Black Women, the Black Church, and the Struggle to Thrive in America*. Maryknoll, NY: Orbis Books, 2012.
Dixie, Quinton, and Peter Eisenstadt. *Visions of a Better World: Howard Thurman's Pilgrimage to India and the Origins of African American Nonviolence*. Boston: Beacon, 2011.
Dorrien, Gary. *The Making of American Liberal Theology: Idealism, Realism, and Modernity*. Louisville, KY: Westminster John Knox, 2003.
Douglas, Kelly Brown. *The Black Christ*. Maryknoll, NY: Orbis Books, 2019.
———. *Sexuality and the Black Church: A Womanist Perspective*. Maryknoll, NY: Orbis Books, 1999.

Douglas, Susan J. *Enlightened Sexism: The Seductive Message that Feminism's Work Is Done*. New York: Times Books, 2010.
Egbuna, Toby. "Black Men, We Must Be Better." *Chezie*, January 17, 2021. www.chezie.co.
Eisenstadt, Peter. *Against the Hounds of Hell: A Life of Howard Thurman*. Charlottesville: University of Virginia Press, 2021.
Erskine, Noel L. *King among the Theologians*. Boston: Beacon, 1995.
Essed, Philomena. *Understanding Everyday Racism: An Interdisciplinary Theory* (Thousand Oaks, CA: Sage, 1991).
Evans, Curtis J. *The Burden of Black Religion*. New York: Oxford University Press, 2008.
Farley, Edward. *Deep Symbols: Their Postmodern Effacement and Reclamation*. Harrisburg, PA: Trinity Press International, 1996.
Ferguson, SallyAnn. "Folkloric Men and Female Growth in *Their Eyes Were Watching God*." *Black American Literature Forum* 21, no. 1/2 (1987): 185–197.
Floyd-Thomas, Stacey, ed. *Deeper Shades of Purple: Womanism in Religion and Society*. New York: New York University Press, 2006.
———. "Katie's Canon: Enfleshing Womanism, Mentoring, and the Soul of the Black Community." *Journal of Feminist Studies in Religion* 35, no. 1 (2019): 101–104.
———. *Mining the Motherlode: Methods in Womanist Ethics*. Cleveland: Pilgrim Press, 2006.
———. "That We May Dare to Suffer: The Moral Muster and Theological Urgency of Human Flourishing." Biola University Center for Christian Thought, March 25, 2019. https://cct.biola.edu.
Fluker, Walter E., and Catherine Tumber, eds. *A Strange Freedom: The Best of Howard Thurman on Religious Experience and Public Life*. Boston: Beacon, 1998.
Frederick, Marla. *Between Sundays: Black Women and Everyday Struggles of Faith*. Berkeley: University of California Press, 2003.
Gathogo, Julius. "John Mbiti's Ubuntu Theology: Was It Rooted in His African Heritage?" *Studia Historiae Ecclesiasticae* 48, no. 2 (2022): 1–22.
Gibson, Ernest L. *Salvific Manhood: James Baldwin's Novelization of Male Intimacy*. Lincoln: University of Nebraska Press, 2019.
Giddings, Paula. *When and Where I Enter: The Impact of Black Women on Race and Sex in America*. New York: Amistad, 2006.
Gilkes, Cheryl Townsend. *If It Wasn't for the Women: Black Women's Experience and Womanist Culture in Church and Community*. Maryknoll, NY: Orbis Books, 2000.
Glaister, Dan. "Abort All Black Babies and Cut Crime, Says Republican." *Guardian*, October 1, 2005. www.theguardian.com.
Glaude, Eddie S. *Begin Again: James Baldwin's America and Its Urgent Lessons for Our Own*. New York: Crown, 2020.
Goff, Phillip A., Brooke A. Di Leone, and Kimberly B. Kahn. "Racism Leads to Push-ups: How Racial Discrimination Threatens Subordinate Men's Masculinity." *Journal of Experimental Social Psychology* 48, no. 5 (2012): 1111–1116.
Grier, Nicholas. *Care for the Mental and Spiritual Health of Black Men: Hope to Keep Going*. Lanham, MD: Lexington Books, 2019.

Griffin, Horace. *Their Own Received Them Not: African Americans and Gays in Black Churches*. Eugene, OR: Wipf and Stock, 2006.
Griffin, Rachel A., and Molly W. Cummins. "'It's a Struggle, It's a Journey, It's a Mountain That You Gotta Climb': Black Misandry, Education, and the Strategic Embrace of Black Male Counterstories." *Qualitative Communication Research* 1, no. 3 (2012): 257–289.
Hallstein, D. Lynn. *White Feminists and Contemporary Maternity: Purging Matrophobia*. New York: Springer, 2010.
Harack, Katrina. "Shifting Masculinities and Evolving Feminine Power: Progressive Gender Roles in Toni Morrison's *Home*." *Mississippi Quarterly* 69, no. 3 (2016): 371–396.
Hardy, Clarence E. *James Baldwin's God: Sex, Hope, and Crisis in Black Holiness Culture*. Knoxville: University of Tennessee Press, 2009.
Harper, Phillip Brian. *Are We Not Men? Masculine Anxiety and the Problem of African American Identity*. New York: Oxford University Press, 1998.
Harris, Trudier, ed. *New Essays on* Go Tell It on the Mountain. New York: Cambridge University Press, 1996.
———. "On *The Color Purple*, Stereotypes, and Silence." *Black American Literature Forum* 18, no. 4 (1984): 155–161.
Hartfield, Jennifer A., et al. "Gendered Racism Is a Key to Explaining and Addressing Police-Involved Shootings of Unarmed Black Men in America." In *Inequality, Crime, and Health among African American Males*, edited by Marino A. Bruce and Darnell F. Hawkins, 155–170. Bingley: Emerald, 2018.
Hartshorne, Charles. *The Divine Relativity: A Social Conception of God*. New Haven, CT: Yale University Press, 1982.
———. *Omnipotence and Other Theological Mistakes*. Albany: State University of New York Press, 1984.
Harvey, Paul. *Howard Thurman and the Disinherited: A Religious Biography*. Grand Rapids, MI: Eerdmans, 2020.
Hemenway, Robert E. *Zora Neale Hurston: A Literary Biography*. Urbana: University of Illinois Press, 1980.
Hernton, Calvin C. *The Sexual Mountain and Black Women Writers: Adventures in Sex, Literature, and Real Life*. New York: Anchor, 1990.
Hicks, Derek. *Reclaiming Spirit in the Black Faith Tradition*. New York: Palgrave Macmillan, 2012.
Hills, Darrius D. "'Admirable or Ridiculous?' The Burdens of Black Women Scholars and Dialogue in the Work of Solidarity." *Journal of Feminist Studies in Religion* 35, no. 2 (2019): 5–21.
———. "Back to a White Future: White Religious Loss, Donald Trump, and the Problem of Belonging." *Black Theology* 16, no. 1 (January 2018): 38–52.
Hobson, Christopher Z. *James Baldwin and the Heavenly City: Prophecy, Apocalypse, and Doubt*. East Lansing: Michigan State University Press, 2018.
hooks, bell. *The Will to Change: Men, Masculinity, and Love*. New York: Washington Square Press, 2004.

Hopkins, Dwight N. *Heart and Head: Black Theology—Past, Present, and Future.* New York: Palgrave Macmillan, 2003.

———. *Shoes That Fit Our Feet: Sources for a Constructive Black Theology.* Maryknoll, NY: Orbis Books, 1993.

Hopkins, Dwight N., and Linda E. Thomas, eds. *Walk Together Children: Black and Womanist Theologies, Church, and Theological Education.* Eugene, OR: Cascade Books, 2010.

Hopson, Mark C., and Mika'il Petin, eds. *Reimagining Black Masculinities: Race, Gender, and Public Space.* Lanham, MD: Lexington Books, 2020.

Hudson-Weems, Clenora. *Africana Womanist Literary Theory.* Trenton, NJ: Africa World, 2004.

Hull, Gloria T., Patricia Bell Scott, and Barbara Smith, eds. *All the Women Are White, All the Blacks Are Men, But Some of Us Are Brave.* New York: Feminist Press, 1982.

Hunter, Andrea G., and James Earl Davis. "Constructing Gender: An Exploration of Afro-American Men's Conceptualization of Manhood." *Gender and Society* 6, no. 3 (1992): 464–479.

Hunter, Andrea G., and Sherrill L. Sellers. "Feminist Attitudes among African American Women and Men." *Gender and Society* 12, no. 1 (1998): 81–99.

Hurston, Zora Neale. *Their Eyes Were Watching God.* New York: HarperCollins, 2000.

Hutchinson, Earl Ofari. *The Assassination of the Black Male Image.* Repr. ed. New York: Simon & Schuster, 1997.

Ivory, Luther D. *Toward a Theology of Radical Involvement: The Theological Legacy of Martin Luther King, Jr.* Nashville, TN: Abingdon Press, 1997.

Janee, Lysaundra. "Who's Going to Ride or Die for Black Women and Girls?" *Medium*, June 9, 2020. https://medium.com.

Jennings, Willie James. *The Christian Imagination: Theology and the Origins of Race.* New Haven, CT: Yale University Press, 2011.

Kane, Emily W. "Racial and Ethnic Variations in Gender-Related Attitudes." *Annual Review of Sociology* 26 (2000): 419–439.

King, Martin Luther, Jr. *The Papers of Martin Luther King, Jr.* Vol. 6. Berkeley: University of California Press, 1994.

———. *Where Do We Go from Here: Chaos or Community?* Boston: Beacon, 2010.

Kornegay, El. *A Queering of Black Theology: James Baldwin's Blues Project and Gospel Prose.* Palgrave MacMillan, 2016.

Leak, Jeffrey B. *Racial Myths and Masculinity in African American Literature.* Knoxville: University of Tennessee Press, 2005.

Leeming, David Adams. *James Baldwin: A Biography.* 1st Arcade ed. New York: Arcade, 2015.

Lemons, Gary L. *Womanist Forefathers: Frederick Douglass and W. E. B. Du Bois.* Albany: State University of New York Press, 2009.

Lightsey, Pamela R. *Our Lives Matter: A Womanist Queer Theology.* Eugene, OR: Pickwick, 2015.

Lloyd, Vincent. "Masculinity, Race, and Fatherhood." *Concilium* 2 (2020): 64–73.

———. *Religion of the Field Negro: On Black Secularism and Black Theology*. New York: Fordham University Press, 2018.
Locke, Alain, ed. *The New Negro: Voices of the Harlem Renaissance*. 1925. New York: Touchstone, 1999.
Lofton, Kathryn. *Consuming Religion*. Chicago: University of Chicago Press, 2017.
Lorde, Audre. *Sister Outsiders: Essays and Speeches*. Berkeley, CA: Crossing Press, 2007.
MacKinnon, C. A. *Toward a Feminist Theory of the State*. Cambridge, MA: Harvard University Press, 1989.
Majors, Richard, and Janet Mancini Billson. *Cool Pose: The Dilemmas of Black Manhood in America*. New York: Simon & Schuster, 1993.
Marion, Jean-Luc. *Being Given: Toward a Phenomenology of Givenness*. Stanford, CA: Stanford University Press, 2012.
Mbiti, John. *African Religions and Philosophy*. London: Heinemann, 1969.
McClintock-Fulkerson, Mary. *Changing the Subject: Women's Discourses and Feminist Theology*. Eugene, OR: Wipf and Stock, 2001.
Miller, Shawn E. "'Some Other Way to Try': From Defiance to Creative Submission in Their Eyes Were Watching God." *Southern Literary Journal* 37, no. 1 (2004): 74–95.
Montgomery, Brint, Thomas Jay Oord, Karen Winslow, eds. *Relational Theology: A Contemporary Introduction*. San Diego, CA: Point Loma Press, 2012.
Morrison, Toni. *Home*. New York: Vintage, 2012.
———. "Home." *Talks at Google*, March 4, 2013. www.youtube.com/watch?v=pBDARw5fdrg&t=1102s.
———. *The Source of Self-Regard: Selected Essays, Speeches, and Meditations*. New York: Random House, 2019.
Muñoz, José Esteban. *Cruising Utopia: The Then and There of Queer Futurity*. New York: New York University Press, 2009.
Myers, Leah Wright. "African American Males Speak: The Lifelong Process." *Journal of African American Studies* 8, no. 3 (2004): 62–68.
Neal, Anthony Sean. *Howard Thurman's Philosophical Mysticism: Love against Fragmentation*. Lanham, MD: Lexington Books, 2019.
Neal, Mark Anthony. "Finding Tea Cake: An Imagined Black Feminist Manhood." *Palimpsest: A Journal on Women, Gender, and the Black International* 1, no. 2 (2012): 256–263.
———. *Looking for Leroy: Illegible Black Masculinities*. New York: New York University Press, 2013.
———. *New Black Man*. New York: Routledge, 2006.
Nelson, James B. *Body Theology*. Louisville, KY: Westminster John Knox, 1992.
Niebuhr, H. Richard. *The Responsible Self*. New York: Harper & Row, 1963.
Oyěwùmí, Oyèrónké. "Conceptualizing Gender: The Eurocentric Foundations of Feminist Concepts and the Challenge of African Epistemologies." *JENdA: A Journal of Culture and Women's Studies* 2, no. 1 (2000): 1–9.
———. *The Invention of Women: Making an African Sense of Western Gender Discourses*. Minneapolis: University of Minnesota Press, 1997.

———. "The Translation of Cultures: Engendering Yoruba Language, Orature, and World-Sense." In *Women, Gender, Religion: A Reader*, edited by Elizabeth A. Castelli, 76–97. New York: Palgrave, 2001.

———. *What Gender Is Motherhood? Changing Yorùbá Ideals of Power, Procreation, and Identity in the Age of Modernity*. New York: Palgrave Macmillan, 2016.

Pally, Marcia. *Commonwealth and Covenant: Economics, Politics, and Theologies of Relationality*. Grand Rapids, MI: Eerdmans, 2016.

Parham, Thomas A., Joseph L. White, and Adisa Ajamu. *The Psychology of Blacks: An African-Centered Perspective*. Upper Saddle River, NJ: Prentice Hall, 1999.

Phillips, Layli. *The Womanist Reader: The First Quarter Century of Womanist Thought*. New York: Routledge, 2006.

Pinn, Anthony B. *Embodiment and the New Shape of Black Theological Thought*. New York: New York University Press, 2010.

———. *Terror and Triumph: The Nature of Black Religion*. Minneapolis: Fortress Press, 2022.

———. *Varieties of African American Religious Experiences: Toward a Constructive Black Theology*. Minneapolis: Fortress Press, 2017.

Pinn, Anthony B., and Dwight N. Hopkins, eds. *Loving the Body: Black Religious Studies and the Erotic*. New York: Palgrave Macmillan, 2004.

Reed, Ishmael. *Writin' Is Fightin': Thirty-Seven Years of Boxing on Paper*. New York: Atheneum, 1988.

Rich, Adrienne. *Of Woman Born: Motherhood as Experience and Institution*. New York: Norton, 1995.

Rivera, Robert J., and Michele Saracino, eds. *Enfleshing Theology: Embodiment, Discipleship, and Politics in the Work of M. Shawn Copeland*. Lanham, MD: Rowman & Littlefield, 2018.

Sanders, Cheryl J., ed. *Living the Intersection: Womanism and Afrocentrism in Theology*. Minneapolis: Fortress Press, 1995.

Sanders, Cody J. *Queer Lessons for Churches on the Straight and Narrow*. Macon, GA: Faithlab, 2013.

Schillebeeckx, Edward. *Jesus: An Experiment in Christology*. Translated by Hubert Hoskins. New York: Crossroad, 1995.

Shults, F. LeRon. *Reforming Theological Anthropology: After the Philosophical Turn to Relationality*. Grand Rapids, MI: Eerdmans, 2003.

Smith, Kenneth L., and Ira G. Zepp. *Search for the Beloved Community: The Thinking of Martin Luther King Jr.* Valley Forge, PA: Judson Press, 1998.

Smith, William A., Man Hung, and Jeremy D. Franklin. "Racial Battle Fatigue and the MisEducation of Black Men: Racial Microaggressions, Societal Problems, and Environmental Stress." *Journal of Negro Education* 80, no. 1 (2011): 63–82.

Smith, William A., Jalil Bishop Mustaffa, Chantal M. Jones, Tommy J. Curry, and Walter R. Allen. "'You Make Me Wanna Holler and Throw Up Both My Hands!': Campus Culture, Black Misandric Microaggressions, and Racial Battle Fatigue." *International Journal of Qualitative Studies in Education* 29, no. 9 (2016): 1189–1209.

Sneed, Roger. *Representations of Homosexuality: Black Liberation Theology and Cultural Criticism*. New York: Palgrave Macmillan, 2010.
Sorett, Josef, ed. *The Sexual Politics of Black Churches*. New York: Columbia University Press, 2022.
Spencer, Stephen. "The Value of Lived Experience: Zora Neale Hurston and the Complexity of Race." *Studies in Popular Culture* 27, no. 2 (2004): 17–33.
Spillers, Hortense J. *Black, White, and in Color: Essays on American Literature and Culture*. Chicago: University of Chicago Press, 2003.
Standley, Fred L., and Nancy V. Burt, eds. *Critical Essays on James Baldwin*. Boston: G. K. Hall, 1988.
Staples, Robert. *Black Masculinity: The Black Male's Role in American Society*. San Francisco: Black Scholar Press, 1982.
———. "The Myth of Black Macho: A Response to Angry Black Feminists." *Black Scholar* 10, nos. 6–7 (1979): 24–33.
Summers, Martin. *Manliness and Its Discontents: The Black Middle Class and the Transformation of Masculinity, 1900–1933*. Chapel Hill: University of North Carolina Press, 2004.
Thurman, Howard. *The Inward Journey*. Richmond, IN: Friends United Press, 1980.
———. *Jesus and the Disinherited*. Repr. ed. Boston: Beacon, 1996.
———. *The Luminous Darkness: A Personal Interpretation of the Anatomy of Segregation and the Ground of Hope*. Richmond, IN: Friends United Press, 1989.
———. *With Head and Heart: The Autobiography of Howard Thurman*. New York: Harcourt Brace, 1979.
Touna, Vaia. *Problem of Nostalgia in the Study of Identity: Towards a Dynamic Theory of People and Place*. Bristol: Equinox, 2014.
———, ed. *Strategic Acts in the Study of Identity*. Bristol, CT: Equinox, 2019.
Townes, Emilie, ed. *Breaking the Fine Rain of Death: African American Health Issues and a Womanist Ethic of Care*. Eugene, OR: Wipf and Stock, 1998.
———. *Embracing the Spirit: Womanist Perspectives on Hope, Salvation, and Transformation*, Maryknoll, NY: Orbis Books, 1997.
———. *Womanist Ethics and the Cultural Production of Evil*. New York: Palgrave Macmillan, 2007.
Tracy, David. *Plurality and Ambiguity: Hermeneutics, Religion, Hope*. San Francisco: Harper & Row, 1987.
Trimiew, Darryl M. *Voices of the Silenced: The Responsible Self in a Marginalized Community*. Cleveland: Pilgrim Press, 1993.
Volf, Miroslav. *Exclusion and Embrace: A Theological Exploration of Identity, Otherness, and Reconciliation*. Nashville, TN: Abingdon Press, 1996.
Walker, Alice. *The Color Purple*. New York: Harvest Books, 2003.
———. *In Search of Our Mothers' Gardens: Womanist Prose*. 1983. Repr. ed. Orlando, FL: Mariner Books, 2003.
Wallace, Maurice O. *Constructing the Black Masculine: Identity and Ideality in African American Men's Literature and Culture, 1775–1995*. Durham, NC: Duke University Press Books, 2002.

Ware, Frederick L. *African American Theology: An Introduction.* Louisville, KY: Westminster John Knox, 2016.

Washington, James M., ed. *A Testament of Hope: The Essential Writings and Speeches of Martin Luther King, Jr.* San Francisco: HarperCollins, 1991.

Watkins, Valethia. "Contested Memories: A Critical Analysis of the Black Feminist Revisionist History Project." *Journal of Pan African Studies* 9, no. 4 (2016): 271–288.

Weisenfeld, Judith, and Richard Newman, eds. *This Far by Faith: Readings in African American Women's Religious Biography.* New York: Routledge, 1996.

Westfield, Nancy Lynne. *Dear Sisters: A Womanist Practice of Hospitality.* Cleveland: Pilgrim Press, 2001.

Whitehead, Alfred North. *Process and Reality.* New York: Free Press, 1929.

Wickware, Marvin E., Jr. "The Labour of Black Love: James Cone, Womanism, and the Future of Black Men's Theologies." *Black Theology* 19, no. 1 (2021): 3–17.

Wilmore, Gayraud S. *African American Religious Studies: An Interdisciplinary Anthology.* Durham, NC: Duke University Press, 1989.

———. *Pragmatic Spirituality: The Christian Faith through an Africentric Lens.* New York: New York University Press, 2004.

Wiredu, Kwasi. "Toward Decolonizing African Philosophy and Religion." *African Studies Quarterly* 1, no. 4 (1998): 17–46.

Yeboah, Amy. 2020. "Why the West Could Not Hear Beale Street: Baldwin's World-Sense of Female Sexuality." *Humanities* 9, no. 1 (2020): article 9. https://doi.org/10.3390/h9010009.

Young, Damon. "Straight Black Men Are the White People of Black People." *The Root*, September 19, 2017. www.theroot.com.

Yukich, Grace, and Penny Edgell, eds. *Religion Is Raced: Understanding American Religion in the Twenty-First Century.* New York: New York University Press, 2020.

INDEX

Africa: diaspora from, 13, 19; Ifá divination in, 135–36, 176n27; Ìyá traditions in, 136–37; matripotency in, 135–37; personhood in, 138; recovery and renewal traditions and, 130–39; relationality in, 139; Western-based gender structures in, 134; women in, 133–35; Yoruba traditions in, 134–37. *See also* African diaspora

African American religious thought. *See* Black religious thought

African diaspora: selfhood among, 19; women of, 13

African Religions and Philosophy (Mbiti), 131

agency: communal, 143; in *If Beale Street Could Talk,* 93; moral, 28, 44

American religion, multidimensionality of, 2

Anderson, Victor, 78, 98, 101, 154

anti-Black male attitudes: in *The Color Purple* (book), 10; as misandry, 80, 114, 148, 151; powerlessness as result of, 20; in womanist-identified literature, 80

anti-Black racism, 20

anti-Black women attitudes, by black scholars, 1

antiracism, Black male identity and, 40

anti-relationality: in *The Color Purple* (book), 57–62; identity formation and, 155; in *Their Eyes Were Watching God,* 72

antisexism, Black male identity and, 40, 44

appropriation, reciprocity as distinct from, 23

Arvidson, P. Sven, 61

Baker-Fletcher, Garth, 24; on Black male identity, 38–39; on Bodyself, 40–43; critique of King, M. L., 120–21; on identity formation, 38; on remythification of Black manhood, 38; on theological discourses, 37–44; *Xodus,* 37–44

Baker-Fletcher, Karen, 14, 24, 35

Baldwin, James, 48, 153; "The Black Boy Looks at the White Boy," 85, 128; on Black church culture, 96–99; on Black male identity, 153; on Black queer religious thought, 96–99; on Black religious life, 84–85; on Black spirituality, 57; critics of, 84; *The Fire Next Time,* 82; "Freaks and the American Ideal of Manhood," 82; on gendered identity, 82; *Go Tell It on the Mountain,* 82–83, 86–92, 96; homophobia and, 82; hypermasculine ethos for, 84; *If Beale Street Could Talk,* 83–84, 92–96; literary masculinism in works of, 83–84, 97, 101; on openness, 99–103; on recovery and renewal, 129; on salvation, 57; soteriology of, 89; "To Crush a Serpent," 57; on White racial imagination, 85; on White supremacy, 85, 128; on writing, 83

Baldwin, Lewis, 116, 121

Beloved Community, 116–23; Black male identity and, 124–25

Between Sundays (Frederick), 141

Beyond Ontological Blackness (Anderson), 154

BF-RHP. *See* Black Feminist Revisionist History Project

Black bodies: Christological framework for, 30; eucharistic solidarity and, 29–34; Eurocentric ideals and, 30; in *Home*, 73; *memoria passionis* and, 30; womanist articulations of, 31

"The Black Boy Looks at the White Boy" (Baldwin, J.), 85, 128

Black culture: as feminine, 5–6; ontological Blackness, 98. *See also* Black queer thought

Black feminism, Black feminists and: Black Feminist Revisionist History Project, 53; on religious studies projects, 2

Black Feminist Revisionist History Project (BF-RHP), 53

Black folk heroes, 66

Black male identity: academic studies on, 11–14; antiracism and, 40; antisexism and, 40, 44; Baker-Fletcher, G., on, 38–39; Baldwin, J., on, 153; Beloved Community and, 124–25; Black masculinity and, 102–3; Black religious thought and, 12; in *The Color Purple* (book), 58; cultural criticism of, 13; expansion of possibilities for, 157–58; feminist theory and, 13; in *Go Tell It on the Mountain*, 90–92; King, M. L., on, 116; masculinity and, 3; methodological approach to, 14–17; in misandrist theories, 11; negotiation of, 12; pathologizing of, 6–8; racist theories and, 11; reconfiguration of, 10; reconstruction of, 106; recovery and renewal and, 129, 142, 144, 160; reimagination of, 14; self-creation of, 12; soul work and, 4, 127; in *Their Eyes Were Watching God*, 72; Thurman on, 112–13; womanism and, 24. *See also* recovery and renewal

Black male theology: Beloved Community and, 116–26; communal manhood and, 116–26; conceptual approach to, 104–7; King, M. L., on, 116–25; liberation theology, 104–5; love labor in, 104–5; National Council of Negro Churchmen on Black theology, 104; realignment of vision in, 125–27; scope of, 105; Thurman on, 107–16, 125–26; womanism and, 105

Black Masculinity (Staples), 19–20

Black masculinity, Black manhood and: analysis of, 151–60; Baker-Fletcher, G., on, 38; Black male identity and, 102–3; Black queer thought and, 96; in Black religious thought, 2; Bodyself and, 40–43; capacity for wholeness, 9; in *The Color Purple*, 51, 63; communal manhood and, 116–26; conceptual approach to, 51–52; fixed representations of, 102; in *Go Tell It on the Mountain*, 86–92; in *Home*, 76; hyperaggression and, 20; identity formation and, 3, 81; in *If Beale Street Could Talk*, 95; meanings of, 78; opportunity structures for, 20; Otherwise, 151–60; recovery and renewal and, 139–40; rejection of, 154; relationality and, 81; remythification of, 38; selfhood as element of, 79; traditional models of, 39–40; Walker's aspirational vision of, 9; White Western deconstruction of, 5; in womanist-identified literature, 55–56

Black men: Black male studies, 11–14; caricaturing of, 49–50; in *The Color Purple* (film), 7; criticism of Walker by, 6–7; dehumanization of, 20, 143; egalitarian gender role attitudes for, 41; as folk heroes, 66; gender regimes' negative impact on, 1; intraracial privileges of, 177n9; methodological relational praxis for, 15; misogyny and, 43; popular perceptions of, 80; religious studies on, 2; sexism and, 43; shared experiences with Black women, 28; socialization of, 19–20; social ostracism of, 5; theological discourses for, 2, 37–48; violence as control mechanism for, 70; womanist-identified literature as influence on, 79. See also Black male identity; Black male theology; Black masculinity; recovery and renewal

Blackpentecostal Breath (Crawley), 156–57

Black queer thought: Baldwin, J., on, 96–99; Black manhood and, 96; critiques of Black church and, 97–98; discourses on, 96; in *Go Tell It on the Mountain*, 96; in *If Beale Street Could Talk*, 96; as insurgency, 100; openness to, 100–103; queer theory and, 96; religion and, 96–99

Black religious thought: Baldwin, J., on, 84–85, 96–99; Black male identity and, 12; Black queer thought and, 96–99; community-building as element of, 19; as feminine, 5–6; in *Go Tell It on the Mountain*, 86–92; identity formation and, 3; in *If Beale Street Could Talk*, 93–96; masculinity in Black males and, 2; as meaning-making process, 3; methodological approach to, 2–3; provincialism of, 2; representative voices in, 168n46. See also religious studies; theological discourses

Black spirituality. See spirituality

Black Theology and Black Power (Cone), 104, 130

A Black Theology of Liberation (Cone), 130

Black Womanist Ethics (Cannon), 44, 54–55

Black women: as anthropological subject in Christianity, 29; consciousness for, 4; dehumanization of, 45; diunital thinking and, 24; egalitarian gender role attitudes for, 41; "the Funk" of, 45; gender politics among, 7; gender regimes' negative impact on, 1; maternal wisdom of, 26, 28; methodological relational praxis for, 15; moral agency for, 28, 44; relational ethos for, 25–26; role in White feminist movement, 124; selfhood of, 45, 47; shared experiences with Black men, 28; social ostracism of, 5; spirituality of, 45, 47–48; Walker on, 25. See also anti-Black women attitudes; femininity; misogyny; womanism

Blain, Keisha N., 124

Bland, Sandra, 31

"Blessed Assurance" (Hughes), 100

Bodyself, 40–43

Breaking the Fine Rain of Death (Townes), 74

Brim, Matt, 96, 101

Buber, Martin, 167n42

Butler, Judith, 4

Byrd, Rudolph, 105

Campbell, James, 82

Cannon, Katie: on actualization of Black people, 125; *Black Womanist Ethics*, 44, 54–55; on Hurston, 71; on identity formation, 3–4; on oppression of Black people, 121; on reciprocity, 23–24; on soul work, 127; on womanism, 27, 106; on womanist-identified literature, 54–55

Carby, Hazel, 7

care ethics, 78

caregiving culture, 170n44; in *Home*, 73–75, 77–78

Carrette, Jeremy, 140

Changing the Subject (McClintock-Fulkerson), 21

Christianity: Black women as anthropological subject in, 29; eucharistic solidarity of Black bodies, 29–34; *Imago Dei* concept, 121

Church for the Fellowship of All Peoples, 108
Clark, Keith, 83
Clark, Septima, 123
Coetzee, Azille, 131
Collins, Patricia Hill, 54, 152–53
The Color Purple (book) (Walker): anti-Black male provincialism in, 10; anti-relational features in, 57–62; Black male identity in, 58; Black manhood in, 51, 63; communal understanding of family in, 59; as cultural benchmark, 7, 79–80; female networking and cooperation in, 59; misandrist claims in, 8; "Natural Man" identity in, 62–63; sexual trauma in, 58; toxic masculinity in, 58
The Color Purple (film), 7
communalism, traditional: Black manhood and, 116–26; dialogical centralism and, 27–29; relationality and, 27; Walker on, 27; womanism and, 27–29
community-building, in Black faith communities, 19
compound subjectivity, in *Their Eyes Were Watching God*, 63–71
Cone, James, 104, 120, 130, 173n27
connectedness, values of, 44, 47–48; Morrison on, 45; Townes on, 46
Constructing the Black Masculine (Wallace), 51–52
Copeland, M. Shawn, 29–34, 136, 167n42, 176n27. *See also* eucharistic solidarity
countermemory, 49
Crawley, Ashon, 156–57
Curry, Tommy J., 1, 11–14, 56, 80, 102

dancing mind (womanist), 22
Dancing with God (Baker-Fletcher, K.), 35
dangerous memory *(memoria passionis)*, 30
Dear Sisters (Westfield), 47
deGregory, Crystal, 121

dehumanization: of Black men, 20, 143; of Black women, 45
dialogical centralism, 15; communalism and, 27–29; dancing mind approach, 22; ethics in, 21, 27–29; eucharistic solidarity and, 29–34; in feminist theology, 21; pluralism and, 22; polyvocality and, 22; process theology and, 34–37; reciprocity in, 21, 23–25; theo-ethics and, 27–29; in Walker works, 25–26
diasporas. *See* African diaspora
diunital thinking, 24
Dorrien, Gary, 110
Douglas, Kelly Brown, 27, 59, 155
Douglas, Susan, 147

Eckhart, Meister, 110
egalitarianism: gender role attitudes and, 41; in *Their Eyes Were Watching God*, 66–70
Enfleshing Freedom (Copeland), 29, 176n27
Enlightened Sexism (Douglas), 147
essential being, notions of, 130–39
ethics: care, 78; Christian, 26; in dialogical centralism, 21, 27–29; of memory, 48–49; womanist approaches to, 8, 26–29, 106; in *Xodus*, 44. *See also* Cannon, Katie
eucharistic solidarity: Black bodies and, 29–34; dialogical centralism and, 29–34; Jesus Christ and, 33–34; *memoria passionis* and, 30; relationality in, 32
Eurocentrism: embodiment and, 30; masculinity influenced by, 39
evangelical liberalism, 118
Evans, Curtis J., 5

family, in *The Color Purple* (book), 59
Farley, Edward, 78–79
femininity, womanhood and, for Black women, White Western deconstruction of, 5

feminism, feminist theory and: Black male identity and, 13; Butler on, 4; covert, 70; in *Their Eyes Were Watching God*, 70. *See also* Black feminism; White feminism
The Fire Next Time (Baldwin, J.), 82
Floyd-Thomas, Stacey, 4, 27
"Freaks and the American Ideal of Manhood" (Baldwin), 82
Frederick, Marla, 47–48, 141

Gandhi, Mahatma, 118
Garth, 14
gender: in Africa, 134; diunital thinking on, 24; identity formation and, 72, 76–77. *See also* gender politics; gender regimes; gender roles; gender theory
gendered racism, 80
gender identity: Baldwin on, 82; in *Home*, 72, 76–77
gender politics: among Black women, 7; in *The Color Purple*, 7; in Hurston works, 64; King, M. L., on, 122–23; for Walker, 6
gender regimes: Black men negatively impacted by, 1; Black women negatively impacted by, 1; in White Western societies, 5
gender roles: in Africa, 134; in *Home*, 73
gender studies, 4
gender theory, 4; racial stratification in, 5; racism and, 6
Gender Trouble (Butler), 4
Gibson, Ernest, 89
Giddings, Paula, 174n59
Gilkes, Cheryl Townsend, 28, 125
God of the Oppressed (Cone), 173n27
Go Tell It on the Mountain (Baldwin, J.), 82–83; autobiographical elements of, 86, 88; Black male identity in, 90–92; Black manhood in, 86–92; Black queer thought in, 96; critiques of, 87; homosexual identity in, 89–90; intimacy as theme in, 86–92; paternal relationships in, 86–87; religious crisis in, 86–92; salvation themes in, 89, 92
Grier, Nicholas, 142–44
Griffin, Horace, 98
Grimes, J. A. "Pick," 114
Guy-Sheftall, Beverly, 105

Hamer, Fannie Lou, 123–24
Harack, Katrina, 73, 76
Hardy, Clarence, 91
Harlem Renaissance: Black male writers during, 54; protest novels of, 64
Harper, Phillip Brian, 102
Harris, Trudier, 7–8, 87, 165n22
Harvey, Paul, 107
healing culture, in *Home*, 73–75, 77–78
Hemenway, Robert, 63
Hemphill, Essex, 99
Hernton, Calvin, 6–7
Hicks, Derek, 73
Hobson, Christopher, 93
holistic masculinity, 103
Home (Morrison), 52, 146; Black manhood in, 76; care ethics in, 78; caregiving and healing culture in, 73–75, 77–78; debasement of female body in, 73; gender identity themes in, 72, 76–77; gender roles in, 73; identity formation in, 78; relationality themes in, 72, 77–78; separatist themes in, 75; traumatic memory in, 73, 76–77; womanist themes in, 75
homophobia, 82, 105
homosexual identity, in *Go Tell It on the Mountain*, 89–90
Hopkins, Dwight, 37, 45–47
Hudson-Weems, Clenora, 138
Hughes, Langston, 100
humanism, 129
humanum, identity formation and, 33

Hurston, Zora Neale: Cannon on, 71; gender politics for, 64; "racial health" themes for, 64; Walker on, 63–64, 160. *See also Their Eyes Were Watching God*
Hutchinson, Earl, 151
hyperaggression, Black masculinity and, 20
hypermasculine ethos, 84
hypersurveillance, 52

identity formation: anti-relationality and, 155; Baker-Fletcher, G., on, 38; Black manhood and, 3, 81; Black religious thought and, 3; Cannon on, 3–4; conceptualization of, 115–16; Farley on, 78–79; gender identity, 72, 76–77; humanum and, 33; in *If Beale Street Could Talk*, 93–94; as nonfixed, 154; personal interests and, 3; in religious studies, 3. *See also* Black male identity; homosexual identity; masculinity
identity politics, 7. *See also* gender politics
If Beale Street Could Talk (Baldwin, J.), 83–84, 92; Black female agency in, 93; Black manhood modeled in, 95; Black queer thought in, 96; Black religious culture in, 93–96; Christian theology in, 94–95; critiques of, 93; identity formation in, 93–94; relationality in, 93; religious crisis as theme in, 96
Imago Dei concept, 121
In Search of Our Mothers' Gardens (Walker), 4, 25
intimacy, as theme, in *Go Tell It on the Mountain*, 86–92
intimate partner violence, 146
The Invention of Women (Oyěwùmí), 133

Jenkins, Barry, 159
Jesus and the Disinherited (Thurman), 36, 112–13
Jesus Christ, 33–34
Jones, Rufus, 110–11

Kagame, Alexis, 132
Kane, Emily, 41
Kenan, Randall, 99
King, Martin Luther, Jr., 104, 106; Baker-Fletcher, G., critique of, 120–21; on Beloved Community, 116–26; on Black male identity, 116; Black male theology and, 116–25; on communal manhood, 116–26; on gender politics, 122–23; *Imago Dei* concept for, 121; moral blind spots of, 122; personalism for, 118, 121; philosophical influences on, 118; *Where Do We Go from Here?*, 116
King, Richard, 140
kinship systems, 131–32
knowing, mechanisms of (womanist epistemology), 4

liberalism, White, romanticism of Black people, 5–6
liberation theology, 104–5
liberatory partnerships, 42–43
Lightsey, Pamela, 97
literary masculinism, 83–84, 97
Lloyd, Vincent, 4, 106
Locke, Alain, 117
Lorde, Audre, 91–92, 158–59
Lynch, Michael, 84

Mailer, Norman, 85, 125
manhood, universal scope of, 6. *See also* Black masculinity; masculinity
The Man-Not (Curry), 11
"Many Thousands Gone" (Baldwin, J.), 48
Marion, Jean-Luc, 170n44
masculinity: Eurocentric approaches to, 39; holistic, 103; literary masculinism, 83–84, 97; toxic, 58. *See also* Black masculinity
"Masculinity, Race, and Fatherhood" (Lloyd), 4
matriphobia, 135
matripotency, 135–37

Mbiti, John, 131
McClintock-Fulkerson, Mary, 21
Mead, Margaret, 84
memoria passionis (dangerous memory), 30
memory: ethics of, 48–49; in *Home*, 73, 76–77. *See also* countermemory
Miller, Shawn, 70
misandry: anti-Black, 80, 114, 148, 151; Black male identity and, 11; in *The Color Purple* (book), 8; in womanist-identified literature, 56. *See also* anti-Black male attitudes; Black male identity
misogyny: Black men and, 43; patriarchy and, 147; violence and, 165n12. *See also* anti-Black women attitudes
Moonlight, 159
moral agency, for Black women, 28, 44
Morrison, Toni: on "the Funk" of Black women, 45; *Home*, 52, 72–78, 146; on spirituality of Black women, 45; *Sula*, 46–47; on values of connectedness, 45; womanist themes for, 22
Muñoz, José Esteban, 101
Myers, Leah Wright, 20
My Sister, My Brother (Baker-Fletcher, K., and Baker-Fletcher, G.), 24
mysticism, 110–12

National Council of Negro Churchmen on Black theology, 104
"Natural Man" identity, in *The Color Purple* (book), 62–63
Neal, Mark Anthony, 139
Nelson, James, 84
New Black Man (Neal), 139
New Black Man trope, 139–40

ontological blackness, 98
Oord, Thomas Jay, 35
openness: Baldwin, J., on, 99–103; to Black queer thought, 100–103

ostracism, of Black men and women, 5
Otherwise (conception of Black masculinity), 151–60
Oyěwùmí, Oyèrónkẹ, 133–35

Pally, Marcia, 36
Parham, Thomas A., 144
pathological masculinity. *See* toxic masculinity
pathologization, of Black communities: of Black male identity, 6–8; racism and, 7–8
patriarchy, patriarchal structures and: misogyny and, 147; rejection of, 142; relationality and, 154–55; sexism and, 147; in *Their Eyes Were Watching God*, 70–72
personalism, 118, 121
personhood, in Africa, 138
Pinn, Anthony, 3, 23
pluralism, dialogical centralism and, 22
polyvocality, 22
process theology, dialogical centralism and, 34–37
protest novels, 64

queer culture. *See* Black queer thought; homosexual identity

"racial health," as theme, 64
racial stratification, in gender theory, 5
racism: abolition of, 105; anti-Black, 20; Black male identity and, 11; gendered, 80; gender theory and, 6; minstrel legacy and, 52; pathologizing of Black communities and, 7–8; powerlessness for Black males as result of, 20. *See also* anti-Black male attitudes; anti-Black women attitudes
reciprocity, 167n42; appropriation as distinct from, 23; Cannon on, 23–24; in dialogical centralism, 21, 23–25; relationality and, 26; in *Their Eyes Were Watching God*, 65–66

recovery and renewal, for Black males: accountability as element of, 145–46; African cultural influences on, 130–39; Baldwin, J., on, 129; Black male identity formation and, 129, 142, 144, 160; Black manhood and, 139–40; communal agency and, 143; conceptual approach to, 128–30; dehumanization of Black males, 143; frameworks for, 139–49; humanism and, 129; kinship systems and, 131–32; New Black Man trope and, 139–40; notions of essential being, 130–39; participatory aspects of, 148; as psychosocial spiritual praxis, 140–41; rejection of patriarchy and, 142; relational identity and, 148; relationality and, 130–39, 148; relational subjectivity and, 132; selfhood through, 130, 144; self-recovery, 148–49; *Ubuntu* concept, 131–32

Reed, Ishmael, 7–8, 79

relationality, as concept: in African traditions, 139; Black manhood and, 81; for Black women, 25–26; communalism and, 27; in eucharistic solidarity, 32; in *Home*, 72, 77–78; in *If Beale Street Could Talk*, 93; methodological relational praxis, 15; patriarchy and, 154–55; reciprocity and, 26; recovery and renewal and, 130–39, 148; in *Their Eyes Were Watching God*, 66; theology and, 34–37; for Thurman, 113–14; Walker on, 10; womanism and, 4, 11, 25–27; in womanist-identified literature, 55; in *Xodus*, 39, 41

relational openness, 34

The Religion of Jesus and the Disinherited. See *Jesus and the Disinherited*

Religion of the Field Negro (Lloyd), 106

religious discourses. *See* theological discourses

religious studies: Black feminist responses to, 2; on Black men, 2; identity formation in, 3; womanist approaches to, 8

Rich, Adrienne, 135

Roberts, J. Deotis, 104

salvation: Baldwin, J., on, 57; in *Go Tell It on the Mountain*, 89, 92

Salvific Manhood (Gibson), 89

Sanger, Margaret, 151

Schillebeeckx, Edward, 33

selfhood: across the African diaspora, 19; Black manhood and, 79; of Black women, 45, 47; recovery and renewal and, 130, 144

self-recovery, 148–49

separatism: in *Home*, 75; womanism and, 10, 29, 75

sexism: abolition of, 105; Black men and, 43; patriarchy and, 147. *See also* anti-sexism; misogyny

The Sexual Mountain and Black Women Writers (Hernton), 79

Shoes That Fit Our Feet (Hopkins), 45

Sneed, Roger, 84, 97–100, 155–56

social gospel, 118

socialization, of Black men, 19–20

soteriology, 89, 111

soul work, 4, 127

spirituality, Black: Baldwin, J., on, 57; of Black women, 45, 47–48. *See also* Black religious thought

Stagolee/Stacker Lee, as Black folk hero, 66

Staples, Robert, 19–20, 165n12, 166n29

Strategic Acts in the Study of Identity (Touna), 3

Sula (Morrison), 46–47

Their Eyes Were Watching God (Hurston), 29–30, 52; anti-relationality in, 72; Black folk hero in, 66; Black male identity formation in, 72; compound subjectivity in, 63–71; covert feminism in, 70; egalitarian themes in, 66–70; feminist interpretations of, 70; partnerships between genders in, 66–70; patriarchal structures in, 70–72; as protest novel, 64; reciprocity in, 65–66; relationality in, 66; violence as control mechanism in, 70; women in masculine spheres, 67

Their Own Received Them Not (Griffin), 98

theological discourses: Baker-Fletcher, G., on, 37–44; for Black men, 2, 37–44; *Xodus*, 37–44. *See also* Black religious thought; religious studies

theology: dialogical centralism and, 27–29; ethics in, 27–29; in *If Beale Street Could Talk*, 94–95; liberation, 104–5; process, 34–37; relational, 34–37; undue separability, 36; womanist approaches to, 8, 26–29, 34–37, 126–27; in *Xodus*, 44. *See also* Black male theology

Thurman, Howard, 36, 106; on Black male identity, 112–13; Black male theology and, 107–16; Church for the Fellowship of All Peoples, 108; church responsibilities for, 110; early family life, 108–9; *Jesus and the Disinherited*, 36, 112–13; mysticism of, 110–12; racial philosophy of, 108; relational paradigm for, 113–14; self-identity for, 109; unity with nature, 108–9

Thurman, Saul, 108

"To Crush a Serpent" (Baldwin, J.), 57

Touna, Vaia, 3

Townes, Emilie, 5, 14, 48–49, 74, 152; dancing mind approach, 22; on womanist connectedness, 46; on womanist-identified literature, 53

toxic masculinity, in *The Color Purple* (book), 58

Tracy, David, 22

traditional communalism. *See* communalism

Traps (Byrd and Guy-Sheftall), 105

Trimiew, Darryl, 19

Turman, Eboni Marshall, 31

Ubuntu, 131–32

undue separability, 36

violence: as control mechanism, 70; misogyny and, 165n12

A Visitation of Spirits (Kenan), 99

Volf, Miroslav, 29

Wade-Gayles, Gloria, 79

Walker, Alice, 1, 165n22; aspirational vision of Black manhood, 9; Black male literary criticism of, 6–7; on Black womanhood, 25; dialogical centralism and, 25–26; gender politics for, 6; on Hurston, 63–64, 160; on relationality, 10; *In Search of Our Mothers' Gardens*, 4, 25; on traditional communalism, 27; womanism and, 6–11, 25–26, 52, 75, 105. *See also The Color Purple*

Wallace, Maurice O., 51–52, 152

Ware, Frederick, 8

Washington, Bryan, 90

Watkins, Valethia, 53

Westfield, Nancy Lynne, 47

What Gender is Motherhood (Oyěwùmí), 135

When and Where I Enter (Giddings), 174n59

Where Do We Go from Here? (King, M. L.), 116

White feminism, White feminists and: Black women and, 124; womanism and, 23

White racial imagination, 85

White (Western) societies: construction of womanhood in, 133–34; gender regimes in, 5; gender structures in, 134; racialized gaze of, 51

White supremacy, 85, 128
Wickware, Marvin, 104–5
Wideman, John Edgar, 129
Wilmore, Gayraud, 126–27
Wiredu, Kwasi, 132
wisdom, of Black women, 26, 28
womanism: Black female consciousness and, 4; Black male identity and, 24; Black male theology and, 105; Cannon on, 27, 106; Christian ethics and, 26; in *The Color Purple* (book), 9–10, 52, 54, 57–63; communalism and, 27–29; as cultural production, 4; dialogical centralist methodology, 21–37; epistemology and, 4; ethics and, 8, 26–29, 106; in *Home*, 75; instructive capacity of, 13; as literary genre, 53–56; in Morrison works, 22; negotiation of identity through, 25; Process theology and, 34–37; relationality and, 4, 11, 25–27; religious studies and, 8; separatism as element of, 10, 29, 75; theology and, 8, 26–29, 34–37, 126–27; Walker and, 6–11, 25–26, 52, 75, 105; White feminism and, 23

Womanist Ethics and the Cultural Production of Evil (Townes), 49

womanist-identified literature: anti-Black male attitudes in, 80; Black Feminist Revisionist History Project and, 53; Black manhood in, 55–56; Cannon on, 54–55; education of Black men through, 79; misandry in, 56; relationality in, 55; Townes on, 53. *See also The Color Purple*; Hurston, Zora Neale; Morrison, Toni; *Their Eyes Were Watching God*; Walker, Alice; *specific authors*; *specific works*

women, womanhood and: in Africa, 133–35; of African diaspora, 13; definition of, 165n12; Western construction of, 133–34. *See also* Black woman; femininity; misandry; *specific topics*

Wonder, Stevie, 6
Wright, Richard, 82

X, Malcolm, 38, 104
Xodus (Baker-Fletcher, G.), 37–38; Black masculinity in, 42; Bodyself in, 40–43; ethics in, 44; relationality in, 39, 41; theology in, 44

Young, Damon, 177n9

ABOUT THE AUTHOR

DARRIUS D'WAYNE HILLS is Associate Professor in the Department of Religious Studies at Grinnell College. His research and teaching have been supported by the Forum for Theological Exploration and the Louisville Institute for the Study of Religion in North America.

www.ingramcontent.com/pod-product-compliance
Lightning Source LLC
Chambersburg PA
CBHW020410080526
44584CB00014B/1266